D1546289

Reason, Revelation, and Devo

Reason, Revelation, and Devotion argues that immersion in religious reading traditions and their associated spiritual practices significantly shapes our emotions, desires, intuitions, and volitional commitments; these in turn affect our construction and assessments of arguments for religious conclusions. But far from distorting the reasoning process, these emotions and volitional and cognitive dispositions can be essential for sound reasoning on religious and other value-laden subject matters. And so Western philosophy must rethink its traditional antagonism toward rhetoric. The book concludes with discussions of the implications of the earlier chapters for the relation between reason and revelation, and for the role that the concept of mystery should play in philosophy in general, and in the philosophy of religion and philosophical theology in particular.

William J. Wainwright is Distinguished Professor of Philosophy Emeritus at the University of Wisconsin–Milwaukee. He has served as Editor of *Faith and Philosophy*, and is past President of both the Society for Philosophy of Religion and the Society of Christian Philosophers. Major publications include *Mysticism* (1981), *Philosophy of Religion* (1988, second edition 1999), *Reason and the Heart* (1995), *Religion and Morality* (2005), and the edited volume *Oxford Handbook of Philosophy of Religion* (2005), as well as over eighty articles and book chapters.

CAMBRIDGE STUDIES IN RELIGION, PHILOSOPHY, AND SOCIETY

Series Editors

Paul Moser, *Loyola University Chicago*
Chad Meister, *Bethel College*

This is a series of interdisciplinary texts devoted to major-level courses in religion, philosophy, and related fields. It includes original, current, and wide-spanning contributions by leading scholars from various disciplines that (a) focus on the central academic topics in religion and philosophy, (b) are seminal and up to date regarding recent developments in scholarship on the various key topics, and (c) incorporate, with needed precision and depth, the major differing perspectives and backgrounds – the central voices on the major religions and the religious, philosophical, and sociological viewpoints that cover the intellectual landscape today. Cambridge Studies in Religion, Philosophy, and Society is a direct response to this recent and widespread interest and need.

Recent Books in the Series

Roger Trigg
Religious Diversity: Philosophical and Political Dimensions

John Cottingham
Philosophy of Religion: Towards a More Humane Approach

Reason, Revelation, and Devotion

Inference and Argument in Religion

WILLIAM J. WAINWRIGHT
University of Wisconsin–Milwaukee

CAMBRIDGE
UNIVERSITY PRESS

CAMBRIDGE
UNIVERSITY PRESS

32 Avenue of the Americas, New York, NY 10013-2473, USA

Cambridge University Press is part of the University of Cambridge.

It furthers the University's mission by disseminating knowledge in the pursuit of
education, learning, and research at the highest international levels of excellence.

www.cambridge.org
Information on this title: www.cambridge.org/9781107650367

First published 2016

Printed in the United States of America by Sheridan Books, Inc.

A catalog record for this publication is available from the British Library.

Library of Congress Cataloging in Publication Data
Wainwright, William J.
Reason, revelation, and devotion : inference and argument in religion /
William J. Wainwright.
    pages   cm. – (Cambridge studies in religion, philosophy, and society)
Includes bibliographical references and index.
ISBN 978-1-107-06240-5 (hardback) – ISBN 978-1-107-65036-7 (pbk.)
1. Philosophy and religion.   2. Inference.   3. Reasoning.   I. Title.
BL51.W1624   2015
210–dc23   2015029264

ISBN 978-1-107-06240-5 Hardback
ISBN 978-1-107-65036-7 Paperback

For William L. Rowe, a firm friend and a fine philosopher

Contents

Acknowledgments

Portions of Chapters 1 and 6 are drawn from William J. Wainwright, *Philosophy of Religion,* second edition © 1999 Wadsworth, a part of Cengage Learning, Inc. Reproduced by permission. www.cengage.com/permissions. Chapter 2 contains extracts from pp. 81–88, ch 5: "Theistic Proofs, Person Relativity, and the Rationality of Religious Belief," by William Wainwright, from *Evidence and Religious Belief,* edited by Kelly James Clark and Raymond J. VanArragon (2011). By permission of Oxford University Press. Chapter 4 contains material adapted from *Reason and the Heart: A Prolegomenon to a Critique of Passional Reason,* by William J. Wainwright. Copyright © 1995 by Cornell University. Used by permission of the publisher, Cornell University Press. Chapter 4 also includes four pages from the *International Journal for Philosophy of Religion,* December 2010, volume 68, issue 1–3, pp. 201–13, "Jonathan Edwards and 'Particular Minds'" by William J. Wainwright. Reprinted with kind permission of Springer Science+Business Media. Chapter 5 is a descendent of William J. Wainwright, "Religious Experience, Theological Argument, and Rhetoric," *Faith and Philosophy* 22 (October 2005: 391–412). Copyright © 2005, Society of Christian Philosophers. Used by permission of the editors. Chapters 6 and 7 contain extracts from pp. 78–102, ch. 4: "Theology and Mystery," by William J. Wainwright, from *Oxford Handbook of Philosophical Theology,* edited by Thomas P. Flint and Michael Rea (2009). By permission of Oxford University Press. Chapter 6 also includes portions of William J. Wainwright, "Christianity," ch. 4 from Charles Taliaferro, Victoria S Harrison, and Stewart Goetz, editors, *The Routledge Companion to Theism,* Routledge, Taylor and Francis Group, 2013 © 2013 Taylor and Francis. Republished with their permission, permission conveyed through Copyright Clearance Center, Inc. Thanks finally to John Wiley & Sons for their permission to include material in Chapter 6 from my "Christianity," pp. 59–66, in Charles Taliaferro, Paul Draper, and Philip L. Quinn (eds.), *A Companion to Philosophy of Religion,* second edition, Wiley-Blackwell, 2010 © Blackwell Publishing Ltd.

Introduction

Rational beliefs can be grounded in perceptual experience, memory, testimony, rational intuitions, or inference. Other things being equal, beliefs grounded in any one of these ways are rational. For example, assuming that my memory is generally reliable and that I clearly remember having had toast for breakfast this morning, my belief that I had toast this morning is rational. The apparent self-evidence of "2 + 2 = 4," or, "A whole is greater than its proper parts," fully justifies my belief that 2 plus 2 *is* equal to 4 and that a whole *is* greater than its proper parts. A number of prominent philosophers of religion have argued that religious beliefs can be justified in a similar fashion. For example, William P. Alston, Richard Swinburne, Jerome Gellman, and I have argued that perceptual or quasiperceptual experiences of God occur and justify the religious beliefs of those who have them. Others such as Alvin Plantinga maintain that in certain circumstances, beliefs in God can be "properly basic." That is, that like many of our memorial beliefs or beliefs in simple necessary truths, they can be fully justified without being grounded in further beliefs. Yet as Jonathan Edwards said in the mid-eighteenth century, "if we take reason strictly – not for the faculty of mental perception in general [which would include sense perception, memory, and rational intuition] but for ratiocination, or a power of inferring by arguments," or *reasoning*, then "reason" refers to the faculty of rational inference and its exercises.[1] The nature and proper role of inference and argument in religion is the subject of this book.

Until quite recently, philosophical studies of religious reasoning and argumentation have tended to focus almost exclusively on the validity of arguments for religious conclusions[2] and the truth of their premises. This is not altogether surprising, since no invalid argument or argument with a false premise is a good argument. But even though truth and validity are *necessary* conditions of a good argument, they aren't sufficient, since an argument can meet both conditions and not be probative.

Arguments are constructed for various purposes, and these purposes must be taken into account when evaluating their success or failure. Furthermore, reasoning is always situated – it does not occur in a vacuum. Arguments are the products of men and women with various needs, hopes, fears, sensitivities, and proclivities, and with diverse individual histories, who are responding to highly specific problems and difficulties. They are not the expressions of a view from nowhere that abstracts from the existential specificity of the reasoner and/or the particularities of his or her concrete situation, although these frequently determine whether an argument is or is not probative in a particular situation or for a particular person. *Reason, Revelation, and Devotion: Inference and Argument in Religion* explores these neglected aspects of religious argumentation in depth.

Chapter 1 introduces four examples of religious reasoning. The first is Samuel Clarke's cosmological proof of the existence of God. Proceeding from the assumption that anything that exists must have a sufficient reason for its existence, Clarke argues that the existence of contingent beings can be explained only by postulating the existence and activity of a necessarily existent being. The second and third arguments discussed in this chapter address the question of what attributes can be properly attributed to the maximally perfect reality that is the intended object of the devotional practices and existential commitments valorized in the major world religions. In what sense can God be said to be omnipotent, for example? If he can do everything that is logically possible for an agent to do, can he do evil? And if he cannot, can he truly said to be omnipotent? Again, is the maximally perfect reality personal, as Christians, Jews, Muslims, and Hindu monotheists believe, or is it necessarily nonpersonal, as Buddhists and others maintain? The chapter concludes by examining a specifically theological controversy: the quarrel between Pelagius and Augustine over the roles played by freedom and grace in human life, as well as some developments of their positions in later Christian thought and analogues of the controversy in Hindu theism. Chapter 1 will bring out the strengths and weaknesses of these arguments. Its primary purpose, though, is to provide the reader with examples of historically important instances of religious reasoning to which she or he can refer in later chapters.

In order for the arguments discussed in Chapter 1 to be good ones, it is not enough that they be valid, noncircular, and have true premises. For as George Mavrodes pointed out, proofs are "person-relative" – a valid, noncircular argument with true premises can prove something to Mary without proving it to John.[3] To take a trivial example, if Mary knows that all the premises of a valid, noncircular argument are true and John does not, the argument can extend Mary's knowledge without extending John's. The proof's relativity in this case depends on the fact that Mary knows something that John does not. Other sources of person-relativity are less obvious, however. Arguments are constructed for various purposes, for example, and these have a bearing on their success. The medieval Hindu theist Udayana, for instance, maintained that his arguments had three aims: to convince unbelievers, to strengthen the faithful, and to honor God by presenting them at his "lotus feet." Chapter 2 explores these and other uses to which religious arguments can be put, and the bearing that the purposes underlying the construction of religious arguments should have on our overall assessment of their success and failure.

Chapters 3 and 4 examine two further sources of person-relativity. Both have a major impact on the character of religious reasoning.

Chapter 3 examines a topic that has been almost totally neglected by analytic philosophers of religion. Paul J. Griffiths and Francis X. Clooney have recently called our attention to the crucial role that the ingestion of central texts plays in classical Buddhism, Christianity, and Vaishnavism. Proper reasoning in these text-centered traditions presupposes that one has so thoroughly absorbed and existentially appropriated the relevant texts that they have become part of one's very being as an intellectual and volitional creature. Moreover, textual traditions affect what their participants regard as good reasons. Because these traditions vary, however, so too does what are regarded as good reasons. The variation of textual traditions thus provides one more source of person-relativity.

Chapter 4 discusses yet another source of person-relativity. The standard view in the West since the rise of modernity in the sixteenth and seventeenth centuries is that reason functions properly only when one brackets what Pascal called our "heart" and William James referred to as our "passional nature" – our temperament, needs, concerns, fears, hopes, passions, and emotions. "Right reason," according to this view, is disinterested reason. Chapter 4 calls this into question. Traditional Christian theology, for example, maintained that in ethical and religious matters, at least, proper reasoning is a function of the state of one's heart as well as of one's logical acumen, and that a valid, noncircular argument about religious matters with true premises can therefore quite properly convince one person without convincing another. Nor is this position peculiarly Christian. Similar views were expressed by Plato and Aristotle and by Chinese Neo-Confucians. Chapter 4 concludes by arguing that appeals to the heart needn't be either unduly subjective or viciously circular.

Chapter 5 reexamines the fraught relations between philosophy and rhetoric. That philosophy should be sharply distinguished from rhetoric has been a commonplace of Western philosophy since Plato. Locke, for example, said that the devices of rhetoric "are for nothing else but to insinuate wrong ideas, move the passions, and thereby mislead the judgment; and indeed are perfect cheats: and therefore … are certainly, in all discourses that pretend to inform or instruct, wholly to be avoided."[4] Locke's judgment is typical. Yet if the views expressed in Chapter 4 are correct, philosophy and rhetoric can't be so neatly separated, and I will argue that a properly chastened rhetoric can and should play an essential role in philosophical reasoning about religion and other value laden matters.

The features discussed in Chapters 4 and 5 are not peculiar to religious rea-soning because they also characterize reasoning about ethics, aesthetics, com-prehensive world views, and other value-laden subject matters. The legitimacy of the textually informed reasoning discussed in Chapter 3, however, depends on the *authority* of religious texts, that is, on revelation, and reason's relation to revelation is discussed in Chapter 6.

Chapter 6 begins with a comparison of Vedanta's and Christianity's accounts of the relation between reason and revelation and continues with an examination of the attacks on revelation mounted by seventeenth- and eighteenth-century deists. The chapter concludes with a detailed case study of the apparently conflicting views of the place of reason provided by seventeenth-century Anglo-American Puritans, on the one hand, and the Cambridge Platonists, on the other. I shall argue that their views on the comparative worth of reason and revelation are not as starkly opposed as might at first seem, and that this is typical of the Christian tradition in general.

Chapter 7 concludes the book by examining Dionysius the Areopagite's and John Chrysostom's claim that reason breaks down when confronted with the overwhelming mystery of God. I shall argue that – unlike the superficially similar claims made by adherents of the Madyamika school of Buddhism, for example – these Christian mystical theologians are not so much rejecting rea-son as (like Plato in the *Republic*) arguing for its absorption in or transcendence by something higher, namely, a kind of "knowing by unknowing." A sense of mystery may chasten reason. It doesn't repudiate it.

I

Four Examples of Religious Reasoning

This chapter examines an influential proof of God's existence, attempts to defend the coherence of the concept of omnipotence, arguments for and against the personhood of ultimate reality, and competing accounts of the relative importance of grace and free will. While this chapter will bring out the strengths and weaknesses of the arguments it examines, its primary purpose is to provide the reader with historically important instances of religious reasoning which he or she can refer to when reading later chapters.

I. Samuel Clarke's Cosmological Argument for the Existence of God

Proceeding from the assumption that anything that exists must have a sufficient reason for its existence, Samuel Clarke (1675–1729) argued that the existence of contingent beings[1] can only be explained by postulating the existence of a self-existent being, that is, a being that is both essentially causeless[2] and self-explanatory or intrinsically intelligible (although not necessarily intelligible to us).[3] If a being is self-existent, however, it is also logically necessary.[4]

We can formulate Clarke's argument as follows:

1. If something exists, it is either self-existent (and hence self-explanatory) or some other being causes it to exist.
2. A contingent being isn't self-existent. Therefore,
3. A contingent being is caused to exist by some other being. (From 1 and 2.)
   Contingent beings are usually caused by other contingent beings. Samuel Clarke's existence, for example, was caused by his parents, their existence was caused by their parents, and so on. Yet what about contingent beings as a whole?
4. Either the series of contingent beings has a first member (a contingent being that isn't caused by another contingent being) or it doesn't (the series is beginningless).

5. If the series has a first member, then a self-existent being exists and causes it. (From 3. Since the first member is *contingent*, another being causes it. By hypothesis, the first member isn't caused by a contingent being. Hence, it is caused by a self-existent being.)

6. If the series of contingent beings doesn't have a first member (and is therefore beginningless), a self-existent being exists and causes the whole series. (From 3. Since the existence of the series is contingent, another being causes it.

    Since the cause of the series of contingent beings isn't part of the series, it isn't itself contingent.)

7. If contingent beings exist, a self-existent being exists and causes them. (From 4, 5, and 6.)

8. Contingent beings exist. Hence,

9. A self-existent being exists and causes contingent beings to exist. (From 7 and 8.)

The argument's most controversial features are the inference from 3 to 6 and its first premise. Why does a beginningless series of contingent beings need a cause for its existence to be intelligible? And why assume that the existence of everything *is* intelligible – that there *is* a reason for its existence? We will discuss these questions in turn.

Many of the cosmological argument's critics believe that its inference from step 3 to step 6 is unsound. Even if every contingent being *is* caused by some other being, it doesn't follow that the *series* of contingent beings is.[5] The series might be beginningless with each member being caused by a preceding member. If it were, each member would be explained (by a preceding member), and so the series as a whole would be accounted for. No further explanation would be required. Thus, a beginningless series of contingent beings may not need an explanation. We therefore can't infer that it has a cause.

This common objection misses the point. The question is not, "Why does this or that member of the series exist, that is, why does member *n* exist, or why does member *n*-3 exist?" and so on for any arbitrarily selected member of the series. Rather, the question is, "Why does *any* member of the series exist – that is, why is there a series *at all*?" The first question can be answered by pointing out that each member is caused by a preceding member. For example, *n* exists because *n*-1 exists, and *n*-3 exists because *n*-4 exists. The second question can't. Since the causes cited in answer to the first question (e.g., *n*-1 or *n*-4) are *members* of the series, they are *part* of what we are trying to explain.

If the series doesn't have an external cause, it is an inexplicable brute fact – something that might not have existed but (for no reason) just happens to do so. Consider an analogy. That Jacob and Rachel begat Joseph satisfactorily explains Joseph's existence. That Isaac and Rebekah begat Jacob satisfactorily explains Jacob's existence. But if what puzzles us isn't Joseph's existence or Jacob's existence but human existence in general, these explanations aren't helpful. Even if we were to learn that every human being is begotten by other human beings and that the series of human beings is beginningless, our question wouldn't have been answered. For we still wouldn't know why there are human beings in the first place. Similarly, if what puzzles us is that any contingent beings exist, we aren't helped by learning that one contingent being is caused by another, that by a third, and so on.[6]

In short, the existence of the series of contingent beings is puzzling whether the series is beginningless or not. If it isn't caused by a noncontingent being, it has no explanation. In effect, step 3 asserts that contingent existence does have an explanation. Step 3 thus implies step 6. Even if there are an infinite number of contingent beings and each of these is caused by another contingent being, a self-existent being is the only thing that can explain the existence of contingent entities.

Samuel Clark's argument's most problematic feature, however, is its first premise. Why would we think that something's existence is either self-explanatory or explained by the activity of another being? Many seventeeth- and eighteenth-century philosophers thought this followed from the "principle of sufficient reason." The principle was often stated like this:

> PSR1: For every contingent fact F, some other fact F' obtains such that, given F', F must obtain.

PSR1 implies that facts are either necessary or fully determined by other facts.

While both Gottfried Leibniz and Jonathan Edwards endorsed PSR1, it should be unacceptable to any theist who believes that the existence of our world is contingent since God freely created it when he could have created another world instead of it or no world at all. If PSR1 is true, God's decision is fully determined by other facts – either facts about his nature or facts about other things. Neither alternative would be acceptable to these theists. If God's decision is fully determined by his nature, other choices aren't possible. God has to make that decision. If he does, his choice isn't free. If God's decision is fully determined by other things, his sovereignty and independence are compromised as well as his freedom. Theists who believe that God could have created a different world or no world at all must therefore insist that at least one contingent fact doesn't have a sufficient reason – namely, the fact that God freely decided to create our world.

However, theists who believe that God was free not to create or to create some other world *can* accept weaker versions of the principle of sufficient reason. We can weaken the principle by narrowing its scope – restricting it to certain *kinds* of contingent facts. We can also weaken it by qualifying the demand for a *sufficient* reason – a set of facts that *fully* determines what we are trying to explain.

For example, we can restrict the principle's scope to the existence of contingent entities:

> PSR2: There is a sufficient reason for the existence of every contingent entity.

PSR2 (which appears to be the version Clarke is using) does not entail that there is a sufficient reason for all of an entity's "accidental" properties (properties that it might or might not have). It therefore doesn't entail that there is a sufficient reason for an entity's freely deciding to do something.

One can also restrict the scope of the principle to contingent facts that don't *require* sufficient reasons:

> PSR3: Every contingent fact that requires a sufficient reason has one.

A contingent fact requires a sufficient reason if and only if (1) it is logically possible that it has a sufficient reason, and (2) it is unintelligible if it doesn't have one. All contingent facts satisfy the first condition. Some may not satisfy the second.

Suppose, for example, that a fair die turns up six. It is logically possible that the die's turning up six has a set of causally sufficient conditions. A request for a specification of the (sufficient) reason for its doing so is therefore logically appropriate. But it is *not* clear that the event's occurrence is unintelligible except upon the supposition that there are sufficient conditions for its occurrence since its occurrence doesn't run counter to the laws of probability.

Or consider a case in which I have good strategic reasons for moving my pawn to king's 4 and freely decide to do so. If my decision is contra-causally free, it isn't fully determined by its causal antecedents. But even though my decision wasn't in fact determined by its causal antecedents, it is logically possible that it was. The first condition is therefore satisfied. The second is not. My decision is intelligible because it expresses intelligible reasons and motives. (The move is strategically sound and I want to win the game.) Nevertheless, because these reasons and motives don't *determine* my decision, my decision doesn't have a sufficient reason.

One can also weaken the principle by dropping the demand that contingent facts must have sufficient reasons. Charles Hartshorne thinks that whether or not everything has a sufficient reason, nothing is "through and through pure chance." Reason discounts the possibility of something whose "inexplicability … would be infinite and total." "Mere chance, as an entire account of a being's existence," isn't admissible.[7] Hartshorne's remarks suggest the following principle:

> PSR4: There is at least *some* reason for every contingent fact.

While some contingent facts may lack causally sufficient conditions, PSR4 implies that they at least have necessary conditions that partly explain them.

Each of the weaker principles is compatible with God's freedom. PSR2 and PSR3 don't apply to contra-causally free decisions. PSR4 does, but doesn't imply that they are fully determined by other facts.

The weaker principles are also strong enough to generate the conclusion that contingent being is caused by a self-existent being. The existence of contingent beings seems to require an explanation. Hence, PSR3 as well as PSR2 imply that contingent being has an explanation. If our earlier discussion was sound, a self-existent being is the only thing that can provide this explanation.

PSR4 is also sufficient to yield the conclusion. If *all* beings are contingent, there is *no* reason for the existence of contingent beings in general. That contingent beings exist is thus "through and through pure chance." Since that violates PSR4, a self-existent being must be at least partly responsible for the existence of contingent beings.

Yet are any of these principles true? The question isn't easily answered – partly because philosophers disagree about their nature. Some think that the principles are empirical generalizations. Others think that one or more of them are presuppositions of rational inquiry. Still others believe that they express necessary truths.[8]

According to the first view, the principle of sufficient reason is an induction from human experience.[9] Impressed with our success in discovering causal explanations, we infer that everything has a cause or explanation. It isn't easy to determine whether this induction is justified. Science has been extraordinarily successful in discovering causes. On the other hand, some phenomena continue to resist explanation. Human behavior is an example. Then, too, because the universe is so vast, our "sample" (the cases in which we have discovered explanations) may simply be too small to justify the sweeping conclusion that *everything* has an explanation. Finally, our sample is restricted to cases in which one spatiotemporal phenomenon is explained by another. It thus provides at best weak support for the claim that contingent reality *as a whole* has an explanation.

Even so, the principle of sufficient reason receives some support from the success of human inquiry, although it should be noted that weaker versions are better supported than stronger ones. For example, there are more cases in which we have discovered *some* reason for contingent facts (necessary conditions, partial causes, and so on) than cases in which we have discovered *sufficient* reasons for them. Hence PSR4 is better confirmed than PSR1 or PSR3.

Other philosophers believe that the principle of sufficient reason is a presupposition of inquiry. For example, W. Norris Clarke argued that (when understood as the claim that being is intelligible) the principle is not merely an expression of the Greeks' "youthful enthusiasm" for reason or of "a belief in a God who was the Logos," but of "an innate drive towards total intelligibility," "an unrestricted desire to know."[10]

This position raises two questions. Is such a drive real? And, if it is, should we trust it?

If Clarke's remarks are treated as straightforward empirical claims, they would appear to be refuted by my grandson's attitude toward algebra. But Clarke's claim is most usefully compared with the claim that we all desire beatitude or moral perfection. The point of the latter is that whether or not we consciously desire beatitude or moral perfection, they are in fact the only things that would truly satisfy or perfect us. Similarly, Clarke's claim is best understood as the claim that "total intelligibility" is the only thing that would truly satisfy our desire to know, even though, in practice, we may content ourselves with less or fail to realize that "total intelligibility" alone would fully satisfy us. The plausibility of this claim partly depends upon whether one is employing stronger or weaker versions of the principle of sufficient reason. Contemporary science offers explanations that aren't deterministic. For example, theories about subatomic particles allow for random events that lack sufficient reasons (causes that fully determine the phenomena under investigation). It seems, then, that reason can be satisfied by accounts that violate PSR1. If so, PSR1 doesn't express a demand of reason. On the other hand, reason presumably *would* be dissatisfied with an account that entailed that quantum phenomena or some other contingent fact had *no* explanation (not even a partial one) and thus violated PSR4.

But should we assume that the demands of reason can be met? Perhaps it is reasonable to trust our mental faculties and endorse their demands in the absence of good reasons for distrusting them. Hence, if some form of the principle of sufficient reason *does* express a demand of the human mind, and if there are no good reasons for thinking it false, it may be reasonable to rely on it.[11]

Samuel Clarke as well as Leibniz thought that the principle of reason is a necessary truth rather than an empirical generalization or a demand of reason. Is this plausible?

David Hume thought not. If a principle is necessarily true, its denial entails a logically impossible proposition. Hume pointed out that the denial of Clarke's version of the principle (PSR2) – "Something exists contingently and has no cause" – isn't self-contradictory. He concluded that it isn't necessarily true.

This inference is illegitimate. Formal contradictions aren't the only kind of logical impossibility. "Something is red and green all over," and, "There is not even a prima facie reason to refrain from torturing children," are not self-contradictory. Even so, they are arguably false in all possible worlds.

Others claim that they can't see the necessity of the principle, but this too is inconclusive. Propositions can be necessary that not everyone sees to be necessary. (Many theists believe that "God exists" is a proposition of this kind. True but complicated mathematical theorems or the claim that there is no set of all sets are other examples.) Still, people's intuitions concerning the necessity of the principle conflict, although weaker versions are more likely to seem necessary than stronger ones. Many, for example, undoubtedly do not see the necessity of (say) PSR4. Even so, it isn't clear that it intuitively seems to them that PSR4 *isn't* necessary (they may have no clear intuitions either way), and a failure to see PSR4's necessity doesn't carry much weight. (A claim to intuit its *non*-necessity would carry more weight, though it, too, would be inconclusive.)

The cosmological argument, then, isn't clearly unsound. Yet as it stands, it doesn't clearly establish *God's* existence – that the self-existent cause of contingent being is a maximally perfect personal agent. How could one show this?

While the causal activity of a self-existent and therefore necessarily existing being may be the only thing that can adequately explain the existence of contingent beings, its *activity* (as distinguished from its existence) must be contingent. For suppose that it is not – that the ground of contingent being necessary exists and (for example) necessarily causes me to exist. Necessary effects of necessary causes are themselves necessary. Hence *I* necessarily exist. But this is absurd. The cause of my existence must therefore act contingently.

In short, if its effect is contingent, the self-existent being's causal act isn't necessitated by its nature or anything else. It thus lacks a sufficient reason. Now one of the more plausible versions of the principle of sufficient reason is PSR3. PSR3 implies that a contingent fact that lacks a sufficient reason doesn't require one. Hence, if RSR3 is true, the self-existent being's causal activity doesn't require a sufficient reason. One of the most plausible candidates for activities that don't require sufficient reasons are free decisions. Hence, if PSR3 is true, the self-existent being's causal act is probably a free decision. If it is, the self-existent being is a personal agent.

Is the personal agent God? Some philosophers think that a self-existent being is necessarily unlimited and hence maximally perfect. If they are right, then the creator established by cosmological argument is maximally perfect as well as personal. If it is, then the self-existent cause of contingent being is God.

II. Is the Concept of Omnipotence Coherent?

God's attributes as well as his existence are also the subject of debate. Consider omnipotence, for example. Few theists think that God can perform logically impossible tasks.[12] A state of affairs such as $2 + 2$'s equaling 5 is logically impossible. Hence *no* one can bring it about. Again, while necessary states of affairs such as $2 + 2$ equaling 4 *are* logically possible, they aren't "producible," that is, can't have causes. Thus *no* agent can produce them.[13] There are also states of affairs that are logically possible and producible but can't be produced *by God*. For example, the state of affairs consisting of my freely choosing to spend the evening reading Roberto Bolano can't be brought about by someone other than myself. (If it were brought about by someone else, then either the action wouldn't really be *my* action or it wouldn't be *free*.) Since the state of affairs consisting of my freely reading Roberto Bolano can't be brought about by someone other than me, it can't be brought about by God.

Thus, omnipotence only includes the power to perform logically possible tasks. This isn't a real limitation, however. Since the tasks in question (bringing about a logically impossible state of affairs, producing an unproducible state of affairs, bringing about another person's free action) can't be performed by *any* possible being, no possible being could surpass God with respect to power by possessing the ability to perform them. These tasks, then, aren't included within the scope of maximally perfect power.

God's *perfection* may also make certain things impossible for him. For example, any being that can appropriately be called omnipotent has the power to create and lift stones of any weight, size, texture, and so on. But if it possesses this power, it can't create stones it is unable to lift. Nevertheless, because its "inability" to create stones that it can't lift is simply a consequence of its *unlimited* power to make and lift stones, it doesn't seem to be a real incapacity.

Furthermore, a maximally perfect being can't have powers whose possession or exercise entails limitation or weakness. Thus God can't destroy himself or divest himself of his knowledge or power. Why not? A maximally perfect being is eternally wise and powerful. It also possesses these properties essentially. *P* is an essential property of something if and only if there are no possible worlds in which it exists and lacks *P*. Suppose, then, that a maximally perfect being could destroy itself or divest itself of its knowledge or power. If it could, then there would be possible worlds in which it does so, in which case it wouldn't be eternally wise and powerful in those worlds. But as we just saw, a maximally perfect being is eternally wise and powerful in *every* world in which it exists. Hence, it can neither destroy itself nor make itself ignorant or weak.

A maximally perfect being's powers may also be *voluntarily* limited. If God creates contra-causally free agents, then what he can do will be limited by their free choices. The fact that the limitation is voluntary doesn't imply that it isn't real. As Jonathan Edwards pointed out, on the view in question, God appears to be subject to a kind of "fate" or "necessity" (namely, the character of the decisions humans freely make) over which he has relinquished control and to which he must therefore submit. But if so, then God isn't fully in charge of things. History is the product of innumerable decisions, only some of which are God's. Sovereignty and power are shared among innumerable agents and, as a consequence, God's own sovereignty and power are limited. This seems objectionable for two reasons. It appears incompatible with traditional understandings of God's omnipotence and sovereignty. It may also undermine the theist's confidence in God's ultimate triumph over evil.

The first objection isn't conclusive. The concepts of divine omnipotence and divine sovereignty are "open textured." While there is rough agreement concerning what is and is not included within the scope of God's power and sovereignty, that agreement is by no means complete. No definitions of these concepts are universally accepted. Given the open texture of the relevant concepts, it isn't enough to show that the constraints imposed by human freedom are incompatible with omnipotence and sovereignty as defined by some philosophers or theologians, for their definitions can be challenged. For example, the constraints are clearly incompatible with divine omnipotence if an omnipotent being is defined as a being that can bring about any logically possible state of affairs. For while it is logically possible that James Madison freely signs the Declaration of Independence, for instance, God cannot bring about that state of affairs. What is less clear is that the traditional notion of God's omnipotence should be articulated in those terms. The idea that God's options are somehow limited by human freedom is as old as the notion that he is sovereign and all-powerful. There is thus a presumption that God's power and sovereignty have usually been understood in a way that accommodates human freedom. There is a presumption, in other words, that the sort of constraint imposed by human freedom has been built into the theist's conceptions of divine power and sovereignty from the beginning. If it has, a consideration of the constraints imposed by human freedom will simply lead to fuller understanding of the traditional concepts rather than to their modification or abandonment.

The second objection is stronger. Unless God is fully in control of events, we have no guarantee that good will triumph over evil. We can perhaps be assured that a maximally perfect being wouldn't have created our world if he hadn't foreseen that the good it contains would, on balance, outweigh its evil. But that is compatible with the possibility that the same ambiguous mixture of joy and sorrow, righteousness and unrighteousness, that has characterized our world's history up to the present will continue until the end of time.

William James argued that the second objection underestimates the extent of God's power and the importance of his decisions. God may be compared to a chess master who is playing against a novice. The chess master can't control the moves of his opponent. Furthermore, it is abstractly possible that the novice will defeat her. (Perhaps by sheer luck the novice will make some extraordinarily good moves.) Nevertheless, given the chess master's experience and skill, we are morally certain that the novice will lose. Similarly, the limitations imposed by human freedom preclude any absolute guarantee of God's ultimate triumph over evil. But given God's enormous power and wisdom and the limitations of creatures, they don't preclude a rational confidence in God's ultimate victory.[14]

James's response implicitly concedes that reason alone can't establish the claim that good will prevail over evil. The belief in God's ultimate victory is based on revelation, not philosophical argumentation. Thus Peter Geach contends that being almighty should be distinguished from being omnipotent. The first implies that God has "power *over* all things," the second that God has the "ability to *do* all things." That God has the power to do all things isn't clearly coherent.[15] That God has power over all things, however, "must be ascribed to God if we are to retain anything like traditional Christian belief in God." What does this involve? "God is not just more powerful than any creature; no creature can compete with God in power, even unsuccessfully. For God is also the source of all power; any power a creature has comes from God and is maintained only for such time as God wills.... Nobody can deceive God or circumvent God or frustrate him, and there is no question of God trying to do anything and failing." The belief that God is almighty in this sense is essential to Christianity because "Christianity requires an absolute faith in the promises of God: specifically faith in the promise that some day the whole human race will be delivered and blessed by the establishment of the Kingdom of God. If God were not almighty, he might will and not do: sincerely promise but find fulfillment beyond his power."[16]

Can a maximally perfect being sin? The answer to this question is especially controversial. At first glance, it would seem that it could not, since moral goodness would appear to be one of a maximally perfect being's essential properties. Nelson Pike has argued that this has an unacceptable implication, however.[17]

Suppose it is morally wrong for God to bring about a particular state of affairs. Suppose, for example, that *s* is a massive flood that causes immense suffering and that God has no morally sufficient reason for producing or permitting it. If God is essentially good, he can't bring *s* about. But an omnipotent being surely has the power to bring about *any* sort of natural disaster, including *s*. (Though if it is good, it won't do so.) If God is essentially good, then, he isn't omnipotent.

Pike concludes that while God *is* good, he isn't *essentially* good. Hence, while God is good in our world, there are logically possible worlds in which he isn't. Suppose that N is the name of the being who is God in the actual world. It is necessarily true that *if* N is God, he doesn't sin. (No sinful being could be called "God.") But it is *not* necessarily true that N *is God* or that N is sinless. N doesn't sin but he could sin if he wished to. There are therefore possible worlds in which N acts badly (although because he does so, he isn't God in those worlds). Since God isn't good in every possible world in which he exists, his goodness isn't essential.

Nevertheless, we may be able to rely on N's goodness. While it is logically possible that N sins, his nature or character may provide "material assurance" that he won't. It would provide that assurance if N's choices aren't constrained by ignorance or by non-rational factors such as sensual desires or nervous impulses. For if they aren't, N has no motive or reason for acting wrongly, and we can therefore rest assured that he won't.[18]

Should classical theists accept Pike's recommendation and abandon their belief in God's essential goodness? Probably not. According to Pike, N sins (and thus isn't God) in some possible worlds although he doesn't sin (and is God) in the actual world. But a being that isn't divine and even sins in some logically possible worlds in which it exists doesn't seem as great or excellent as a being that is divine and sinless in every possible world in which it exists. Hence, if Pike is right N isn't maximally perfect. But in that case, N isn't God.

It thus seems that a maximally perfect being must be essentially good. If it is, it can't bring about *s* even though beings that aren't essentially good may be able to do so. God's power is thus limited by his goodness. But a limitation of this sort may not be as significant as it appears. While God can't bring floods about when doing so would be morally wrong, he can bring about flooding of any magnitude when doing so would be morally permissible. God's inability to bring *s* about thus isn't a consequence of a deficiency in his flood-producing powers but, rather, of his own inherent goodness. Hence, the limitation in question doesn't seem to involve real weakness.

Another difficulty is potentially more damaging, however. Freedom is a necessary condition of moral agency. It would therefore seem that if God is a moral agent (as theists believe), he must be able to sin even if (being God) we can be assured that he will not. God's inability to sin thus seems incompatible with his moral agency.

One's response to this problem may depend upon whether one is a "compatibilist" or "incompatibilist." Compatibilists believe that determinism is consistent with freedom. Incompatibilists do not. Although compatibilists and incompatibilists agree that an action is free only if the agent who performed it could have refrained from doing so, they interpret this condition in very different ways. The compatibilist thinks that in order for this condition to be met, it need only be true that *if* the agent had chosen to refrain from performing the action, he or she would have done so. Suppose, for example, that someone deliberately fails to rescue a drowning child. His failure to rescue her is free provided that if he had chosen to rescue her, he would have done do. And this conditional is true if he knew how to swim, was not too far from her, and so on. The fact that his decision not to rescue the child was causally determined is irrelevant, for even though his decision was causally necessary, it is nonetheless true that if he *had* chosen to rescue her, he would have done so. It is thus true that he *could* have rescued her. His failure to rescue her was therefore free. The incompatibilist, on the other hand, argues that unless the agent's choice was contra-causally free (that is, underdetermined by its causal antecedents), there was no *genuine* alternative to the agent's action. The agent could not *really* have refrained from choosing as he did, and so his action wasn't free.

Compatibilists, in short, argue that it is the nature or character of its causes that determine whether an act is free. Such things as duress, lack of opportunity or ability, psychological disorders, and so on are incompatible with an agent's freedom. But other causes (a normal genetic makeup, for example, or a good home environment) are not.

Incompatibilists, on the other hand, argue that the issue is not so much the *nature* of the causes at work as whether those causes *determine* the choices that an agent makes. The intuition behind their claim is that if an agent's choices aren't contra-causally free but are ultimately necessitated by factors over which the agent has no control (the past history of the universe, for example, or God's eternal decrees), then the agent's choices aren't really under its control. If they aren't then the agent isn't genuinely responsible for them.

Jonathan Edwards believed that three conditions are necessary and sufficient for moral agency. A moral agent must (1) be a rational being who perceives "the difference between moral good and evil." The agent must also (2) have "a capacity of choice ... and a power of acting according to his choice," and (3) be capable "of being influenced in his actions by moral inducements or motives."[19] God clearly satisfies the first and third conditions. His moral knowledge is perfect and his behavior is guided by moral considerations. It is because God, who is by nature good, sees that it would be morally wrong or unfitting to do certain things that he does not, and indeed cannot, do them. Yet does he satisfy the second condition? That is, does God have "a capacity of choice and a power of acting according to his choice"? Compatibilists such as Edwards believe that this condition is met because God's actions are expressions of his reflective inclinations.

Incompatibilists think that freedom is incompatible with *any* kind of necessitation and that more is therefore required – that if God had a real capacity for choosing good over evil, it must be possible for him to have chosen evil. Yet if it is, he isn't essentially good.

But the sort of necessitation involved in God's case shouldn't be confused with another. Classical theists believe that the sources of God's actions lie in his own nature. God is genuinely independent, neither determined nor causally affected by other powers. His activity is therefore fully autonomous. If, on the other hand, the choices of human agents are causally necessary consequences of conditions that ultimately extend beyond their control, human agents aren't genuinely independent and their activities are not autonomous. The two sorts of necessity are thus significantly different. Consequently, even if the second sort of necessity is incompatible with a capacity for free moral choice, it doesn't follow that the first is. Classical theism may entail that moral freedom is compatible with some sorts of necessitation (and, in particular, with the necessity of God's choices being determined by his essential goodness). It does not entail that *causal* necessitation is compatible with *human* freedom.[20]

III. Is Ultimate Reality Personal?

Paul J. Griffiths has argued that "if there are any transcultural universals in the sphere of religious thinking, it is probable that ... the attempt to characterize, delineate, and, if possible, ... exhaustively define maximal greatness" is "among them."[21] But as Griffiths is well aware, attempts to do so vary significantly from one tradition to another.

Medieval Christians, for example, distinguished pure perfections from mixed perfections and imperfections. Imperfections included limitations such as a normal human being's inability to lift one thousand pound weights as well as defects such as blindness or unrighteousness. Mixed perfections were good-making qualities that entailed an imperfection or defect – repentance, for example, which presupposes a sin of which one repents, or the ability to ride a bicycle, which involves corporeality with its attendant limitations. Pure perfections, on the other hand, are good-making properties that entail no defect or limitation. Traditional examples were being or actuality, unity, independence, goodness, power, creative activity, love, and knowledge. But the last three at least imply that a maximally perfect being, while transcending all finite realities, would be more like a person than anything else. They believe, in other words, that a maximally perfect being should be understood as God – an infinitely wise, good, powerful source and ruler of all that is.

Theistic Hindus make similar claims. One of the most interesting examples is Vishishtadvaita Vedanta, which, in many ways, resembles classical Western theism. God is "the sum of all noble attributes." "He, the supreme one, is unique, transcending in character every other entity because his nature is opposed to all evil and is of the sole nature of supreme bliss. He is the abode of countless auspicious attributes unsurpassed in their perfection." He is omnipotent, omniscient, and all-loving. "His grandeur is inconceivable."[22] Salvation is a consequence of his grace, and consists in an eternal loving union with God himself.

Some high religious traditions are nontheistic, however. Theravada Buddhism[23] and Advaita Vedanta, for example, believe that the maximally perfect reality is nonpersonal. They don't think of it as God.

Theravada Buddhists believe that a person is nothing more than a collection of interrelated experiences and body states called "dharmas." The dharmas are causally conditioned and transient. (They last for at most a few moments.) Consciousness is as conditioned and impermanent as the other dharmas. There is no self or permanent substance underlying these states.

The no-self (*anatman*) doctrine may appear to conflict with the karma doctrine common to all Indian schools, including Buddhism. According to the law of karma, a person's present situation is the causal result of her deeds in her past lives, and her present deeds determine her situation in her future lives. And this seems to presuppose the persistence of the self – that one and the same self persists through a set of past, present, and future lives. How, then, is personal identity or the apparent persistence of the self understood? In three related ways. First, the persistence of the self is identical with the persistence of a series of mental and physical states. To say that a person, B, is a reincarnation of person A is to say that the series of states making up the life of B is a continuation of the series of states which made up the life of A. A and B are, so to speak, earlier and later segments of one and the same causal series. Second, there is a continuity of character (temperament, desire, tastes, outlook, and the like). Adjacent lives resemble each other (as do earlier and later stages in a single life). Finally, it is believed that B can, in principle, remember what A did and experienced.

Just as a chariot is nothing over and above its parts (axel, wheels, frame, etc.) put together in a certain way, so the self is nothing over and above the psychological and bodily dharmas that constitute it. Since there is no permanent self, the maximally perfect reality can't be one. Nor can it be a self in the attenuated sense in which the series of transient and causally conditioned states that constitute my life is a self. For the realm of the transient and causally conditioned (*samsara*) is the realm of suffering or unsatisfactoriness (*duhkha*). One cannot therefore construe a maximally perfect reality as a person. To do so would imply that it was impermanent, causally conditioned, and unhappy.

Yet why would one think that the no-self doctrine is true? Buddhists often argue that there would be a reason for believing in the reality of the self only if the self was perceived, and it is not. When we turn our attention inward and introspect, all we find are particular perceptions, sensations, thoughts, momentary volitional states, and the like. We find nothing, in other words, but the dharmas. Neither ordinary introspection nor the kind of self-knowledge involved in advanced stages of meditation reveal anything over and above the dharmas that could be appropriately called a self or soul or "transcendental ego."[24] So why do we persist in believing in the reality of a permanent self? Because doing so is an expression of our will to live and of our self-assertion and self-attachment.

In the last analysis, the truth of the no-self doctrine can be grasped only in meditation from which we come to *see* that the self is nothing but a flow of dharmas. The *point* of the doctrine (or of an existential appropriation of it) is to break one's attachment to the self, thereby escaping *samsara* and attaining nirvana.

What is nirvana? The term's primary original meaning was the blowing out of a fire, and from that secondary meanings developed, namely, cooling or the dying down of a fever, and ultimately a state of health or well-being.[25] How, though, do Theravadins use the term? It is sometimes characterized as the cessation of the process of becoming (*bhava*) or, more fundamentally, as the extinction of the "thirst" (desire) and illusion that underlie the process.

Positive terms are sometimes applied to it. It is called, for example, auspicious, good, safety, purity, peace, tranquility, protection, the other side or opposite shore (of *samsara*), the island (in the ocean of *samsara*), or the refuge.[26] (Note that these terms don't tell us what nirvana is *in itself* but only what it is *for us* who are bound to the wheel of *samara*.) More often, nirvana is described negatively. "There is, monks, that plane where there is neither extension nor … motion or the plane of infinite ether … nor that of neither-perception-nor-non-perception, neither this world nor another.… Here, monks, I say that there is no coming or going or remaining or deceasing or uprising, for this is itself without support, without mental object … this is … the end of suffering."[27] (Note that the only positive thing said of nirvana in this passage is that it is the end of woe.)

Nirvana is not a being or substance for, if it were, it would either be a dharma or constructed of them (like tables or rocks or persons) and would therefore be causally produced and impermanent. (Note that for this reason, modern interpretations of nirvana as a psychological state are mistaken. If nirvana were a psychological state, it would be a dharma and thus caused and fleeting, whereas nirvana is "without source [cause]" and is not of "short duration" but is, rather, "unaging and undying."[28])

What is it, then? It can't be identified with a psychological state or anything else in *samsara*.[29] Nor is it a transcendent substance or power or force such as God, or the Brahman, or the Tao. Trevor Ling thinks it is best thought of as a kind of transcendent condition or state,[30] although apparently not as a condition or state *of* anything. The fact that it is often compared with empty space (which is not, of course, an entity), that we can be said to enter into it, and the use of metaphors such as "the island" or "the opposite shore," suggest that it can also be thought of as a kind of transcendent place or realm. It does, then, have a genuine ontological reality; it isn't a mere fiction.[31]

The persuasiveness of Theravada's position depends, among other things, on the plausibility of its controversial analysis of personhood.[32] It also depends on its belief that ordinary personhood is unavoidably egocentric and self-seeking, and on the high value it places on experiencing the space-time world as "empty" – viewing the flow of dharmas without attempting to conceptualize it and without attachment to it. The position's persuasiveness, though, may ultimately depend upon whether or not one trusts the words of the Buddha – whether, that is, one believes that he has the words of life.

Advaita Vedanta's rejection of theism is a consequence of its emphasis on ultimate reality's unity and incomprehensibility. Advaita believes that Brahman (the first principle) is an absolute unity. "Brahman is without parts or attributes … one without a second. In Brahman there is no diversity whatever." "All difference in Brahman is unreal."[33]

The Brahman contains no plurality and transcends every distinction. It thus has no properties. Why is this the case? If the Brahman had properties, we could *distinguish* between the Brahman and its properties. This would be incompatible with its absolute unity. Moreover, because Brahman has no properties and we can understand things only by grasping their properties, it is incomprehensible. "It is the reality beyond all thought … outside the range of any mental conception."[34]

If ultimate reality transcends *all* properties, it transcends the property of being a person. Nevertheless, even if the Brahman isn't *literally* a person, it might be more like a person than anything else. So why does Advaita reject theism?

Persons are rational agents – beings who have beliefs about themselves and the world and who act on the basis of their beliefs. Believing and willing are essential to personhood. The major theistic traditions describe ultimate reality as an omniscient mind and an omnipotent and active will and thus as personal. Advaita Vedanta is nontheistic because its emphasis on the divine unity forces it to deny that the Brahman is either a knower or a causal agent.

Knowledge presupposes a distinction between the knower and what it knows. Even self-knowledge involves a distinction between the self as knower and the self as known. Advaita concludes that thought and knowledge are incompatible with Brahman's unity: "All specific cognition such as seeing, and so on is absent."[35]

Why can't the Brahman be a causal agent? If the Brahman is maximally perfect, it must be unlimited. It is limited, however, if something exists outside it. The Brahman must therefore be identical with the whole of reality. But if the Brahman is identical with the whole of reality and if the Brahman contains no plurality, then reality as a whole must be an undifferentiated unity. The

space-time world, with its distinctions among times, places, and events, is therefore unreal. Since a real causal relation is a relation between two real things,
the Brahman is not the cause of the space-time world or of the events in it.
The Brahman is therefore neither the world's creator nor its ruler. "The Lord's
being a Lord, his omniscience, his omnipotence, etc., all depend on … ignorance; while in reality none of these qualities belong to the Self [Brahman]….
In reality the relation of ruler and ruled [creator and created] does not exist."[36]
The Brahman is the "ground" of the world, but only in the sense that it is the
real thing on which people project the illusion of spatiotemporal reality. (This
is compared to the way in which a person who mistakes a rope for a snake
projects the illusory idea of the snake onto the rope.)

   Advaita does contain what might be called "theistic elements." For example, it
distinguishes the *nirguna* from the *saguna* Brahman. The former is the Brahman
without attributes. The latter is the Brahman with attributes, and is roughly
described the way theists describe God – as all knowing, all powerful, all good,
the sovereign lord of heaven and earth. The *nirguna* Brahman is the Brahman
as it really is, however, while the *saguna* Brahman is ultimately illusory.[37] The
concept of the *saguna* Brahman is a useful tool for those who are still on their
spiritual journey, but is finally cast aside by the fully enlightened. Yet even
though Advaita believes that (like all conceptualizations of the Brahman) the
idea of an omnipotent, omniscient, and all-good cause of the space-time world
is ultimately false, it does regard it as superior to other conceptions.[38] Moreover,
Advaita describes the real Brahman as an infinite, joyous consciousness (albeit
a consciousness that has no contents or objects and is thus "empty").[39] But
because Advaita refuses to ascribe either knowledge or activity to ultimate
reality, it remains essentially nontheistic. Its maximally perfect reality isn't the
God of the theistic traditions but, rather, an "infinite ocean of joyous empty
consciousness" – impersonal, inactive, and anonymous. The Brahman is "pure
consciousness and infinite bliss" – "beyond all attributes, beyond action."[40]

   Some schools of Vedanta are theistic, however, and their response to
Advaita is instructive. Vishishtadvaita Vedanta, for example, maintains that
the Brahman is not only personal but the *supreme* person (*paramatman*) – creator and lord (*ishvara*) who leads the world's creatures to salvation. Far from
being devoid of attributes, the Brahman (whom Vishishtadvaita identifies with
Vishnu) is the sum of all "noble" attributes, omniscient, omnipotent, omnipres-
ent, and all merciful.

   What accounts for the difference? In part, the suspicion is that the Advaitin
account of a maximally great reality is incoherent. Ramanuja (1017?–1137?),
for instance, argued that Advaita's conception of the Brahman is logically incoherent because it conceives of the Brahman as a substance without properties, whereas, by definition, a substance is what *has* or *underlies* properties.
Furthermore, because cognitively grasping something involves classifying or
identifying it as a thing of a certain kind, and things are classified or identified
on the basis of their properties, one can't cognitively grasp a thing without

properties. It follows that the Advaitin's Brahman can't be known, and that Advaita itself therefore doesn't know it. Finally, Ramanuja argued that the denial of the reality of distinctions undercuts Advaita's appeal to scripture. If the scriptures they acknowledge are valid, then some language accurately describes reality (for scriptural language does so). But language necessarily involves distinctions (between subject and verb, noun and adjective, and the like) and so, if any language accurately describes reality, some distinctions must be real. Therefore, if distinctions are *not* real (as Advaita maintains), the scriptures it appeals to aren't valid.

Advaitins aren't without recourse, of course. For example, they will deny that they are construing Brahman as a substance without properties. Since, in their view, *no* concept applies to the Brahman, neither the concept of a property *nor* the concept of substance applies to it. Again, even if *conceptual* cognition necessarily involves classification or identification, they will insist that not all cognition is conceptual. The fact that Brahman can't be conceptually cognized thus doesn't entail that it can't be known. Finally, Advaitins will concede that, in the final stage of enlightenment, even scripture, with its words and names, must be transcended.

The important point for our purposes is that the Vishishtadvaitin's and Advaitin's disagreements are rooted in fundamental differences in metaphysics and epistemology – whether a reality without properties is possible, for instance, and whether cognition must involve at least some conceptual content.

Other differences are even more fundamental. All the Vedantin schools profess to elucidate the true meaning of a common set of scriptures – the *Brahma* (or *Vedanta*) *Sutras*, the *Bhagavad Gita*, and, preeminently, the *Vedas* (especially their last part, namely, the *Upanishads*). In practice, though, both theistic and nontheistic Vedantins privilege some texts over others. Advaitins privilege the *Isha* and other nontheistic Upanishads, and interpret theistic-sounding texts in their light. Theistic Vedantins, on the other hand, privilege the *Bhagavad Gita* and theistic Upanishads such as the *Shvetashvatara Upanishad*, taking these texts pretty much at face value while explaining away apparent inconsistencies between their privileged texts and other scriptural texts that, on their face, seem clearly nontheistic.

These differences in turn are rooted in fundamental differences in spiritual practice. Advaitins, for example, emphasize ascetic practices designed to appropriate existentially the truth of the "great words" of scripture such as "Thou art that [you are the Brahman]," "All that is is one only," or, "All is one without distinction," and place a high value on "monistic" mystical experiences – joyous states of consciousness in which the mind is emptied of contents and distinctions disappear. While these experiences aren't the aim of the Advaitin's quest, they are more or less explicitly regarded as a model of the unifying and transfiguring Brahman-knowledge that is the goal of their religious journey. Theistic Vedantins such as Ramanuja, on the other hand, were Vaishnavas (devotees of Vishnu), and their attitudes, outlook, and actions were profoundly shaped by devotional practices designed to express and cultivate love of, and surrender to, Vishnu. While they did not deny the reality of monistic mystical consciousness, they downplayed its significance, for, in their view, the ultimate aim of the religious life is an ecstatic and permanent loving union with God (Vishnu).[41]

In short, while Advaitins and theistic Vedantins such as Ramanuja agree that the proper object of ultimate concern is maximally great, they disagree on just how maximal greatness should be construed. This disagreement is, in turn, rooted in metaphysical and epistemological disagreements, in differences in scriptural interpretation, and in differences in religious practice and aspiration. The most fundamental difference, however, is, arguably, a difference in evaluation. Theistic Hindus prize love in a way in which Advaitins do not. Since love is a relation between persons, it is not surprising that, in their view, maximal greatness includes personhood.[42]

IV. What Is the Relation between Grace and Free Will?

Our fourth example of religious reasoning is provided by disputes over the nature of grace and free will. The seminal dispute on this issue was between Pelagius and Augustine.

Pelagius clearly thought of himself as an orthodox theologian who had "no intention other than to think in and with the Catholic Church."[43] What was his position?

As rational beings, men and women have a capacity to acknowledge God and know themselves as his servants, to distinguish the morally good from the morally evil, and to recognize their obligation to pursue the former and reject the latter.[44] Moreover, men and women are able to choose autonomously. They are free either to act in accordance with the "law of nature" (the moral law) or refuse to do so. (They have, in Pelagius's phrase, "the capacity for either direction.") Because of their autonomy, men and women aren't bound by natural necessity as animals are, nor can they be forced to sin by the promptings of their own flesh.

This has an important consequence. Because men and women possess the capacity for either direction, it lies within their own power to be without sin. Their autonomy and capacity for sinlessness is a gift from God. Why, then, do they so often fail to exercise this capacity?

History, according to Pelagius, is divided into three periods: "the time of nature, extending from Adam to Moses; the time of the law, extending from Moses to Christ; and the time of grace inaugurated by Christ."[45]

Adam is the first sinner, and Pelagius doesn't hesitate "to agree with the words of the Apostle Paul that sin entered the world through … Adam."[46] But Adam's sin spread through imitation – the fact that people freely chose to follow Adam's example. Their sin was not the result of any kind of inherited corruption or guilt.[47]

During the first period, some succeeded in following the law of nature and living sinlessly. Among them were Abel, Noah, Melchizedek, Abraham, and Job. These were, as Pelagius said, "gospel men before the gospel," "disciples of the apostles." They were not warned by a revealed command as Adam was, but simply consulted their own nature, the law written on their hearts. They were exceptions in their own time, however, and men and women eventually became so corrupt that they lost the ability to effectively use their God-given power to avoid sin. Their corruption chiefly consisted in ignorance of their own nature (the law written on their hearts) and of their ability to act sinlessly.

The remedy was the law.[48] The Mosaic legislation was a file for removing the rust of ignorance from human nature. When it was removed, people were once again able to live sinlessly, and Pelagius thought that some did so. Two points should be noted: (1) Having received and accepted the law, the Jews were fully capable of fulfilling it, and if they had done so would have won eternal life. (In explaining Paul's claim that the law didn't justify those who were under it, Pelagius said that the reason it didn't was simply because most of those under it didn't keep it.) (2) The law was grace, an unearned gift of God by means of which human nature could be cleansed.

By the end of this period, however, humankind was once again thoroughly entrapped by sin. The power of sin was "the power of habit ... which builds itself up through successive acts of sinning," and is closely connected to example. Men and women "learn to sin by their existence from childhood alongside others who sin." As a consequence, "habit infects us from childhood and gradually corrupts us more and more through many years." (Pelagius goes so far as to say that habit holds the sinner "as if by a certain necessity of sinning," a "necessity" which the sinner "has prepared for himself," however.)[49] Sinful habit in turn produces ignorance, and because our reason is again clouded, we once more lose our understanding of our nature.

At this point, the law of Moses can no longer help us. While it can "stir the sense of guilt and make man aware that sin is sin," it is unable to make us see that the law of Moses is the law of our own nature.[50] We perceive it as strange, alien, and foreign to us, and so fail to recognize that, because it is the law of our own nature, action in accordance with it will fulfill us.

When the power of sin was strongest, however, Christ appeared and broke the bounds in which it held us. His redeeming work had three aspects.

The first was his redeeming death. Christ died "an undeserved death on behalf of men," enduring "the condemnation of death that is due to men because of their sin." He, "for whom there was no judgment of death, and no cause of enduring either the cross or curse [since he is without sin] submitted to the curse for us, because we were all guilty of death; as standing under a curse, we were deserving of the tree ourselves in that we did not abide by all the things which were written in the law."[51] Christians receive the benefit of Christ's redemptive death "as the forgiveness of sins in the sacrament of baptism." Past sins are forgiven. We are "freed of guilt and pronounced wholly righteous." (Pelagius can thus say that Christ makes us "righteous without our labor," or that he makes us "acceptable and pleasing" to himself.)[52]

But Christ is also the revealer. He reveals both the will of God (the law) and God's promises. Pelagius sees no antithesis between law and gospel. He speaks of Christ giving commandments and giving laws, asserts that grace is law, proclaims that the New Testament as a whole is law, and so on. The difference between the law of Moses and the gospel is simply that between a less perfect and a more perfect law. (The two are related as child to the adult which it will become or the seed to the fruit which develops from it.) Yet Christ not only reveals the law, he also reveals the "rewards and punishments which await men in the judgment." Thus Pelagius says that Christ "opens the eyes of our hearts, in that he makes clear to us the things to come lest we be occupied in things of the present." He "rouses us, by the greatness of future glory and by promises of rewards, from our devotion to earthly desires and from that love by which we delight only in the things of the present."[53]

Finally, Christ serves as a model or example – most generally as an example of someone "who consistently put to death sinful desire and thus revealed to men that of which their nature is capable," but also "as an example for a number of concrete modes of behavior. By his taking upon himself the form of a servant and remaining obedient unto death," Christ provides an example of "humility and obedience." By his "bearing of our infirmities," he teaches us to bear with the infirmities of others. From his humble birth we learn to despise riches. And so on.[54]

Christ's redemptive death embraced in baptism wipes our slate clean, so to speak, and his teaching and example dispel the ignorance that has overlaid human nature, thereby breaking the power of the sinful habits that have held us in thrall.[55] As a result, salvation once again becomes possible for us.

So what does "grace" mean for Pelagius? It includes at least five things: (1) our God-given ability to freely choose the good (and thus live sinlessly); (2) the law of Moses; (3) the forgiveness of sins received in baptism in virtue of Christ's redemptive death; and (4) the teaching of Christ and (5) his example, which have the power to dispel ignorance and destroy sinful habits. Each was a free gift, for God was under no obligation to provide it. In no case does grace compel or force the will, however, or impose any sort of necessity upon it. One must freely respond to the redeeming death in faith if one is to receive the grace of forgiveness, and one must respond to the grace of teaching and example by freely chosen good works if one is to receive the promised rewards. Pelagius thinks his doctrine thus coherently affirmed both the necessity of grace and the freedom of the human will. The question of course is: Does it?

Augustine thought not. Adam fell because of pride – because, as Paul Tillich said, Adam wanted "to be autonomous and to stand upon himself."[56] Pride in turn draws concupiscence and ignorance in its wake. "Concupiscence" has two meanings. Most fundamentally, it refers to a movement of the will away from the highest good toward lower goods One turns away from what is eminently worthy of love and unduly loves what has comparatively little value. As such, it is a perversion or disorder of love. But the term also refers to sexual desire, which is accompanied by shame.[57]

Pride's second consequence is ignorance – not primarily an ignorance of significant facts but an existential ignorance, a distorted understanding of the true nature of reality (including one's own). By closing oneself off from goodness and light, one falls prey to self-deception, bad faith, and illusion.

Sin as Augustine understands it is not so much an act or pattern of acts as a state or condition of the self that precedes and expresses itself in morally wrong acts. It is fundamentally a sickness of the will or disorder of love, something wrong at the very core of one's being.

Sin's essential punishment is the loss of the highest good – other punishments are secondary. "If God is everything positive, the ultimate good, or the power of being overcoming non-being, [then] the only real punishment ... is the intrinsic one of losing this power of being, of not participating anymore in the ultimate good.... Augustine described it thus: 'The soul dies when it is left alone by God, as a body will die when it is left by the soul'."[58]

How is Adam's sin related to our own? Adam's sin is the pattern or prototype of our own. Each of us sins *as* Adam sinned. And in this, Augustine agrees with Pelagius. But more is involved than Pelagius recognized. "We all existed potentially in Adam's procreative power, and in this way we participated in his free decision and thus are guilty."[59] The "hereditary taint" is passed from parents to children in the act of physical procreation – an act that is morally tainted because it involves libido, untoward desire, or concupiscence.[60] "From this concupiscence whatsoever comes into being by natural birth is tied and bound by original sin."[61]

"Because of original, hereditary sin everybody belongs to ... a unity of negativity" – what Augustine in one place calls "the ruined mass" and, in another, a "mass of perdition." Since each of us belongs to the ruined mass, we can be saved only by "a special act of God."[62] Sin thus becomes a tragic destiny that belongs to us in so far as we are human. It is similar in this respect to the Fate that forms the dark background of the Greek tragic heroes, but with this difference: we guiltily participate in forging our own destiny. The Greek tragic hero is not responsible for Fate.

If our predicament has been correctly described, grace can't be reduced to the pardon of past sins and the help provided by teaching and example. It must also involve the healing of a corrupted nature and of a will that has lost its liberty (its power to do well). "It is not by law and doctrine uttering their lessons from without, but by a secret, wonderful, and ineffable power operating within that God works in men's hearts not only revelations of the truth but also good dispositions of the will.... By such grace is is effected, ... not only that we ... believe what ought to be loved but also ... love what we have believed."[63]

The forgiveness of past sins, teaching, and example might be an adequate remedy for the human plight as understood by Pelagius. It is not an adequate remedy for the human plight as it exists in reality. One's understandings of the human plight and of grace go together. Because Pelagius failed to recognize the seriousness of our condition, he failed to appreciate the fact that much more than pardon and instruction are needed if we are to be healed.[64]

It is sometimes thought that "free choice is the condition of grace. By striving, struggling and searching for God, man's will gains merit, and grace is merely the gift which crowns that merit."[65] Or if (and this is more common) it is admitted that we can't make the first movement toward God, that God must turn to us *before* we can turn to him, it is nonetheless asserted that our *response* to God's gracious movement in faith and trust is our own work, and not God's. Augustine himself at one time believed this. "That we should consent when the gospel was preached to us, I thought was our own doing and came from ourselves … but that even the merit itself of faith was God's gift, I neither thought of inquiring into, nor did I say." He came to the conclusion, however, that "it is impossible to withstand the most manifest divine testimony, by which faith … is shown also to be the gift of God."[66]

Is Augustine's understanding of grace compatible with human freedom? He agrees that we are endowed with free (voluntary) choice. But this admission doesn't amount to much. For Augustine equates free choice and the will, where to will something is to choose it because one loves it, desires it, delights in it, or is attracted to it.[67] Will or free choice, in Augustine's view, is thus nothing more than love or desire – an unconstrained movement of the soul toward something that attracts it. Since it is clear that all of us love or delight in, or move toward, many things, it is clear that each of us has will or free choice.[68] The problem, according to Augustine, is not whether we have free choice, since we clearly do, but whether we have *liberty* or the power to love and adhere to the highest good.[69]

Free choice and the will are thus equated, and will is defined as a spontaneous or unconstrained movement of the soul toward what attracts it. Grace changes the direction of the will so that where it once spontaneously moved toward lower goods and away from higher ones, it now spontaneously moves toward God, the Highest Good. Hence, grace doesn't destroy free choice or will; it merely alters its direction. Even though a person's desires were altered by grace so that she now seeks God where formerly she did not, she can be said to be free because she is doing what she wants. Furthermore, in bestowing the gift of right love and right action on the sinner, the sinner regains her power to do the good. Thus not only is grace compatible with our freedom, it restores our liberty.[70]

(It is worth noting that Augustine uses "liberty" in two different though related senses. Adam enjoyed liberty but lost it. The liberty that he lost, however, was the *power* to act well. The liberty conferred on us by grace is "the good use of free choice" [the exercise of that power], and this is something better than what Adam lost. "Whereas the first liberty of the will [that lost by Adam] was to be able not to sin, the last [which is a consequence of the grace bestowed through Christ] was much greater, not to be able to sin ... the first was the power of perseverance, to be able not to forsake the good – the last was the felicity of perseverance, not to be able to forsake the good."[71])

There is certain appropriateness in speaking of an unerring will of the good as liberty. An ordinate (properly ordered) love of the good was a feature of human nature as it was created or intended to be, and as such it belongs to the human essence.[72] Insofar as we choose the good, we are therefore acting in accordance with our nature. To be truly free, though, is just to act according to our nature rather than against it, since it is only then that we are doing what we really want to do, that is, what we would want if we were fully rational and thus true to our own nature.

Nevertheless, while those who have received grace may be free in the two senses we have considered,[73] it remains true that the good use of their free choice is wholly wrought by God. Whether this is compatible with genuine freedom is a moot point.[74]

What were Augustine's reasons for his doctrine of grace?[75] First, in many cases it is apparent that God bestows his grace on those who have in no way merited it. St. Paul is converted after he has persecuted the church. And Augustine was convinced that God's grace had searched him out in "his wildest aberrations and deepest misery."[76] Second, grace is by definition a free, gratuitous gift. Grace that was a response to merit would be merited grace or grace that was owed, and thus no grace at all. Finally (and arguably most important) was Augustine's own experience. "For many long years he had known the law without being able to carry it out. And not only did he know the law, ... he saw it carried out by others, and although he longed with his whole soul to imitate them, he had to admit that he was unable to do so."[77] As long as he relied on himself, Augustine found he was powerless to do the good.

The first two reasons are not fully convincing. The first shows that God can act graciously toward those who have hitherto rejected him, and the second shows that grace can't be regarded as something owed or as any kind of payment. They are neither individually nor jointly sufficient to justify the claim that salvation is through grace alone.

The third is another matter. Augustine's experience is by no means idiosyncratic but occurs cross-culturally. The individual acknowledges the validity of the Torah, the Dharma, the Noble Eightfold Path, or some other standard by which she believes that life as a whole should be assessed, and recognizes that when judged by that standard her own life falls woefully short. She makes deeply serious attempts to meet the standard, but after prolonged and strenuous efforts finds herself totally unable to do so. As a result, she feels that she is at the end of her rope, deploring her utter failure and weakness of will. Only after she realizes that no amount of conscious striving will heal her spiritual and ethical sickness, and "lets go" of her own efforts, abandoning herself to Christ, the Lord Vishnu, the Buddha of the Western Paradise, the motion of the Tao, the Suchness of things, or whatever else she believes to be the ground of reality can she meet the standard whose rightness she has always acknowledged. Where one comes down in the dispute between Pelagius and Augustine may largely depend on whether or not one has had (or at least valorizes) experiences such as Augustine's.

Similar issues are at stake in the sixteenth-century debates between Protestant reformers and Roman Catholics. Consider, for example, the conflicting views of John Calvin and the Council of Trent on justification and faith.

Calvin defines justification "as the acceptance by which God receives us into his favor as if we were righteous."[78] If we picture humanity as brought before the bar of God's justice, justification can be regarded as God's acquittal of sinful humanity. "To justify, therefore, is nothing else than to acquit from the charge of guilt, as if innocence were proved."[79] The ground of God's acceptance or acquittal is his own goodness. Nothing in the sinner warrants it. "God of his mere gratuitous goodness is pleased to embrace the sinner, in whom he sees nothing that can move him to mercy but wretchedness, because he sees him altogether naked and destitute of good works. He therefore seeks the cause of kindness in himself."[80]

Even so, we can't be restored to God's fellowship as long as we remain sinful. For God is holy and "to have any intercourse with sin is repugnant to his righteousness."[81] We are restored to righteousness and made acceptable through the forgiveness of sins and the imputation of Christ's righteousness. And Calvin approvingly quotes Augustine, who says, "The righteousness of the saints consist more in the forgiveness of sins than the perfection of virtue,"[82] and asserts that "a man will be justified by faith when, excluded from the righteousness of works; he by faith, lays hold of the righteousness of Christ, and clothed in it appears in the sight of God ... as righteous."[83] The sinner, in other words, is deemed righteous because Christ's righteousness is *imputed* to him, regarded as if it were his own. As Jacob put on the garments of his brother Esau and received Isaac's blessing "under the person of another, so we conceal ourselves under the precious purity of Christ ... [so that] we may obtain an attestation of righteousness from the presence of God."[84] In short, in spite of the fact that we have no righteousness of our own, we are regarded *as if* we possessed the righteousness of Christ by a kind of legal fiction.

Faith does include regeneration, however – a conversion or turning in which "withdrawing from ourselves we turn to God, and laying aside the old, put on a new mind."[85] It involves a "transformation not only in external works but in the soul itself,"[86] by which "the image of God, which was ... all but effaced by the transgression of Adam," is "form[ed] in us anew."[87] Conversion includes both a rejection of evil, a liberation from the sinful dispositions that have become natural to us and held us in thrall, and "new thoughts and affections," "sentiments of justice, ... and mercy" which are instilled into our souls by the Holy Spirit.[88] Its "fruits" are "offices of piety towards God, and love towards men, general holiness and purity of life."[89]

Calvin is careful to insist, however, that these works and the new holy dispositions from which they spring are merely *consequences* or *expressions* of faith. They are in no sense the *basis or ground* of our justification or acceptance. Nor do they *merit* salvation or any other kind of reward. In short, Christ's righteousness alone justifies us – not our own.

The "Decree Concerning Justification" and "Canons Concerning Justification" that were promulgated at the Council of Trent on January 13, 1547, were the Roman Catholic Church's official response to Calvin and the other Protestant reformers.

According to Trent, justification consists in the healing and sanctification of sinful humanity. Justification is "not only a remission of sins but also the sanctification and renewal of the inward man ... whereby an unjust man becomes just and from being an enemy becomes a friend."[90] Canon 11 anathematizes those who (like Luther and Calvin) say that "men are justified by the sole remission of sins" and God's acceptance of the unacceptable. While justification includes those things, it also includes the Holy Spirit's infusion of love into the human heart.[91]

Furthermore, human beings cooperate with God in the work of salvation. Grace is necessary for justification. It is false that "man can be justified before God by his own works ... without divine grace."[92] Nevertheless, Adam's sin did not destroy our free will, and those who, like Luther, maintain that free will is a fiction, "a name without a reality," are anathematized.[93] Our free will, "moved and aroused by God," can assent to "God's call and action."[94] "While God touches the heart of man through the illumination of the Holy Ghost," it is false that "man ... does absolutely nothing while receiving the inspiration since he can ... reject it."[95] God has the initiative and grace is indispensable, but men and women must freely assent to, and cooperate, with God's grace.

Works are not "merely the fruits and signs of justification." They are also "*the cause of its increase.*"[96] Furthermore, "those who work well unto the end" receive eternal life "as a *reward* promised by God himself to be faithfully given to their good works and *merits*." Although it is true that our good works proceed from the supernatural strength that Christ infuses into those who are incorporated in him, God's bounty is "so great that He wishes the things that are His gifts to be their merits."[97]

There are at least two substantive issues between classical Protestants such as Luther and Calvin, on the one hand, and Trent on the other. The first is this: Trent maintains that begraced men and women can act meritoriously and cooperate in the work of their own salvation. Through God's favor, they can be *creative* – a *source* of good. Classical Protestants reject this view for two primary reasons. First, it detracts from God's infinite majesty and unlimited sovereignty. God enjoys a *monopoly* of creative power. He *alone* is the source of being and value. Any other view is unworthy of him.

Second, Classical Protestants appeal to the deeply felt experience of their own inability to act as they ought.

Defenders of Trent can (and do) counter the first by arguing that in ascribing worth and dignity to creatures, we *cannot* detract from God's dignity and majesty. For no matter how much dignity creatures enjoy and how much worth they possess, they are *creatures* and hence their dignity and worth is infinitely exceeded by God's. The second reason can be (and sometimes is) countered by pointing out that the dramatic conversion experiences of a Paul, Augustine, or Luther are atypical of Christian experience and hence an insufficient sample on the basis of which to construct a perfectly general theory of the nature of grace, justification, sanctification, and the like. Classical Protestants, in turn, counter this response by arguing that those who take this line fail to appreciate how radical and unconditional God's demand really is and overestimate their own strength and ability.

The second substantive issue is this. Both Trent and Protestants such as Calvin agree that salvation is life with God. They disagree on what is required for admission to that life. According to Calvin, all that is needed is forgiveness and the legal imputation of Christ's righteousness. God is absolutely sovereign and can therefore admit whoever he pleases into his presence. According to Trent, however, we can't be admitted to God's presence before our nature has healed and restored to what it was intended to be. Friendship presupposes a certain likeness or equality between the friends. This likeness or "equality" is effected by God's pouring his love or charity into our hearts, thus making us like himself.

It is important to note that disputes such as those between Pelagius and Augustine or the Reformers and Trent are not restricted to Christianity. Thus the Shri Vaishnavas split into two sects: the Northern school (*Vadagalai*) and the Southern school (*Tengalai*). According to the former, God's relation to the human soul is like the relation of a mother monkey to its baby. The baby monkey is playing on the floor of the jungle. When danger approaches, its mother descends from the tree tops. The baby clings to her, and she carries her child to safety. Just so, "when the soul is lost in Maya, the Lord in grace descends. The soul clings to the Lord, and the Lord carries the soul to heaven." The act by which the soul clings to the Lord, like that by which the baby monkey clings to its mother, is wholly voluntary. According to the Southern school, on the other hand, God's relation to the soul is like a mother cat's relation to her kitten. "When the kitten is in danger, the mother cat picks up the kitten by the scruff of the neck and carries it to safety." Similarly, salvation is wholly God's work. The human soul, like the baby kitten, contributes nothing.[98]

V. Conclusion

We have now examined four historically important instances of religious reasoning. Some will find some of the arguments we have discussed convincing and others will not. For example, I find suitably qualified versions of Clarke's cosmological argument persuasive, while the author of the finest book on Clarke's argument (William Rowe) does not. Some find Pelagius's account of grace and free will more persuasive than Augustine's, while others find Augustine's account the more persuasive of the two. What accounts for such differences? Not, in the most interesting cases, differences in intelligence, information, training, or philosophic-theological acumen. Rowe and I, for instance, were trained by the same teachers, are intimately familiar with one another's take on Clarke's argument, and have discussed the differences between us over many years. Yet if differences of intelligence, training, information, and the like don't account for the fact that we have arrived at different conclusions, what does? Various answers to this question will be addressed in the following chapters.

2

The Purposes of Argument and the Person-Relativity of Proofs

Until quite recently, philosophical studies of religious argumentation have almost exclusively focused on the validity of the arguments[1] and the truth of their premises. This is not altogether surprising since no invalid argument or argument with a false premise is a good argument. But while truth and validity are necessary conditions of good arguments, they aren't sufficient since an argument can meet both conditions and not be probative.

Arguments are constructed for various purposes, and these purposes must be taken into account when evaluating their success or failure. Moreover, reasoning is always situated – it does not occur in a vacuum. Arguments are the products of men and women with various needs, hopes, fears, sensitivities, and proclivities, and with diverse individual histories, who are responding to highly specific problems and difficulties. They are not the expressions of a view from nowhere that abstracts from the existential specificity of the reasoner and/or the particularities of his or her concrete situation. Yet the latter frequently determines whether an argument is or is not probative in a particular situation or for a particular person.

In order for arguments such as those discussed in Chapter 1 to be good ones, it is not enough that they be valid and noncircular and have true premises. For as George Mavrodes pointed out, proofs are "person-relative"[2] – a valid, noncircular argument with true premises can prove something to Mary without proving it to John. To take a trivial example, if Mary knows that all the premises of a valid, noncircular argument are true and John does not, the argument can extend Mary's knowledge without extending John's. The proof's person-relativity in this case depends on the fact that Mary knows something that John does not. Other sources of person-relativity are less obvious, however.

I. The Purposes of Religious Arguments

Arguments are constructed for various purposes, for example, and these have a bearing on their success. Consider Udayana's, Madhva's, and Ramanuja's contrasting attitudes toward proofs for the existence of God.[3] All three were theists. Udayana was an adherent of the Nyaya-Vaisesika school, which identified God with Shiva. Madhva and Ramanuja were Vedantists who identified God with Vishnu. All three accepted the authority of the Vedas. Udayana thought that their validity was not "self-authenticating" but "derived ... from their general trustworthiness as shown in part by the success of the theistic proofs by which means the existence of *Ishvara* [the Lord] can be demonstrated ... with certainty." Madhva, on the other hand, believed that while the theistic proofs "had no independent power to convince the sceptic or doubter, ... they could ... be used to confirm the faith of one who had already affirmed the authority and uncreatedness of the Vedic scriptures." By contrast with both, Ramanuja regarded proofs of the existence of God "as illicit attempts to establish something rationally which can be known through scripture alone."[4]

Ramanuja's and David Hume's critiques of design arguments for the existence of God are quite similar. Their purposes in proffering these critiques were strikingly different, however. Hume's aim was arguably to justify skepticism or agnosticism. Ramanuja's aims were religious – to protect the transcendence of the God revealed in the scriptures. Vishnu's perfections are infinite and thus radically unlike the limited and imperfect properties of creatures. "The needs of the design argument," on the other hand, "based as it is on analogical reasoning require significant similarity between the cause of the world and human agency." Any "god" it could succeed in establishing would therefore not be the God of the Vedas.[5]

Historically, proofs of God's existence and other theologically significant matters have served a variety of purposes. Proofs are sometimes directed toward unbelievers as well as to the faithful. Anselm's *Monologion*, for example, is addressed to his fellow monks. But it is also directed toward the "ignorant" who don't believe, and whom he hopes to persuade, through reason alone, that God exists, is the source of all good, and himself the Good that alone can truly satisfy us. And Udayana's arguments were addressed not only to Hindus but also to Buddhists who rejected the Vedas and denied that God exists or that the world was created.

But proofs have also been used in interreligious contexts to establish common ground. Thomas Aquinas's *Summa Contra Gentiles*, for example, was at least in part directed toward Muslims who already believed in God's existence. In that context, philosophical proofs of God's existence, omniscience, and the like were designed to secure a common foundation upon which to argue for specifically Christian tenets. Aquinas and his Dominican patrons "may [also] ... have thought that the *Summa Contra Gentiles* was precisely the sort of work needed by Christian missionaries ... who were faced with the high intellectual culture of" Muslim Spain, "and especially" with "Arabian Aristotelianism."[6] Or to cite another example, the Jesuit missionary Roberto de Nobili (1577–1656) used a version of Aquinas's five ways to establish common ground with (primarily theistic) Hindus.[7]

Moreover, theistic proofs have often been used *within* a tradition to resolve intramural disputes – for example, by using philosophical arguments to help determine the meaning of jointly accepted sacred texts. The dispute between Augustine and Pelagius discussed in Chapter 1 is an example. Another example is this. Udayana's theistic proofs were not only directed toward Buddhists but also toward Mimamsikas who were Hindu and therefore shared allegiance to a common body of scriptures (most notably, the Vedas). In that context, the function of his arguments was to convince Mimamsikas that their atheistic interpretation of the Vedas was mistaken. Yet another example is provided by the dispute between al Ghazali and the "philosophers" (preeminently Ibn Sina [Avicenna] and Ibn Rushd [Averroes]). Ghazali and his opponent Ibn Sina employed "kalamic" and Aristotelian causal proofs,[8] respectively, to show how Sura 10 of the Quran ("Surely your Lord is God, who created the heavens and the earth in six days") should be interpreted – namely, literally in the first case and metaphorically in the second.[9] The "philosophers" taught that the created world was eternal, and that relevant passages of the Quran should be interpreted so as to accommodate this fact. Ghazali responded by attempting to show that the world must have had a beginning. The importance of the dispute lay in the fact that in the Aristotelian framework that the philosophers were employing, eternity and necessity were co-implicative. That God eternally generates the universe therefore entails that he necessarily does so. Necessity excludes (free) will, however, and a God without will is not a person and, hence, is not the God of theism.[10]

(As the last two examples indicate, one and the same argument can be deployed to achieve different ends in different contexts. Another example is this. The third argument discussed in Chapter 1 has been used within Vedanta to settle a dispute between theistic and nontheistic Vedantins. But it can also be deployed in extramural disputes between theists and nontheists who are not members of a common tradition but agree that ultimate reality is maximally perfect.[11])

Theistic proofs are sometimes also employed to strengthen the faithful. Thus Ghazali's *Jerusalem Tract* (which contains a proof of the existence of God) was "traditionally … said to have been written at the request of members of the Jerusalem mosque to bolster their courage as they made themselves ready for the arrival of the first Christian crusaders."[12]

Furthermore, theistic proofs can be employed devotionally. For example, there is a dominant rabbinic tradition in which "rational legal argument pursued according to recognized principles and processes is the most highly commended path to encounter and engagement with God."[13] Its "classical literature" comprises "records of debates … [recording] arguments and opinions on all sides of an issue, including minority opinions." Because "the debates … are essentially open-ended …, they provide the foundation for further debate as circumstances and cases may require.… The pattern of training was (and still is in traditional *yeshivot*) interactive; … it required the interaction of three persons: the rabbi, the student (*talmid*) and his 'companion' or 'associate' (*chaver*). The minds of the student and his associate were trained through engagement in vociferous oral argument over some part of the tradition which ultimately crystallized in the Talmud." The rabbi "was the assessor of the students' progress and he assessed his students by himself engaging with them in Talmudic argument."[14] This process was not only a *mitzvah* and an act of worship but a form of *imitatio Dei*, for God Himself engages in the study of Torah."[15]

Moreover, Hasidic rabbis argued not only with each other but occasionally even with God himself. For example:

a terrible famine once occurred in the Ukraine and the poor could buy no bread. Ten rabbis assembled at the house of the "Spoler Grandfather" for a session of the Rabbinical Court. The Spoler said to them: "I have a case in judgement against the Lord. According to Rabbinical law, a master who buys a Jewish serf for a designated time (six years or up to the Jubilee year) must support not only him but also his family. Now the Lord bought us in Egypt as his serfs, since he says: 'For to me are the sons of Israel serfs,' and the prophet Ezekiel declared that even in Exile, Israel is the slave of God. Therefore, O Lord, I ask that Thou abide by the Law and support thy serfs with their families." The ten judges rendered judgement in favor of the Spoler Rabbi.[16]

There were precedents for this in the Hebrew bible and in earlier Rabbinic literature. For example,

R. Kahana said on the authority of R. Ismael b. R. Jose: What is meant by ... *Sing praises to Him who rejoices when they conquer Him* [i.e., prevail upon Him to rescind intended punishment]. Come and see how the character of the Holy One, blessed be He, is not like that of mortal man. The character of mortal man is such that when he is conquered he is unhappy, but when the Holy One is conquered He rejoices, for it is said *Therefore He said that He would destroy them, had not Moses His chosen stood before Him in the breach, [to turn back his wrath].*[17]

It should be noted, however, that Hasidic argument with God was "not common," and when it did occur was "always on behalf of the Jewish people and for God to find good in them and save them from suffering. The person who argues is motivated by his love of his people and so, feeling an intimacy with God, turns to God out of desperation or great worry."[18]

Theistic proofs are also used "as aids to prayer or devotion or as a basis for meditation." Thus, Bonaventure's *The Soul's Journey to God* "leads the reader nearer and nearer to the object of devotion, pausing briefly to review" the reasons for what we believe, "before entering mystically into the being of God."[19] Again, on Aquinas's view, our ultimate happiness lies in the joyous vision of God's own essence, when we thus "see" him face to face. When we succeed in demonstrating some of the things we formerly took on faith, we see to be true what we formerly only believed to be true. This rational seeing is an important step in the contemplative life that begins with mere belief and ends in the vision of God himself.[20]

One of the most interesting examples is Udayana's. Udayana's theistic proofs are designed to establish the existence of the God of the Nyaya-Vaisesika system. God is one soul among others "albeit ... the 'supreme soul' or *paramatman*.... As one cause among several, God makes the world from eternally pre-existing 'atoms' (*paramanus*) and other 'substances' (*davuyas*), including the also eternally pre-existing souls." The law of karma, too, is simply given. Yet God desires the liberation of all of the souls bound to the wheel of *samsara* (the wheel of birth and rebirth). Therefore, within the limits imposed upon him by the eternal structure of the world and the law of karma, God creates a world that is conducive to the liberation of at least some souls (by teaching "the first embodied souls the Vedas," for example, and enjoining them to "pass on what they heard (*sruta*) to the next generation ..., and so on"). However, while some will listen and achieve liberation, others will not, and so eventually (after "one hundred Brahma years"[21]) the world will dissolve back into its constituents "at a precise moment of God's own" choosing.[22] But then, after another one hundred Brahma years, God will create the world anew, and this process will continue "until all souls have been freed from the round of existence."[23] This is the God whose existence and nature Udayana believed he had established in a number of works but "principally in the *Nyayakusumanjali*."[24]

The title is instructive. "*Nyaya*" means arguments. "'*Kusuma*' means a bunch of flowers, and '*anjali*' is the ... gesture of reverential greeting when the hands are cupped together and held before the face, and [also] the gesture of pious supplication when, for example, flowers are brought to the altar and offered in worship to God." So the title means "a bouquet of arguments offered to God." The theistic proofs are offered to Shiva for his "sake alone, and not just for any benefit which may accrue to ... one who hears and understands and meditates on them." The three concluding verses make this clear. The first is a prayer on behalf of unbelievers who remain unpersuaded by the arguments offered for their benefit. The next verse is a prayer for mercy on those who believe but may sometimes "waver in their certainty or wander in their concentration." These verses imply that Udyayana's book was designed both to persuade unbelievers and to strengthen the faith of those already committed. But the third verse subordinates these purposes to another, "namely, to the loving worship of Shiva for Shiva's sake alone." It does not matter, in the end, whether "the flowers of logic perfume the 'right' hand' or the 'left' – the pure or the impure, ... the believer or the unbeliever – so long as they are acceptable as a gift to the Lord Shiva, so that [he] ... 'may be pleased by my presenting it as an offering at his footstool.' "[25]

A final example of a devotional use is provided by Anselm. As noted earlier, Anselm's *Monologion* was addressed to unbelievers as well as to his fellow monks. His *Proslogion*, by contrast, is written in the form of a prayer addressed *to God* by someone who strives to lift his "mind to the contemplation of God, and seeks to understand what he believes."[26] Moreover, Anselm insists that without faith, understanding is impossible. ("Unless I believe, I should not understand.") He prays to God, who gives "understanding to faith," that God may give him "to understand that thou art as we believe, and thou art that which we believe." And at the conclusion of his famous ontological argument, Anselm exclaims: "I thank thee gracious Lord, I thank thee; because what I formerly believed by thy bounty, I now so understand by thy illumination, that if I were unwilling to believe that thou dost exist, I should not be able not to understand this to be true."

It is important to note that the arguments Anselm deploys in the *Proslogion*[27] are not based on premises that can be known to be true only by revelation. Anselm regards them as universally accessible and uses them to construct proofs that employ ordinary canons of logic. Even so, their setting is very different from that of the theistic proofs offered by Descartes, for example, or by Samuel Clarke. In the first place, Anselm's whole enterprise is framed by a desire to *see* God. Because God has created us to enjoy him as our highest good, "a rational creature ought to devote all its powers and will to remembering and understanding and loving the Highest Good – the [end] for which it knows itself to exist."[28] In pursuit of this goal, Anselm's project has two "interrelated goals: to 'contemplate God,' 'see God's face'; and to understand what he or she believes.... Of the two ... the aim of seeing God's face dominates and frames the project of understanding," since the latter "is both subordinate to and partially constitutive of the former."[29]

In the second place, the *Proslogion*'s inquiry is a divine–human collaboration. "The soul begins by asking questions of, putting puzzles to, and/or begging help from, God. Then God 'illumines the soul that it may see,' 'teaches so that it may understand'.... It then belongs to the soul to articulate what God has revealed, usually expressing the reasoning and the statement of results in a second person address to God, punctuating it with exclamations of thanks and praise."[30] Throughout the investigation, the inquirer is placed "in a position analogous to that of a philosophy student who seeks the teacher's help in refuting arguments for solipsism or proving the existence of other minds." The student doesn't really doubt the existence of other minds. (For one thing, her appeal to her teacher presupposes belief in the existence of at least one other mind, namely, that of the teacher.) Rather, what she is trying to do – with her teacher's help – is find reasons for what she already believes that do not themselves depend on the truth of "other minds exist." Her goal here is similar. The soul that prays the *Proslogion* doesn't doubt God's existence or goodness. (Anselm's belief in God's existence and goodness is presupposed by his plea for help.) What it is seeking from God is help in finding reasons for God's existence and goodness that don't themselves depend on the truth of "God exists" or "God is good."[31]

Finally, if the enterprise is to be successful, volitional and emotional discipline is as necessary as intellectual discipline. Anselm shares the Christian-Platonist assumption that God is Goodness itself, and that, "where values are concerned, what you love affects what you see." Thus he assumes "that even the unbeliever's natural human desire for goods could motivate his *Monologion* search for the source of the goods perceptible to the senses or reason." And the "*Proslogion* alternates" rigorous argumentation with "prayer exercises designed to stir the emotions and will." Again, Anselm's *Epistola de Incarnatione Verba* argues that a clear view of the matters to be discussed requires "faith, humble obedience to the divine precepts, and discipline to resist carnal passions."[32] (This notion has its roots in Plato. In his seventh letter, Plato argues that "it is barely possible for knowledge to be engendered of an object naturally good, in a man naturally good; but if his nature is defective … and if the qualities he has have been corrupted then not even Lynceus could make such a man see. In short, neither quickness of learning nor a good memory can make a man see when his nature is not akin to the object … so that no man who is not naturally inclined and akin to justice and all other foms of excellence … will ever attain the truth that is obtainable about virtue [and the Good]."[33]

In some well-known passages from the *Pensees*, Blaise Pascal asserts that, at best, "proofs only convince the mind" (252).[34] They make "little impression" upon the heart (542). A successful theistic proof might establish the existence of "a God considered as great, powerful, and eternal." It would not prove the existence of "the God of Abraham, the God of Isaac, the God of Jacob." God is indeed great, powerful, and eternal. But he is also "a God of love and comfort … who fills the soul and heart of those whom he possesses" (555). *This* God's existence cannot be established by philosophical arguments. More than two centuries later, William James claimed that philosophical proofs of God's existence, nature, and so on "prove nothing rigorously." At most, "they only corroborate our preexistent partialities." "*Feeling* is the deeper source of religion and … philosophical and theological formulas are secondary products like translations of a text into another tongue."[35]

Pascal and James express a widely held view. Philosophical proofs are, at best, religiously useless. At worst, they are inimical to the religious life.[36] I believe that cases such as those that I have been considering show that this view is seriously mistaken. Proofs can be, and often are, an integral part of some styles of piety and ways of living a religiously engaged life. Nor is this style of piety or way of living the religious life confined to a few religious intellectuals.

Austin Warren has argued that Harriet Beecher Stowe's *Oldtown Folks* and *The Minister's Wooing* "are the best [extant] recreations of [New England] theocracy's last days." Consider, then, her description of the latter's heroine, Mary:

Had she been born in Italy under the dissolving influences of that sunny dreamy clime, beneath the shadow of cathedrals, and where pictured saints and angels smiled in clouds of painting from every arch and altar, she might like fair St. Catherine of Siena, have seen beatific visions in the sunset skies and a silver dove descending upon her as she prayed; but unfolding in the clear keen cold New England clime, and nurtured in its abstract and positive theologies, her religious faculties took other forms. Instead of lying entranced in mysterious raptures at the foot of altars, she read and pondered treatises on the Will, and listened in rapt attention, while her spiritual guide, the venerated Dr. Hopkins, unfolded to her the theories of the great Edwards on the nature of true virtue. Womanlike, she felt the subtle poetry of these sublime abstractions which dealt with such infinite and unknown quantities – which spoke of the universe, of its great Architect, of man, of angel, as matters of intimate and daily contemplation.

Stowe then comments as follows: "It is not in our line to imply the truth or the falsehood of these systems of philosophic theology which seem for many years to have been the principal outlet for the proclivities of the New England mind." But "he who does not see a grand side to these strivings of the soul cannot understand one of the noblest capabilities of humanity.... These hard old New England divines were the poets of metaphysical philosophy, who built systems in an artistic fervor, and felt self exhale from beneath them as they rose into the higher regions of thought." Or consider this brief exchange between Deacon Twitchell and Doctor Hopkins:

"Well," said Deacon Twitchell, "Brother Seth ... says you deny depravity. He's all for the imputation of Adam's sin you know; and I have long talks with Seth, every time he comes to see me; and he says that, if we did not sin in Adam, it's given' up the whole ground altogether.... I wish Seth could talk with you sometime, Doctor. Along in the spring, he was down helpin' me to lay stone fence – it was when we was fencin' off the south-pastur' lot – and we talked pretty nigh all day; and the longer we talked, the sotter Seth grew. He's a master hand at reading; and when he heard that your remarks on Dr. Mayhew had come out, Seth tackled up o' purpose and came up to Newport to get them, and spent all his time last winter studyn' on it and makin' his remarks; and I tell you Sir, he's a tight fellow to argue with. Why, that day, what with layin' stone wall and what with arguin' with Seth, I come home quite beat out.[37]

A good deal of evidence supports the general accuracy of Stowe's picture. New England sermons were typically "sequentially written and closely reasoned," and parishioners would sometimes take notes while they were being preached to refer to later.[38] "The Reverend Convers Francis – transcendentalist and professor at Harvard – says of Dr. Osgood, pastor at Medford," though his sermons "contained a considerable share of learned criticism, I remember my father, a mechanic with but a slender education, was always delighted with them and used to talk about them after meeting."[39] Something of the flavor of New England piety is indicated by the fact that the missionary to the Algonquins, John Eliot, translated a treatise on logic into their language "to initiate the Indians in the knowledge of the Rule of Reason," and in that way help them to read their bibles properly.[40]

The upshot is that precise argumentation and abstruse journeys into philosophical theology are an essential feature of some forms of authentic religiosity. But notice that for arguments to play the roles assigned to them in this context, they must be sound. Bad arguments won't persuade intellectually sophisticated nonbelievers. Arguments designed to establish common ground fail if those to whom they are addressed reject their premises or doubt their validity. Although Anselm's ontological argument for God's existence is developed in a devotional context, his reply to Gaunilo makes it clear that he thought that even unbelievers should recognize its soundness. Nor will bad arguments help Anselm achieve his interrelated goals of contemplating God – "seeing his face" and understanding what he had formerly only believed. Finally, offering God a bad argument is like offering him a blemished lamb; it dishonors him (cf. *Malachi* 3). In short, contextualizing arguments by situating them in the lives of the people who employ them and the persons to whom they are addressed in no way absolves their makers or recipients from the responsibility of assessing their validity, the truth of their premises, and their probative force.

II. The Person-Relativity of Religious Arguments

Suppose that we grant that theistic arguments can play a useful role in both the search for truth and in discussions with nonbelievers. What makes arguments of this sort *good* ones? George Mavrodes addresses this question in "On the Very Strongest Arguments."[41]

Alvin Plantinga and Richard Swinburne articulate similar versions of a widely held view. Plantinga has suggested that a good argument is not only valid but "draws its premises from the stock of propositions accepted by nearly every sane man, or perhaps nearly every rational man." Swinburne thinks that a good argument is a valid argument "whose premises are known to be true by those who dispute about the conclusion." Plantinga and Swinburne thus implicitly assume that universality is an important good-making characteristic of arguments, and this isn't implausible. For "an argument that had this property would" provide "an epistemic good for a whole lot of people.... It would provide them with a way of knowing something that they did not know before (or at least that they might not have known before)."[42]

It may be a mistake to place too much weight on the value of universality, however. For the "strength" of an argument is also important. Strength, though, "is more a matter of quality than quantity." Strong arguments are arguments which "establish" or "demonstrate" or "prove" their conclusions – "they make their conclusions secure," and arguments that fall far short of universality may possess "maximal epistemic security."[43] This can be true, for example, when a noncircular argument validly proceeds from premises *I* know to be true but others don't even though they understand them or would understand them if they were to study them. For what could be more secure *for me* than a conclusion I base on a valid noncircular argument that proceeds from premises *I* know to be true? And what this suggests is that arguments are "person-relative" in the sense that a good argument for one person may not be a good argument for another.

The notion of a proof's person-relativity was introduced by Mavrodes in his seminal *Belief in God*. He began by distinguishing two sorts of "propositional concepts."[44] Subjective propositional concepts "have psychological implications or content." Examples are "believed," "doubted," and the like. Objective propositional concepts "have no psychological [implications or] content." "Important examples" are the terms "'truth' and 'falsity.'" Propositions incorporating subjective psychological concepts are person-relative. A proposition can be believed by me, for example, without being believed by you, or doubted by you without being doubted by me. Propositions incorporating only objective propositional concepts are not person-relative. A proposition can't be true for me and not true for you, although you may, of course, not recognize its truth. An important consequence of these definitions is that the concept of knowledge is also person-relative. Because a necessary (though not sufficient) condition of A's knowing *p* is that A believes *p*, if the latter is person-relative, then so too is the former.[45]

How does this bear on the notion of proof? To answer this question, Mavrodes distinguished between an argument's soundness, its "cogency," and its "convincingness." "An argument is cogent for a certain person N if and only if (1) it is sound and (2) N knows it to be sound."[46] "An argument is convincing for N if and only if (1) it is cogent for N and (2) N knows that each of its premises is true without having to infer any of them from its conclusion or from any other ... statements that he knows only by an inference from that conclusion."[47] Soundness isn't person-relative.[48] But cogency and convincingness are since their definitions contain subjective propositional concepts. Because we ordinarily reserve the word "proof" for cogent or convincing arguments, the concept of proof, too, is person-relative.

While I think there is something profoundly right about Mavrodes's contention, it does raise two questions.

The first is this. Philosophy has traditionally made claims on universal assent. Philosophers have believed that at least *some* arguments and *some* claims *ought* to be accepted by *all* rational or properly disposed subjects. In their view, a proof, properly so-called, is an argument that all rational or properly disposed subjects *ought* to find cogent or convincing whether they in fact do so or not. Call arguments that meet this condition "probative." We may grant that cogency and convincingness are person-relative. It is less clear that probativeness is. For the concept of probativeness incorporates an epistemic ought, and epistemic oughts, like moral oughts and truth, aren't obviously person-relative. If I morally ought to do x, then anyone in my situation ought to do x. Similarly, if I ought to believe *p* or accept *a* (where *p* and *a* take propositions and arguments as values, respectively), then anyone in my situation ought to believe *p* or accept *a*. Note that the fact that A ought to believe *p* or accept *a* does not imply that A does believe *p* or accept *a*. Subjective propositional concepts such as believe and accept are indeed part of the content of the epistemic ought in the sense that, in unpacking the latter, we introduce hypothetical or counterfactual conditionals that include them (for example, "if anyone were in my situation, she should believe *p*"). But unlike Mavrodes's standard examples of "mixed concepts" (knowledge, proof),[49] the application of the relevant concepts ("ought to believe," "ought to accept") to a subject doesn't ascribe a psychological state to that subject, and so isn't person-relative in Mavrodes's sense.

The second and more important question, though, is this: What exactly accounts for the person-relativity of proofs? In some cases, the answer is differences of education, intelligence, or training. A trained physicist, for example, may know certain truths in physics, or be able to follow certain scientific demonstrations, which the untrained lay person doesn't (and perhaps cannot) know or follow. Again, since what a person knows is partly determined by his or her temporal and spatial location, one person may know things that others do not. Thus, glancing out my window, I may know that it is now raining on Milwaukee's east side although my cousin in Arizona does not. Or again, I may be privy to information that is unavailable to others. The culprit may have confessed to me, for instance, but to no one else. Or God may have revealed something to Israel that he didn't reveal to other nations.

There are other, more interesting, sources of person-relativity, however. It is plausible to suppose that a good argument is a sound noncircular argument that accomplishes its purpose. Yet as we saw in Section I, these purposes can vary. Theistic proofs, for example, may be used to convince nonbelievers, to strengthen the faithful, as instruments of contemplation or as offerings to God. A good argument for one person may not be a good argument for another if the latter doesn't share the former's purposes. If an argument is designed to establish common ground, for instance, or to further the project of contemplation, or as an offering to God, it may be of little or no interest or use to a person who doesn't share these aims – even if the argument is sound and noncircular. Thus, while Samuel Clarke's version of the cosmological argument is arguably sound and noncircular, and can play a useful role in furthering one's understanding of God and his relation to the world, it has comparatively little value if one's aim is to convince nonbelievers since the latter can (and usually will) reject one or more of the its premises.[50]

Furthermore, even if one sees no flaws in an argument, one may dismiss it from one's mind, give it little or no weight in one's practical or theoretical deliberations, or treat it as at most an interesting intellectual curiosity. William James thought that we regard something as real only when we have use for it,[51] and something similar may be true here. Arguments are taken seriously only when they seem to have some important bearing on how we should think, act, or feel. Whether or not they appear to us to have that bearing depends importantly on our purposes, however. An argument may thus fail to be a good argument for someone because she doesn't have the interests and concerns needed for her to take the argument seriously.[52] If our interests are confined to this world, for example, God's existence or nonexistence will seem of comparatively little importance to us. Jonathan Edwards, for instance, argued that an exclusive focus on immediate affairs makes us impervious to even the strongest arguments for immortality and a final judgment. And Plato thought that an undue focus on the world of matter and becoming was likely to blind us to considerations pointing to the reality of eternal things.

There is an even more important source of the person-relativity of arguments, however. Not all good arguments are sound deductive or inductive arguments. For conclusions are sometimes warranted even when they are not entailed by one's premises and can't be derived from the evidence by inductive extrapolation (by generalizing from the character of a fair sample, for example, or by inferring that an event will occur because similar events have occurred under similar conditions in the past). Cumulative case arguments or inferences to the best explanation are examples.[53] Moreover, sound deductive or inductive arguments are themselves often embedded in cumulative case arguments. Modal versions of the ontological argument and Samuel Clarke's cosmological argument are cases in point. Both arguments seem to me to be sound, for I believe that their premises are true and entail their conclusions.[54] In practice, however, these proofs are no more that parts of larger arguments within which they are embedded. These larger arguments include reasons supporting the proofs' premises, and responses to the more telling objections to them and to the proofs' claims to validity and noncircularity. For in the final analysis, our assessment of the proofs will express our best judgment as to the cumulative force of all the considerations bearing on their overall adequacy. Clarke's argument provides an example.

His first premise (if something exists, it is either self-existent or some other existent being causes it to exist), and his inference from his third step (a contingent being is caused to exist by some other existent being) to its sixth (if a series of contingent beings doesn't have a first member, a self-existent being exists and causes the whole series), are controversial and are unlikely to convince every intelligent and well-trained person. Yet as we saw in Chapter 1, the strong version of the principle of sufficient reason that underlies Clarke's first premise can be replaced by weaker ones that yield essentially the same result, and his inference from step 3 to step 6 can be supported by refuting the standard objections to moves of this kind. And of course responses such as these may in turn require still further support. Our sense of the adequacy of Clarke's cosmological argument will thus ultimately depend on our sense of the comparative weights of *all* the conflicting considerations bearing on the proof's soundness and noncircularity.

Several things make universal agreement as to a proof's overall adequacy unlikely, however. In the first place, our assessment of the premises and of the reasons offered in their support will be unavoidably affected by our experiences and by what William James called our "willing" or "passional" nature – our temperament, needs, desires, and concerns, our hopes and fears, our passions, and our deepest intuitions. As we saw in Chapter 1, for example, theistic Vedanta's construal of maximal greatness as personal is arguably rooted in the high valuation it places on mutual love – an evaluation not shared by its

Advaitin opponents. Again, our assessments of cosmological arguments such as Clarke's may be partly determined by our craving for explanatory completeness or a lack of it, or by the presence or absence of sheer wonder at the fact that contingent being exists when it might not have.[55] Other things being equal, a person who craves explanatory completeness, or is struck by sheer wonder at the very existence of contingent being, is more likely to be persuaded by cosmological arguments than someone who is devoid of this craving and experience of wonder.

In the second place, a person's assessment of the strength of the claims offered in support of these premises or inferences is often a function of his or her evaluation of the comparative plausibility of comprehensive explanatory systems that include these claims as parts. That God is self-existent (and hence self-explanatory) and the creative ground of everything other than himself is part of classical Western theism, for example. Disagreements over a proof's adequacy can ultimately involve a clash of world views, and world views are supported by cumulative case arguments.

Third, our final assessments of the comparative weight of the numerous considerations bearing on the adequacy of Clarke's cosmological proof, or any other interesting philosophical argument, are paradigm examples of informal reasoning. In assessing an inference to the best explanation, for example, we have to decide which hypotheses should be taken seriously and which dismissed as nonstarters, what evidence is relevant and what is not, which comparative weights to place on various kinds of evidence, and so on. We must also make judgments or prior probability. Some hypotheses and opinions are legitimately dismissed without argument, but those we can't dismiss must be assigned a certain antecedent probability. Each of us approaches arguments with his "own view concerning" the likelihood of the conclusion "prior to the evidence," however, and "this view will result from the character of his mind.... If he is indisposed to believe he will explain away very strong evidence; if he is disposed to believe he may be willing to "accept very weak evidence."[56]

Finally, and perhaps most important, each reasoner must make an assessment of a cumulative case argument's overall force and determine how strongly the argument's "antecedents" (its premises and the considerations bearing on them) support its conclusion.

There are no mechanical decision procedures for making these assessments. Judgment is called for, and, in the last analysis, each of us must form her own best judgment concerning these matters. Our judgments, however, are irredeemably personal since, when all is said and done, each of us can view the various pieces of evidence only "in the medium of [her] primary mental experiences, under the aspects which they spontaneously present to [her], and with the aid of [her] best" efforts to do justice to them.[57]

The construction and assessments of interesting and existentially significant philosophical arguments thus invariably reflect our personal histories. An important way in which they sometimes do so is by reflecting our immersion in a particular textual tradition. Consider Anselm, for example. His *Proslogion* contains numerous allusions to scripture.[58] These allusions are integral to his text. For as Philip Clayton points out, the *Proslogion* was the product "of the form of life that was cultivated in the monastic (Benedictine) community at Bec," the "quintessential activity" of which was "meditating on the meaning of" scripture. But while "'scripture' for Anselm would have meant the whole of the Christian Bible and the bulk of the Fathers, the Hebrew Psalms" would have had "special import, owing to the preeminence given to the Psalter in the devotional life laid down by Benedict's Rule." This Rule minimally required chanting "through the entire Psalter at least once a week," although it "expected more than this from diligent monks" and "Lanfranc demanded more than this from the monks at Bec."[59]

Now "the Fool" is encountered in two Psalms, the fourteenth and fifty-third. This means that, at a minimum, Anselm would have encountered the Fool twice a week. "The Fool is [thus] not simply a foil ... against whom Anselm could test the strength of his own reasoning," but rather the source of something like a hermeneutical dilemma: "We believe God to be a being whose non-existence cannot be conceived. But we read in scripture about some Fool who appears to deny God's being. How can this be? ... Anselm prayed and meditated [on this question] until the argument [of the *Proslogion*] came to him. And ... fittingly," it "came to him one night at Matins as he meditated on the meaning of the Psalms that were set for that office."[60] Whether a person immersed in a radically different textual tradition[61] would find his arguments convincing is rather doubtful, however.[62]

Assessments of interesting and existentially significant philosophical arguments also reflect our passional nature. This is not necessarily a bad thing. As I shall argue in Chapter 4, certain dispositions of the heart may be needed to reason rightly about value-laden subject matter. That certain dispositions and attitudes are needed to reason rightly about moral matters, for example, is a commonplace in classical Chinese and Western moral philosophy. Thus, as we saw, Plato thought that "no man who is not naturally inclined and akin to justice and all other forms of excellence, even though he be quick at learning and remembering this or that ... will ever attain the truth that is attainable about virtue," while Aristotle believed that the first premises of ethical reasoning are general propositions about what is good for people in general, for certain kinds of people, or for people in certain circumstances. General propositions of this kind are partial articulations of the good life. Men and women whose natures have been warped by bad education or circumstances, however, will have a perverted sense of the good (identifying it with the life of pleasure, say, or the life of worldly honor). These people (as Plato says) have a "lie in their soul," and are therefore incapable of reasoning correctly about moral matters. A properly cultivated emotional nature is thus essential to sound ethical reasoning.

Now classical Christian theism identified God with Goodness itself. If this identification is correct, it is not surprising that the proper dispositions and feelings should also be thought to be necessary to reason correctly about God.

But the relevance of my remarks is even more general than my application of them to classical ethics and Christian theism might suggest. The most obvious instances of the thesis that basic philosophical disputes often reflect different passionally inflected assessments of more or less the same body of evidence is furnished by conflicts over comprehensive world views. Some of these world views are religious, but many are not. It is at least arguable, however, that *all* comprehensive world views integrally incorporate or reflect values.

Contemporary naturalism, for example, is typically reductive, incorporating a taste for "desert landscapes." It valorizes science as the only source of truth and dismisses any epistemic claims made by religion, poetry, or the arts. In some cases, a preference for naturalism may also reflect a desire that the world not contain "spooky" realities. Thomas Nagel, for instance, exclaims, "It isn't just that I don't believe in God.... It is that I hope there is no God! I don't want there to be a God; I don't want the universe to be like that."[63] Plato, on the other hand, thought that materialism was rooted in an undue preoccupation with bodily pleasure and pain. The *Phaedo* argues that "no man's soul can feel intense pleasure or pain in anything without also at the same time believing that the chief object of these his emotions is transparently clear and utterly real."[64] If this is correct, then what pains and pleases us will affect our judgments of what is and is not real. Bodily pleasures and pains, for example, drive "a rivet into the soul, pinning it down to the body and so assimilating it thereto that it believes everything to be real which the body declares to be so," and regards everything else as comparatively unreal.[65]

Again, Pierre Hadot has maintained that ancient metaphysical systems such as Stoicism and Epicureanism are rooted in distinct existential attitudes, "affectively toned" pre-theoretical senses of what the world is like and what things are important. "The role of theory is to provide a picture of the world which will help inculcate [or sustain] the [preferred] attitude by showing how it is rationally appropriate." Mark Wynn argues that not only do deep-seated and pervasive existential attitudes of this sort "direct our attention to a certain subject matter, and lead us to put certain questions to" it, "they also control our reading of the [nature of] the world in [a] more fundamental kind of way."[66]

If world views do incorporate values, and values can't be grasped in the absence of the right feelings and attitudes, then appropriate dispositions of the heart will be needed to discern the truth of any world view. Wrong dispositions, on the other hand, will result in false judgments and intellectual blindness.

Yet if these considerations are correct, then arguments are person-relative in an even deeper sense than those discussed earlier. Since an argument's cogency and convincingness can depend on the state of one's heart, and the states of people's hearts vary, an argument that is cogent or convincing for one person may not be cogent or convincing for another.

Some of these arguments may nevertheless be probative, however. Proofs are relative to persons because they differ in education, training, and intelligence; because they differ in their spatiotemporal location or the information available to them; or because they differ in purpose or in the state of their hearts. Many of these differences are epistemically innocent. Variations in education, training, and intelligence, or in spatiotemporal location or available information, are examples. Other differences are less obviously so. It is arguable, for instance, that *all* men and women *ought* to exhibit the dispositions and motions of the heart needed to reason rightly about moral matters and the things of religion, or to share certain purposes. If they should, then any person-relativity derived from variations in purpose or in dispositions of the heart ought not to exist; and (other things being equal) proofs whose cogency and convincingness depend upon having the right dispositions or sharing the right purposes *should* be cogent and convincing to everyone who can understand them. They are therefore probative in the sense defined earlier whether everyone or even most people accept them or not.

Immersion in different textual traditions and variations in the state of one's heart are thus among the most important sources of the person-relativity of religious proofs.[67] Chapters 3 and 4 will discuss them in depth.

3

Religious Reading and Theological Argument

Anselm's *Proslogion* is not only cast in the form of a prayer, it is larded with passages from the Psalms and other portions of scripture. The two are connected. As Sr. Benedicta Ward notes, "when [Anselm] uses the language of the psalms, he is not quoting; he is speaking with the language of the scriptures." Verses from the psalms "are woven together with Anselm's own thoughts, and are prayed spontaneously by him. This is the traditional monastic use of the psalter, where the words of the Hebrew psalms become the prayer of Christ." [1] As Alcuin wrote to Charlemagne, "if you come to the psalms with a serious mind, and look with the spirit of understanding, you will find there the word of the Lord incarnate, suffering, risen, and ascended." [2]

For Anselm and his fellow monks, reading, meditation, and prayer "were different aspects of the same thing, not separate exercises in their own right. Reading was an action of the whole person, by which the meaning of a text was absorbed, until it became a prayer. It was frequently compared to eating." [3] Thus Anselm's "Meditation on Human Redemption" opens with the words, "Taste the goodness of your Redeemer, burn with love for your Savior. Chew the honeycomb of his words, suck their flavor, which is more pleasing than honey, swallow their health-giving sweetness. Chew by thinking, suck by understanding, swallow by loving and rejoicing. Be happy in chewing, be grateful in sucking, delight in swallowing." [4] And indeed, "the text 'O taste and see how gracious the Lord is' was applied more often to the reading of the scriptures than to the Eucharist before the twelfth century." [5]

These views were by no means peculiar to Anselm. For example, Bernard's Thirty-Fifth Sermon on the *Song of Songs* says that the Bible is "the wine cellar of the Holy Spirit," and calls it "a tasty matter for rumination that fattens his stomach, ... and makes all his bones sing with praise.... And in the *Vajracchedikasutra*," the Buddha says that "learning or teaching" one of its four-line verses "produces more merit than giving away whole world-systems filled with jewels." [6]

In short, the ingestion of religious texts was widely believed to be essential to spiritual development. These texts were not only transmitted by books or other physical instruments, however, but perhaps most often orally. In the first thousand years of the Christian era, for example, "Buddhist and other Indian 'texts' were principally stored in the memories of monks and pandits." The major monasteries contained impressive libraries, and copying them (or having them copied) was a meritorious work. Moreover, a major purpose of the pilgrimages of Chinese Buddhists to Indian monasteries during this period was to secure copies of important manuscripts. Even so, evidence suggests that they did not play a central role in pedagogy.[7] "The principal significance of manuscripts" at the famous monastery of Nalanda, for instance, "(and throughout Buddhist India) ... had ... not to do with their pedagogical use but with the significance of their presence. Whether stored in a library, enshrined in a stupa, or lying on the lap of teacher, they represent the word of the Buddha by their presence. They are the *buddhavaccana* [Buddha's voice]," and are thus "a mode of the Buddha's presence." The training of the monks "did not occur by way of manuscripts," however, "at least not principally: it occurred by hearing, memorizing and pondering."[8]

Or consider catechetical instruction in early Christian North Africa and in Jerusalem. It consisted of four stages. In the first, "a petitioner or inquirer who had professed interest in becoming a Christian" was tested for his sincerity and, "if all went well, ... was admitted to formal catechetical instruction," though without having "yet asked for (or been promised) baptism." The second stage typically lasted three years. Instruction was "largely oral," mostly took place during communal worship, and "took the form of exegetical commentary upon scriptural texts. These [meetings] occurred at least weekly and may at some places and at some times have been daily." If, at the conclusion of this process, it "seemed good both to the catechumen and to the Church, baptism was requested and promised. This usually happened at the end of the season of Epiphany." At this "point the catechumen became one of the elect, someone who has been judged competent to receive baptism." This third stage was constituted by "a period of still more intensive oral instruction in the Bible." Describing the process at Jerusalem "at the end of the fourth century, Egeria says that it took three hours a day seven days a week, and that the catechist" (often the bishop) "'goes through the whole Bible ... first relating the literal meaning of each passage, then interpreting its spiritual meaning.'" Instruction here, too, "was entirely oral." Baptism itself was bestowed "at the dawn of Easter Sunday." The fourth and final stage took up the week immediately following baptism," in which "they had explained to them the ritual mysteries (especially the Eucharist) from which until then they had been barred."[9]

Historically, oral instruction and memorization were important for at least two reasons. The first and most obvious was widespread illiteracy. It is probable "that no more than fifteen percent of Christians were literate ... during the first five centuries of the Christian era," and "the percentage was almost certainly lower in both medieval India and medieval Europe."[10] The second and more interesting reason was this: through the memorization of what is read or heard, one "becomes textualized (an embodiment of the work)." The text enters "into the fabric of [one's] intellectual and emotional life in a way that makes deep claims upon that life, claims that can [henceforth] only be ignored with effort and deliberation."[11]

Anthologies and commentaries are typical products of religious reading traditions, and are both closely connected to memorization. An anthology's excerpts are often short. When they are, the anthology may be "intended for use as a tool in memorization." Cyprian's *Ad Quirinum,* for example, "is an anthology of biblical excerpts," most quite short and self-contained, which were designed to be memorized. Cyprian himself describes his purpose as follows: he collected "what is necessary [essential for a Christian to know] in connected excerpts placed under subject heads.... Brevity of this sort is very useful for readers ... for a longer work would dissipate the reader's understanding and comprehension while a tenacious memory holds on to what has been read in a cleverly ordered compendium."[12] Furthermore, when (as was often the case) little or only minimal information is given about an excerpt's source,[13] the reader is encouraged to focus on the excerpt itself, extracting whatever spiritual nourishment it provides. Again, commentaries on religious texts typically take as their "initial object" one of the small sections "into which the work has been subdivided for memorization ... and only then, if at all, take up ... larger units or ... the work as a whole.... A comment on any one of these [excerpts] will typically presuppose [memorial] knowledge of them all, and may be incomprehensible without such knowledge."[14]

Reading traditions incorporate "acknowledged constraints" on what should and should not be read, as well as "upon what and how religious readers should read and compose as well as (by entailment) upon the kinds of conclusions that can be properly drawn and taught" from what has been read. This is evinced in various ways. One is the importance of commentary in these traditions, which "implies a reverence for the text that is studied, a recognition of the truth it passes down, and a willingness to subordinate personal interests, [idiosyncrasies], and novelty to the wisdom of the tradition that has preserved and cared for the texts in which that wisdom is" enshrined.[15]

Humility before the commentarial tradition is closed tied to reverence toward one's teacher. "Apprehension of the true doctrine is said to be the service and respect due those reciters of the doctrine who are entirely involved in religious practice and who explain the sacred works in the proper ways. It is sitting near them; getting up before them; bowing and doing homage to them; obeying them; protecting them, receiving them; giving them the necessities ...; giving them reverence, protecting them as your master; praising them, and protecting them from criticism."[16] The received wisdom of the tradition provides the standard by which all other claims to truth are to be assessed. Thus Augustine's scathing criticism of the teachers of grammar and rhetoric is grounded in his conviction that whatever intrinsic beauties Virgil, Ovid, and the other poets may have, when they "are loved for themselves rather than for the usefully decorative place they may have in ornamenting and complementing a Christian account of things, the result will be idolatry, and (usually) the improper inflaming of the passions and desires."[17] (More on this in Chapter 5.)

As John Clayton has pointed out, reading traditions inflect their participants understanding of what is and is not rational. "Every day of the lives of" figures such as Ghazali, Udayana, and Anselm "was in large part filled with 'listening to,' 'thinking about,' and 'meditating on' sacred texts as a path to holiness." Moreover, and as we have seen, these texts, or significant portions of them, "would have been committed to memory. Texts in this way were internalized and became part of them. They not only *cited* the texts, they *thought* and *spoke* the texts, they *lived* the texts." It thus isn't surprising "that their rational reflections should have been ... prompted and guided by their tradition's authoritative texts." Nor should it be surprising that their traditions affect what they regard as good reasons. "The choice and the construction of theistic arguments in the writings of Ghazali and Udayana [and Anselm, too, we might add] were controlled by the specific teachings about the divine nature and activity in their respective religious traditions.... Nor do they ever adduce ... any reasons" for their conclusions, "which are not reasons for their own religious communities, though they do introduce as warrants reasons that would not be regarded as such" by some of the targets of "their particular proofs."[18]

The insistence on the necessity of reasoning from within a tradition is by no means peculiar to these figures. In his comparative study of St. Francis de Sales and the Vaishnava theologian, Sri Vedanta Dasika, Francis Clooney points out that "as a corrective to ordinary thinking and speaking," both "recommend that religious people become deeply imbued with the language and images of scripture, ... its emotions, and imposing and inspiring images of people who have lived concretely the ideals which scripture announces."[19] Moreover, both believe that when reason and argument are dissevered from scripture and tradition, they invariably go astray. "'Whosoever understands the seers' teaching of the dharma with the help of reasoning, not contrary to the Vedas and instructive scriptures – only that person understands the dharma, no one else.' [*Manu* 12.106] Mere reasoners who have recourse to arguments inconsistent with the Vedas strip away its authentic meaning."[20]

It is worth noting that reading traditions are not peculiar to religion. They were also characteristic of the philosophical schools of antiquity. As Pierre Hadot has pointed out:

... it was believed that the truth had been "given" in the master's texts, and that all that had to be done was to bring it to light and explicate it. Plotinus, for example, writes: "These statements are not new; they do not belong to the present time, but were made long ago, although not explicitly, and what we have said in this discussion has been an interpretation of them, relying on Plato's own writings for evidence that these views are ancient." ... Each philosophical or religious school or group believed itself to be in possession of traditional truth, communicated from the beginning by the divinity to a few wise men. Each therefore laid claim to being the legitimate depository of the truth.[21]

Moreover, in each case the transmission and proper interpretation of the tradition's authoritative texts was designed to effect a moral and spiritual transformation in the lives of those who existentially appropriated them.

The appeal to texts is neither incidental nor superfluous. The full meaning of explicitly or implicitly value-laden propositions or assertions typically *includes* their emotive connotations and the associated metaphors and narratives that express them. As a result, arguments that employ these propositions can't be fully understood unless one appreciates their connotations and associations – an appreciation that is typically engendered by an immersion in the textual practices of the arguments' authors and audiences. Consider "God is a maximally perfect being, 'a being greater than which none can be thought,' " for example, or, "God is the creator of every contingent being, 'of all things in heaven and on earth.' " The first proposition is a crucial premise of ontological proofs and the second is the conclusion of most modern versions of the cosmological argument. A person who fully understands these propositions – and thus sympathetically appreciates them – is more likely to be predisposed to accepting them and, as a consequence, to require a lower standard of proof than someone who does not.

On the face of it, though, traditional practices such as these run directly counter to the insistence on neutrality enjoined by an Enlightenment project that continues to dominate most modern thought. Yet modern intellectuals, too, ingest and are shaped by texts and by the standards and models of rationality that they explicitly or implicitly endorse. Academically trained Western philosophers like me, for example, master certain texts, acquire certain skills, and share many logical and dialectical techniques. But in addition to all the things we have in common, we ingest and are molded by very different philosophical models – Plato versus Aristotle, for instance, or Descartes versus Hume, or continental idealism versus the Anglo American analytic tradition, and so on – and these affect and inflect our work. Nor is there a neutral or non-question-begging stance or point of view from which these competing standards of rationality could be impartially assessed. This does not imply that these competing textually inflected models of rationality aren't properly exposed to rational scrutiny by outsiders, or that they don't have certain features in common (rules of formal logic, for example, shared agreement on certain empirical facts, and the like) but it does imply that these shared features aren't by themselves sufficient to adjudicate adequately between rival systems of philosophical (or religious) belief.

Note, however, that the justification for embracing a *religious* tradition typically involves an appeal to that tradition. The authority of the Vedas, for example, is said to be a consequence of their "intrinsic luminosity," and we know that they are intrinsically luminous because the Vedic commentarial traditions vouch for it.[22] Yet this creates three problems. In the first place, supporting tradition by appealing to tradition is obviously circular (although as we shall see in Chapter 4, circles aren't always vicious). In the second place, the authority of religious traditions ultimately rests on claims to revelation.[23] Claims to revelation are contentious, however, and will be discussed in Chapter 6. A more immediate problem, though, is these traditions' insularity.[24]

A good example of the problem is provided by a nineteenth-century Sanskrit debate between the Christian John Muir and three Hindu pandits. The pandits' reaction to Christianity was almost entirely negative. Among other things, they accused Christianity of fostering "contempt for and abuse of animal life" because of its failure to acknowledge the role animals play in the reincarnation of souls, and its doctrine of creation *ex nihilo* was faulted because it seemed to directly implicate God in the world's evils. Furthermore, the pandits rejected Christianity's doctrines of original sin and forensic justification as illogical and unjust and insisted that it was wrong to think that humanity's "basic defect" was moral rather than epistemological.[25]

Two things made it especially difficult for Muir and his adversaries to find common ground: the fact that the authority of the Vedas was assumed by the pandits to override any incompatible non-Vedic doctrine, and the fact that "in so far as [the pandits'] interpretations of Christianity enabled them to apprehend it accurately, Muir's exposition of that religion propounded little or nothing that hadn't been discussed at some time in Hinduism and rejected by the mainstream of orthodoxy."[26]

Francis X. Clooney and James L. Frederick believe that one can overcome insularity, however, without abandoning one's deep commitment to one's own religious tradition by practicing what they call "comparative theology."

Comparative theology is interreligious. "There is no good reason today to keep theological traditions separate from one another," both because "almost all of what counts as theological thinking is shared across religious boundaries," and because a common reason makes "it possible for believers in many different traditions to at least understand one another and ... to agree on [at least some] topics."[27]

A second feature is closely related to the first. Interreligious theology is necessarily comparative. "Since traditions and their key components are neither identical nor entirely dissimilar, an intelligent interreligious theology is already a comparative theology where similarities and differences are taken into account."[28] It is essential that one's comparisons be detailed and specific, however. One must engage in the study of concrete others such as Shri Vaishnavism or Jodo Shin Shu or Madhyamika in all their rich particularity. And one must do so on a long-term basis without either (1) relying on abstract theories of "religious experience or religion in general to provide a foundation for comparison" or (2) employing the doctrines of one's home religion to interpret the doctrines of the alien religion,[29] since doing so "usually leads to systemic distortions in the reception of the [religious] Other, ... in which the threat of the Other, as well as its transformative power, is muted."[30]

Comparative theology should also be dialogical, and this is its third feature. One must take one's counterparts in other traditions as one's theological peers, thereby including them among the voices to which one is answerable. In *On Liberty*, John Stuart Mill argued that the best test of the truth of one's opinions is how well they come off in untrammeled debates with intelligent, well-informed, and morally – and one could add, spiritually – sensitive adherents of opposed views. What is true in general is also true of comparative theology. If it is to be effective, one's dialogue partners must be real people and not ideal constructs. In spite of good intentions, Nicholas of Cusa's *De Pace Fidei* fails because the "Greek," the "Arab," and other parties to his debate aren't real persons but "intellectual powers" that were "established by the King of the Universe ... over each of the mundane provinces, and over each of the religious sects."[31] His fictional disputants turn out to agree in essentials but only because each is committed to a brand of Neo-Platonism remarkably similar to Nicholas's own. (In this respect, *De Pace Fidei* resembles Ralph Cudworth's *True Intellectual System of the Universe* and other attempts to show that the "ancient theology [philosophy]" was implicitly Christian,[32] and thus, one might argue, were not genuinely open to the religious Other.)

The fourth and most contentious feature of comparative theology is that it is "confessional." "Even after initial comparisons and during dialogue, theologians should be able to affirm the content of their faith as true, render it intelligible to those who believe it already, and venture to put persuasive arguments before outsiders in order to demonstrate the truth of the faith, which might even lead some outsiders to believe and convert."[33] Yet even if it does not, all participants will have learned not to misrepresent each other's positions, will have become acutely aware of striking agreements and resemblances, and may even end up modifying their own positions in subtle and not so subtle ways.

Clooney's comparative examination of de Sales and Desika on loving surrender to God exemplifies what he means by "(inter) religious reading." One is vulnerable "to both texts," refusing "to reduce either to a component of some later and settled 'higher' viewpoint." Repeatedly reading the two texts together generates a "spiritual power" that draws "the mind into a situation it cannot control and that illumines and ignites the heart. Each text has this power, and so too both together, as their worlds" become "open to us, neither preempting the other."[34]

Comparative theology's confessional stance has an important implication. While it draws on "the methods ... and findings" of comparative religion, it doesn't pretend to be neutral. Comparative religion is most usefully regarded as "a discipline within the secular study of religions ... [that] holds up for itself the scholarly ideal of detached inquiry, and seeks, as its primary public, the academic community of scholars." "Comparative theology," on the other hand, "does *not* proceed from a religiously neutral starting point," and is *not* merely descriptive but "normative, constructive and revisionist." Moreover, even though it "includes the academy of scholars as a public to be addressed," it is typically addressed by believers to believers in both the home religion and the relevant alien religion. "Unlike comparative religion, comparative theology entails a 'faith seeking understanding.'"[35]

This is fully consistent with comparative theology's placing a high value on the search for objective truth. Indeed, while its penultimate aim is mutual understanding, comparative theology's ultimate aim is to discover truth and thereby learn to "know God [the divine?] more fully."[36] Moreover, in pursuing this aim, an "honest acknowledgement of [one's] own normative commitments and interests, ... when coupled with a willingness to submit [them] to critique and revision," is more likely to correct "bias and distortion" than "the vain pursuit of the chimerical ideal of scholarly objectivity and neutrality."[37]

There is of course a certain unavoidable tension between comparative theology's confessional stance and its search for truth. For "when all is said and done," its "theological method comes down to a balancing act between openness and commitment, or as Clooney puts it, 'between a necessary vulnerability to truth as one might find it, and the truth as one has already found it.' The crucial question ... is just where to draw the line between a sincere openness to another religious perspective and a compromise of one's core convictions."[38] There are no mechanical decision procedures for drawing these lines, however. Like the good physician's diagnoses, wisely doing so is a matter for trained and informed judgment.

Agreement is desirable. But whether it is secured or not, the proper practice of comparative theology is transformative. "Every theological position can [and should be] brought into the comparative theological framework by rereading it in the light of positions taken by" theologians from the other "traditions involved in the conversation." "My model of theology ... might be described ... as moving from a confessional base through intervening intellectual activities to a renewed and transformed expropriation of confessional views. Neither theological comparison or confession can flourish in separation from the other, and each constantly transforms the other."[39]

Precisely how, though, does it do so? How, for example, has Clooney reread the Christian doctrine of the Incarnation in the light of the two theistic Hindu views of divine embodiment he discusses in Chapter 4 of *Hindu God, Christian God*? Both Shaiva Siddhanta and the Vaishnavas believe that God freely "externalizes himself and assume[s] a body ... out of love" so that humans can know and experience him. They differ on the nature of those bodies, however. For the Shaivites, a body is essentially an instrument through which one communicates and produces effects. Divine bodies thus include revealed mantras that are employed "in meditation aimed at visualizing Shiva," and "intermediate beings ranging from gods to gurus through whom Shiva creates lesser beings." Ultimately for the Shaivites, however, God is "without form."[40] For Vaishnavas, on the other hand, God is embodied in the ten descents (*avataras*), the most important of which are Rama and Krishna. God's bodies are real but without the imperfections of ordinary human bodies.[41] In spite of appearances, these descents are not limited and do not really suffer. Their apparent sufferings are "*abhinya*, a term which commonly refers to theatrical performances and gestures, that is, the physical movements made by an actor or dancer in the course of a performance to express emotions." Just as "a powerful theatrical performance can be truly transformative or wrenching even if no one is 'really' drowned or murdered or saved, so the deeds of Krishna and Rama are deeply" engaging and affecting "because of the powerful way in which God communicates through these actions and [thereby] transforms the 'audience' of devotees"[42] But what one would like and doesn't receive is an account of just how a consideration of views like these has transformed Clooney's understanding of and commitment to a Christian view of God's embodiment, for which the reality and intensity of the embodiment's sufferings are essential.

While comparative theology arguably escapes the insularity that has characterized most textual traditions, it does have problems of its own.

First, while Clooney admits that the dialogue should, in principle, include participants from all traditions, this is impossible in practice because it would require each participant to examine and reflect upon each tradition in depth.

Second, comparative theology's method works very well when one's dialogue partners are drawn from similar traditions.[43] But it is unclear how well the method will work when the participants' views and practices are more distant from one another (a more or less traditional Roman Catholic, for example, and a Shri Lankan Theravada Buddhist, or a Muslim fundamentalist and a Neo-Confucian).

Third (and most important) does comparative theology truly respect the religious Other? Hugh Nicholson doubts that abandoning abstract or a priori interpretative frameworks and "integrating theological reflection with knowledge of the actual teachings of other traditions" (as both Clooney and Frederick do) are sufficient to solve "the problem of theological hegemonism." By the very fact that it stresses "interreligious solidarity and interreligious friendship," comparative theology is in danger of excluding "*oppositional* discourses" and those who engage in them.[44] Moreover, as John Cobb has pointed out, there may well be "a fundamental tension between the imperative to dialogue and the insistence on already possessing the one absolute religion," since the latter "encourages the assumption that the Christian faith [for example] is the final destiny in which the others can be fulfilled.[45] The implication of Cobb's remarks is that, because it is confessional, comparative theology is ultimately nothing more than a somewhat more open and generous form of doctrinal exclusivism.[46]

Just what, though, is *wrong* with doctrinal exclusivism? Cobb has argued that entering dialogue with a prior commitment to the truths of one's home religion is unacceptably arrogant since it antecedently disqualifies the other religions when "in every fiber of [their] being" they refuse "to be disqualified."[47] Yet note that precisely the same charge can be leveled at even the most irenic *philosophical* exclusivists.

Consider, for example, disputes between physicalists or materialists and Platonic idealists, between determinists and indeterminists, or between Kantian moralists and consequentialists. The analogy is important, for philosophical disputes of this sort are paradigmatic examples of dialogues typically marked by mutual respect, a willingness to learn, to make and respond to criticism, and (in principle at least) to abandon one's view if the argument demands it. Moreover, dialogue of this sort is essential to the practice of philosophy. Something is lacking if compatibilists, for example, talk only to each other. And this remains true even if compatibilists are pretty good at envisaging incompatibilist alternatives and objections to their own position. For other things being equal (intelligence, knowledge, etc.), alternatives and criticisms are most effectively presented and pressed home by those who actually subscribe to them.

Yet is there any reason to expect that, as a result of such a dialogue, either member of one of these pairs of opposed philosophical positions will be radically transformed and not merely transformed around the edges? Is there any reason to think that either of them *should* be? And if so, how? In the face of unresolved philosophical disagreements, the "equal weight view"[48] would arguably require agnosticism or skepticism. Agnosticism or skepticism doesn't *transform* the opposed positions, however; it *abandons* them. And a third position combining the insights of determinism, say, and indeterminism is hard to imagine. (Compatibilism is still a form of determinism, and a two-level or noumenal-phenomenal view like Kant's is, if coherent at all, still indeterminist.) Furthermore, in the cases in which the competing philosophical positions are clearly incompatible if taken at face value, finding a significant common core or modifying the competing positions in a way that eliminates the inconsistency without essentially abandoning at least one of them will seldom be a plausible option. Is there any reason to think, then, that at the end of the dialogue between determinists and indeterminists, most adherents of one of these opposed positions won't (quite properly given their reasons, perspective, and the like) continue to judge the other opinion to be false, that is, remain philosophical doctrinal exclusivists?

If there is not, then why balk at *religious* doctrinal exclusivism? Perhaps the two sorts of disagreement are relevantly different. But if so, how? One possible outcome of *philosophical* disagreement is suspension of judgment. A similar move in the case of *theological* disagreement would involve abandoning one's faith stance, and one might think that this is problematic in a way that suspending judgment on a purely philosophical issue is not. But any difference here is at best one of degree. Not all theological issues carry heavy existential freight, and many philosophical issues do. William James, for example, confessed that he desperately needed to believe in the freedom of his will, while Plato thought that physicalism or materialism had deleterious moral and spiritual consequences. It is also true that religious intolerance can have horrendous consequences, while entrenched positions on the status of universals (for example) do not, but here too the differences can be exaggerated. The fact that doctrinal exclusivism is often combined with salvific inclusivism and a commitment to liberal social and political values suggests that doctrinal exclusivism by itself doesn't necessarily lead to deleterious consequences. And philosophical views, too, can have problematic social and political consequences. (Witness the role played by Rousseau's *Social Contract* in constructing the views of the authors of the Reign of Terror during the French Revolution, or the questionable impact of consequentialism on contemporary bureaucratic institutions.)

The upshot is that it is at least arguable that the most intellectually honest response to irresolvable confessional differences is either agnosticism or skepticism, or a suitably modest form of doctrinal exclusivism such as Clooney's and Frederick's. I have argued that if one isn't prepared to embrace agnosticism or skepticism with respect to basic philosophical disputes,[49] then it isn't reasonable to embrace them with respect to fundamental religious disagreements. But if it isn't, then views such as Clooney's and Frederick's arguably provide the most attractive alternative to the insularity of some traditional positions.

4

Passional Reasoning

In *An Essay concerning Human Understanding*, John Locke defined reason as "the discovery of the certainty or probability of such propositions or truths, which the mind arrives at by deduction made from such ideas, which he has got by the use of its natural faculties; viz. by sensation or reflection" (4.18.2). Rational belief is proportionate to the strength of the evidence at one's disposal. "The mind, *if it will proceed rationally*, ought to examine all the grounds of probability, and see how they make more or less for or against any proposition, before it assents to or dissents from it; and upon a due balancing of the whole, reject or receive it, with more or less firm assent, proportionably to the preponderancy of the greater ground of probability on one side or the other" (4.15.5). What is true of beliefs in general is true of religious beliefs. They are rational only if they are (1) properly basic (by being immediately grounded in the mind's intuitive awareness of its own ideas, for example), (2) inferred from those ideas by sound deductive or inductive reasoning, or (3) the content of a revelation whose credentials are certified by beliefs meeting the first or second condition. Although modern intellectuals may doubt whether religious beliefs meet these standards, Locke did not. God's existence can be demonstrated, and the evidence at our disposal makes it probable that the Bible is God's revelation,

Locke's view is sometimes called evidentialism. Evidentialism has much to be said for it. Like scientific beliefs, religious beliefs appear to be "evidence essential" – they are rationally held only if one is entitled to believe that someone in one's intellectual community has good evidence for them. (I am entitled to believe there are quarks, for example, but only because I have good reason to believe that physicists have evidence for them.)[1] Religious beliefs are also controversial. Responsible inquirers have called them into question, and some doubts about them are not unreasonable. Under these conditions, one can appropriately be asked what entitles one to believe. The only entitlement that is likely to convince others of one's right to believe is good evidence. But finally (and most important), Christians, at least, have often assumed that there *is* good evidence for their position and that those who examine it without prejudice will be persuaded by it.

These considerations do not entail that a person does not have an epistemic right to believe unless she can provide good evidence for her belief. But they do imply that she must at least believe that there *is* good evidence for them, and that some people (the community's theologians or saints, perhaps) have it.

Two interrelated facts, however, have contributed to a recent tendency to downplay the importance of evidence in the formation and retention of religious beliefs. The first is the obvious absence of evidence that would compel the assent of any fully informed, sufficiently intelligent, and adequately trained inquirer. The second is the fact that religious belief seems to depend more directly on the state of one's heart or moral temperament than on one's evidence. How else to explain why two equally intelligent and informed inquirers can arrive at such different assessments of the same evidence? (Compare Richard Swinburne's and J. L. Mackie's evaluation of the evidence for design, for example.)

My *Reason and the Heart*[2] offered a different account of these facts, namely, that mature religious belief can, and perhaps should, be based on evidence, but that the evidence can be accurately assessed only by men and women who possess the proper moral and spiritual qualifications.

This view was once a Christian commonplace; reason is capable of knowing God on the basis of evidence – but only when one's cognitive faculties are rightly disposed. It should be distinguished from two other views that have dominated modern thought. The first claims that God can be known by "objective reason," that is, by an understanding that systematically excludes passion, desire, and emotion from the process of reasoning. The other insists that God can be known only "subjectively," or by the heart.[3] Both views identify reason with ratiocination or calculation. They also assume that reasoning is objective only when unaffected by wants, interest, and desires. The tradition I discussed steers between these two extremes. It places a high value on proofs, arguments, and inferences, yet also believes that a properly disposed heart is needed to see their *force*.

This epistemic view is deeply embedded in important strands of the Christian tradition. Calvin, for example, thought that rational arguments for the authority of scripture "will not obtain full credit in the hearts of men until they are sealed by the inward testimony of the Spirit."[4] And even though Aquinas believed that there is good evidence for the divine origin of Christian teaching, he did not think that it was sufficient to compel assent in the absence of an inward movement of a will grounded in a "supernatural principle."[5] Similarly, seventeenth-century Anglican divines argued that "the gospel can only obtain, 'a free admission into the assent of the understanding, when it brings a passport from a rightly disposed will.'" The notion that a proper disposition is needed to appreciate the force of rational arguments for the authority of the gospel can be easily extended to rational arguments for the truths of "natural religion" when these too, come under attack. John Spurr has argued that this process was well under way by the end of the seventeenth century.[6]

I. Four Accounts of Passional Reasoning

Jonathan Edwards

One of the most carefully articulated versions of this position is Jonathan Edwards's. His view is briefly this. "Actual ideas" are ideas that are lively, clear, and distinct. Thought has a tendency to substitute "signs" (words, images) for actual ideas. This tendency is useful and normally quite harmless. But it impedes reasoning when "we are at a loss concerning a connection or consequence [between ideas], or have a new inference to draw, or would see the force of some new argument."[7] Now if accurate reasoning about a subject matter involves attending to actual ideas of it, as both Locke and Edwards believe, then one can't accurately reason about religion if one lacks the appropriate actual ideas. To have an actual idea of God, for example, one must have actual ideas of the ideas that compose it. But most of us do not. Those parts of the idea of God that everyone has (ideas of power, knowledge, and justice, for instance) either aren't attended to or, when they are, fail to elicit the proper affective reactions. Other parts of the idea of God are simply missing. Without the simple idea of "true beauty" (the radiance or splendor of true benevolence), we can't understand God's holiness and the facts that depend on it such as the infinite heinousness of sin (and of the consequent necessity of atonement). And because we can't properly understand ideas of affections if we haven't experienced them, we can't understand God's benevolence if we aren't benevolent ourselves. True benevolence remedies each of these deficiencies.[8] Because the desires of the truly benevolent are properly ordered, they are suitably affected by the ideas of God's attributes and activities that everyone has. (They fear his wrath, for example, and are properly grateful for his benefits.) They also understand God's benevolence since their own benevolence mirrors it. Finally, the truly benevolent delight in the benevolence in which holiness consists; that is, they "perceive" or "taste" or "relish" its beauty. Edwards's claim, then, is that to reason accurately about God one must possess an actual idea of God, and to have that one must be truly benevolent. Right reasoning about religious matters requires right affections.

Edwards speaks of the savingly converted's ability to perceive God's beauty as a new "spiritual sense." The "immediate object" of this sense is "the beauty of holiness," "true moral or spiritual beauty" – "a new simple idea" that cannot be produced by the "exalting, varying, or compounding of that kind of perceptions or sensations which the mind had before."[9] But the spiritual sense also has an indirect object – spiritual facts or truths. There are two cases to consider.

In the first, the spiritual sense enables us to recognize the truth of propositions that are logically or epistemically related to the excellence of divine things. For example, our apprehension of Christ's beauty and excellency produces a conviction of his sufficiency as a mediator. Moreover, to grasp the appropriateness of God's end in creation, namely, the communication of his glory *ad extra*, one must perceive its beauty. Again, one must see the beauty of holiness to appreciate the "hatefulness of sin" and thus be convinced of the justice of divine punishment and our inability to make satisfaction.[10]

But it also helps us grasp the truth of the gospel scheme as a whole. A conviction of the gospel's truth is an inference from the beauty or excellency of what it depicts, namely, "God and Jesus Christ ... the work of redemption and the ways and works of God." "There is a divine and superlative glory in these things" that distinguishes "them from all that is earthly and temporal," and a spiritual person "truly sees" this glory; his perception of it is as immediate and direct as a perception of color or the sweetness of food.[11] (This was not a new idea. Richard Sibbes, for instance, said, "God ... causeth him to see a divine majesty shining forth in the scriptures, so that there must be an infused establishing by the Spirit to settle the heart in this first principle ... that the Scriptures are the word of God." Or again, "How do you know the word to be the word? It carrieth proof and evidence in itself. It is an evidence that the fire is hot to him that feeleth it, and that the sun shineth to him that looks on it; how much more doth the word ... I am sure I felt it, it warmed my heart and converted me.")[12]

A conviction of the gospel's truth is thus "an effect and natural consequence of this perception."[13] The perception and conviction are nonetheless distinct. The mind *infers* the truth and reality of the things depicted in the gospel from its *perception* of their spiritual beauty. There is, however, no "long chain of arguments; the argument is but one, and the evidence direct; the mind ascends to the truth of the gospel but by one step, and that is its divine glory." And because only one step is involved, we can truly say that the divinity or reality or truth of the gospel is "as it were" known intuitively, that "a soul may have a kind of intuitive knowledge of the divinity [or truth or reality] of the things exhibited in the gospel."[14]

The mind's object differs in the two cases, however. In the first, it is a comparatively specific doctrinal proposition that is logically or epistemically connected with other propositions that affirm that some person or characteristic or activity or state of affairs is truly amiable or beautiful or excellent. Our spiritual sense enables us to *perceive* the truth of the latter, and from this we *infer* the truth of the former. In the second, the mind's object is the content of the gospel as a whole – what Paul Ricoeur has called "the world of the text." The central or controlling features of this world – God, Christ, and the scheme of salvation – are *perceived* to be truly beautiful. On the basis of this perception one immediately concludes that the biblical world is not fictional, like the ones depicted in *The Brothers Karamazov* or *Moby Dick*, but *real*.

If this is correct, then the new spiritual sense does not typically involve a direct or immediate or quasiperceptual awareness of God himself. Rather, God's reality is inferred from the excellency and beauty of the things depicted in scripture. Yet as we have just seen, the inference "is without any long chain of argument; the argument is but one, and the evidence direct." Because of the inference's spontaneity and immediacy, a person can even be said to have "a kind of intuitive knowledge" of divinity. Edwards's interpretation of the redeemed's knowledge of God's reality is thus strikingly similar to Descartes's and Locke's account of our knowledge of other minds and physical objects. While other minds and physical objects aren't directly perceived on their view, their reality *is* spontaneously and immediately inferred from sensations or impressions that *are* directly apprehended. Edwards thinks our knowledge of God is similar. Even though God is not directly perceived, his reality is no more remote or uncertain than other minds or physical objects are on views such as Descartes's and Locke's.

Why, though, trust the deliverances of the new spiritual sense? Edwards addresses this issue in the final chapter of *The Nature of True Virtue,* where he attempts to show that "the frame of mind, or inward sense ... whereby the mind is disposed to" relish divine things for their spiritual beauty is not "given arbitrarily," but agrees "with the necessary nature of things."[15] Now the "frame of mind" that disposes a person to delight in true beauty (that is, to be pleased with true benevolence) is true benevolence itself. Edwards thinks that it will therefore be sufficient to show that *true benevolence* agrees with the nature of things.

Edwards's strategy, in other words, is this. True benevolence is the "mechanism" underlying the new spiritual sense. If we can show that true benevolence has a foundation in the nature of things, we are entitled to conclude that the spiritual sense, too, is aligned with reality. Edwards's task, then, is to prove that true benevolence agrees with the "necessary nature of things," and he offers four arguments to show that it does.[16] They vary in their persuasiveness, however, and a more convincing argument can be derived from his doctrine of the indwelling of the Holy Spirit.

Like his medieval and Reform predecessors, Edwards thinks that God is present to his creatures in virtue of his knowledge, his causal activity, and his substance. Yet because he is an occasionalist like Malebranche, a subjective idealist like Berkeley, and a mental phenomenalist like Hume, God's presence is even more intimate on Edwards's view than on more traditional accounts. What are "vulgarly" called causal relations are mere constant conjunctions. True causes necessitate their effect. Because God's will alone meets this condition, God is the only true cause. He is also the only true substance. Physical objects are collections of "corporeal ideas" (ideas of color, for example, solidity, resistance, and so on). Minds are series of "thoughts" or "perceptions." Now any substance underlying perceptions, thoughts, and corporeal ideas would be something that "subsisted by itself, and stood underneath, and kept up" mental and physical properties. But God alone subsists by himself, and stands underneath, and keeps up thoughts, perceptions, solidity, color, and other corporeal qualities (ideas). "The substance of [minds and] bodies," therefore, is either "nothing, or nothing but the Deity acting in that particular manner ... where he thinks fit." The only real cause and the only real substance are thus God himself. "How truly, then is it in him that we live, move, and have our being."[17]

God's relation to his elect is even more intimate, however. The Holy Spirit "dwells" in the saints "as a vital principle in their souls [and] there produces those effects wherein he exerts and communicates himself *in his own proper nature*."[18] "True saving grace is no other than the very love of God; *that is, God in one of the persons of the Trinity*, uniting himself to the soul of a creature as a vital principle, dwelling there and exerting himself by the faculties of the soul of man, in his own proper nature, after the manner of a principle of nature." The saints are thus "not only partakers of a nature that may in some sense be called Divine, because 'tis conformed to the nature of God; *but the very Deity does in some sense dwell in them*."[19] (There were several Puritan precedents for this view.)

Edwards is making two claims. First, the new spiritual disposition and tastes that God bestows on the soul are divine. The difference between God's love and joy and the love and the joy that he bestows on his saints is a difference of degree, not of nature or kind. Second, God does not act on the soul from without, but dwells within it, as the principle of a new nature, living, acting, and exerting itself in the exercise of the soul's faculties. The "mechanism" underlying the new spiritual sense is thus ultimately God himself. Hence, because God in some sense *is* reality or "being itself,"[20] it follows that the spiritual sense is necessarily aligned with reality.

All of this works, however, only if the saint's acts (or love) are literally God's acts (or love), and Edwards himself sometimes expresses doubts on the matter. Thus, shortly after claiming that in communicating "divine love to the creature ... God's spirit or love doth but communicate of itself; 'tis the same love, so far as a creature is capable of being made partaker of it," Edwards qualifies his claim by saying: "The scripture seems in many places to speak of love in Christians as if it were the same with the Spirit of God in them, *or at least* as the prime and most natural breathing and acting of the Spirit in the soul."[21]

Moreover, just *how* can the saints' acts be God's acts? Not in the way an ambassador's acts are the king's acts, or a viceroy's acts are his emperor's, or my agent's acts are mine, for the relation in these cases is juridical,[22] and we are looking for something more ontological. A closer analogy may be provided by cases in which the principal's intentions, purposes, and desires *become* the intentions, purposes, and desires of his or her ambassador, viceroy, or agent, that is, don't merely *preempt* the intentions, purposes, and desires of the latter but are *existentially appropriated* by them. But even this yields no more than a relation of imitation, not the identity relation that Edwards characteristically insists on.

Still, a sufficiently close resemblance relation might be enough not only to distinguish God's relation to the saints from his relation to the ungodly, but also to explain why true benevolence is grounded in the nature of things. For the saints' actions and temper mirrors God's action and temper in a way in which the actions and temper of the ungodly do not. The saints' benevolence is appropriately related to objective reality because it resembles or is an image of it. Nature's activity, on Edwards's view, is really *God's* activity. Love is thus a "natural" or fitting response to reality since it imitates the action of nature itself.

John Henry Newman

Newman calls our faculty of informal reasoning the "illative sense."[23] It is principally employed in three ways: (1) in conducting an argument, (2) in assigning prior probabilities, and (3) in evaluating an argument's overall force.

Consider a dispute between two historians. In conducting their arguments, each has first to decide which "opinions ... to put aside as nugatory, "what evidence is relevant, "what has prima facie authority," and the relative weights to be placed on various kinds of evidence ("tradition, analogy [with familiar historical phenomena?], isolated monuments and records, ruins, vague reports, legends," etc.). "Then arguments have to be balanced against each other." Finally, each historian must decide whether a conclusion can be drawn and how certain it is. "It is plain how incessant will be the call ... for the exercise of judgment." Although these things can be done well or badly, "it is plain ... how little that judgment well be helped on by logic [i.e., by formal principles] and how intimately it will be dependent on the intellectual complexion of the" reasoner.[24]

Our illative sense is also responsible for judgments of antecedent probability. We legitimately dismiss some hypotheses and opinions without argument.[25] Those we can't dismiss as irrelevant or absurd are assigned a certain probability. But these assignments will "vary according to the particular intellect" that makes the assessments.[26] Not only do we assign conflicting probabilities to the premises, each of us also has a "view concerning" the likelihood of the conclusion "prior to the evidence.... If [one] is indisposed to believe he will explain away very strong evidence; if he is disposed, he will accept very weak evidence."[27]

For example, one historian finds the proposition, "No testimony should be received, except such as comes from competent witnesses," more plausible than, "Tradition, though unauthenticated, being ... in possession, has a prescription in its favor." Another does not. As a result, the historians assign different initial probabilities to the same events.[28] Again, Pascal's cumulative case argument for Christianity depends "upon the assumption that the facts of Christianity are beyond human nature" and that it is thus antecedently unlikely that human beings would have invented them. Hence, "as the powers of nature are placed at a high or low standard," the force of his argument "will be greater or less; and that standard will vary according to the respective dispositions, opinions, and experiences, of those to whom the argument is addressed."[29]

One of the illative sense's most important functions, however, is assessing an argument's overall force. It determines, that is, how strongly an argument's "antecedents" (all the factors bearing on the truth or falsity of the argument's conclusion) support its conclusion. These assessments, too, reflect the histories and tempers of the persons who make them. For when it comes to "the question, what is to become of the evidence being what it is," each must decide "according to (what is called) the state of his heart."[30]

Just as there are no formal rules for producing or recognizing good poetry, so there are no formal rules for determining the truth in concrete matters. In "concrete reasonings," the "ultimate test of truth or error in our inferences" is "the trustworthiness of the Illative Sense that gives them its sanction."[31] The ultimate test, in other words, is our own best judgment. My judgment, however, is irredeemably personal, for I can only view the various pieces of evidence "in the medium of *my* primary mental experiences, under the aspects which they spontaneously present to *me*, and with the aid of *my* best illative sense."[32]

Formal reasoning (whether deductive or inductive) isn't a real alternative to illative inference. The mind's acts of concrete reasoning are too subtle, varied, and intricate to be fully verbalized. Try, for example, to articulate the mental acts involved in arriving at the conclusion that the emendations of an early commentator on Shakespeare's *Henry V* are reliable, or to verbalize adequately the grounds of one's impression that whatever the medieval mind could or could not do, it could not produce the *Aeneid*, or the "delicate and at first invisible touches" in an anonymous publication that point to a certain author.[33] Because our reasoning in cases such as these can't be fully symbolized, formal principles can't get a firm grip on it.

But (and this is the more important point) even if our concrete reasonings *could* be adequately symbolized, our illative sense would remain indispensable. Formal inference and concrete reasoning are not real alternatives since the former is an abstraction from the latter. One must employ illation in deploying formal arguments, for one's assessment of the premises' plausibility and of the relevance of the argument's conclusion to the question at hand rest on assumptions and tacit understandings that can't be reduced to formal principles.

Their illative senses often lead people to opposed conclusions. They do so because "the intuitions, first principles, axioms, dictates of common sense, presumptions, presentiments, prepossessions, or prejudices" with which we approach a body of evidence are reflections of our experiences.[34] Because the latter vary, so too will the former.

Our impression of an argument's overall force is also affected by what could be called "personal" factors. People sometimes withhold assent from an argument through "a vague feeling that a fault" lies at its "ultimate basis" or because of "some misgiving that the subject matter [is] beyond the reach of the human mind." Or we may remain unpersuaded because "we throw the full *onus pobandi* on the side of the conclusion," refusing to assent until the arguments are not merely good but conclusive.[35] These attitudes and vague convictions are rooted in our characters and individual histories. Because these differ, so too will our estimates of an argument's force.

The illative sense does not, then, provide "a common measure between mind and mind."[36] "Explicit argumentation" concerning the merits of competing principles, assumptions, points of view, and other "starting points" and "collateral aids" to argument is "sometimes possible to a certain extent." But "it is too unwieldy an expedient for a constantly recurring need."[37] Even when we do resort to it, agreement is unlikely. For our supporting arguments, too, must be assessed by the illative sense, and the latter reflects "personal characteristics in which men are in fact in essential and irremediable variance with one another." The most we can do is "point out where the difference ... lies, how far it is immaterial, when it is worthwhile continuing an argument ..., and when not."[38]

Yet doesn't this give the game away by revealing the illative sense's subjectivity? *Truth* may not be relative (Newman clearly thinks it isn't), but illative reasoning surely is. Because *all* reasoning involves illation, even the most rigorous thinking appears tainted by subjectivity.

This is clearly not Newman's intention. Newman believes, for example, that good cumulative case arguments for the faith are "valid proofs." Although they cannot be "forced on the mind[s] of anyone whatever," they *are* capable of convincing anyone who "*fairly* studies" their premises.[39] And in general, if one's argument is good, one will find "that, allowing for the difference of minds and of modes of speech, what convinces him does convince others also.... There will be very many exceptions but those will *admit of explanation.*"[40] Some opposed "intuitions," for example, can be discounted because they have been created by "artificial and corrupt" social codes and practices. Others can be dismissed as expressions of raw and uncultivated human nature.[41] The important point is that our illative sense can be well or badly employed. If everyone were to use it rightly, most major disagreements would disappear.

How does one know when one is using one's illative powers properly? There are (at least) three indications that one is doing so. The first is "the agreement of many private judgments in one and the same view."[42] Newman says, for example, that his argument from conscience[43] would not be "worthwhile my offering it unless what I felt myself agreed with what is felt by hundreds and thousands besides me."[44] In matters of religion, ethics, metaphysics, and the like, "each of us can [ultimately] speak only for himself ... [Each of us] brings together his reasons and relies on them, because they are his own, and this is his primary" and indeed his "best evidence." Nevertheless, if it "satisfies him, it is likely to satisfy others," providing that his reasoning is sound and his conclusion true. "And doubtless he does find ... that allowing for the difference of minds and modes of speech, what convinces him does convince others also." The agreement of others is "a second ground of evidence."[45] (The first ground of evidence is one's own reasons.) *Universal* agreement should not be expected because people's illative senses are often undeveloped or misemployed. A failure to secure *extensive* agreement, however, indicates that one's illative powers are being used idiosyncratically.

Other signs that one has drawn the right conclusion are "objections overcome ... adverse theories neutralized ... difficulties gradually clearing up," consistency with other things known or believed, and the fact that "when the conclusion is assumed as an hypothesis, it throws light upon a multitude of collateral facts, accounting for them, and uniting them together in one whole."[46] A sign that one has reasoned rightly, in other words, is that one's argument satisfies the criteria for inferences to the best explanation.

Successful practice is a third indication that our reasoning is sound. In the absence of other indicators sufficient to warrant certainty, "our only test is the event or experience. Hence the proverbs 'The proof of the pudding,' etc., etc."[47]

An examination of the way in which we actually think shows that illative reasoning is natural, for "that is to be accounted a normal operation of our nature, which men in general do actually instance."[48] Our illative capacities, in short, are part of our natural noetic equipment. Yet even if they are, why should we trust them? For three reasons. The first is "necessity." "Our being, with its faculties ... is a fact not admitting of question, all things being of necessity referred to it, not it to other things." Indeed, "there is no medium between using my faculties, as I have them, and flinging myself upon the external world according to the random impulse of the moment."[49]

The second is "interest." "It is a general law that, whatever is found as a function or attribute of any class of beings, or is natural to it, is in its substance suitable to it and subserves its existence." Each species thus finds its "good" in the use of its "particular nature."[50] Because illative reasoning is natural to us, its proper use subserves our existence and contributes to our good.

The third reason is providence. "The laws of the mind are the expression, not of a mere constituted order, but of His will."[51] "*A Good Providence* watches over us" and "blesses such means of argument as it has pleased Him to give us ... if we use them duly for those ends for which He has given them."[52] Confident in the divine providence, "we may securely take them as they are, and use them as we find them."[53]

Newman's contribution to the tradition that Edwards represents is his demonstration that the way in which the mind reasons when influenced by religious sentiments, images, and ideas is identical with the way in which it reasons on ordinary occasions. "Moral evidence and moral certitude are all we can attain, not only in the case of ethical and spiritual subjects, such as religion, but of terrestrial and cosmical [i.e., scientific] questions also."[54] In both cases, reasoners employ cumulative case arguments or inferences to the best explanation. Although it is true that "the moral state of the parties inquiring or disputing" is not relevant in subjects such as astronomy,[55] its relevance is not restricted to "spiritual subjects." For passional factors play a role in historical inquiry, philosophy, and everyday reasoning. If the way in which theists assess evidence is suspect, then so too is the way in which historians, philosophers, and ordinary practical reasoners do so, for the procedures of the latter are essentially the same.

William James
One of James's earliest philosophical essays sounded a note that echoed throughout his writing. Criticizing Spencer's definition of truth as ("mere") correspondence, James asserts that a "correspondence" between the mind and reality is a "*right* mental action," and rightness is determined by "pure *subjective interests* ... brought ... upon the scene and corresponding to no relation already there."[56]

It is important to appreciate how pervasive interest is. Science itself is an expression of it. Its concepts are formed by abstracting selected aspects of reality, and selection is determined by interest. The "essences" or "kinds" of philosophy and science are "purely teleological weapons of the mind. The essence of a thing is that one of its properties which is *so important for my interests* that in comparison with it, I may neglect the rest."[57] Scientific values – "usefulness ... 'elegance' ... congruity with our residual beliefs," the desire for a "cleaner, clearer, more inclusive mental view" – are "subjective qualities."[58] Even the demand for successful predictions ("uniformity of sequence") is "as subjective and emotional" as my other demands because it is an expression of the practical need "in a general way at least, [to] banish uncertainty from the future."[59]

Assessments of scientific evidence are also affected by interests. Two scientists may draw different conclusions from the same body of evidence because each "is peculiarly sensitive to evidence that bears in some one direction." In such cases, each of the differing conclusions ultimately reflects "a sort of dumb conviction that the truth must lie in one direction rather than another."[60]

James's point here is not that science serves an interest (the acquisition of new truths, technical mastery, and so on), although it does, but that the scientific enterprise is intrinsically infused with them. Even so, science *is* dominated by our "theoretic needs," and it differs in this respect from other forms of human inquiry.

The theoretic need is "but one of a thousand human purposes,"[61] however, and some of these play a more prominent role in disciplines such as metaphysics.

The "objective" facts are not decisive. Comprehensive metaphysical systems such as idealism and materialism conflict, and "objective nature[62] has contributed to both sides impartially."[63] If we can "suppose for a moment that both give a conception of equal theoretic clearness and consistency, and that both determine our expectations equally well," our choice will be determined by passion and interest.[64]

In the final analysis, our visions of the world are "accidents more or less of personal vision,"[65] for they express our "temperament" – our "individual way of just seeing and feeling the total push and pressure of the cosmos."[66] Monism or Absolute Idealism, for example, rests on a "generous vital enthusiasm about the universe" and a will that things "*shall* cohere ... *shall* be one."[67] A pluralism[68] that places great importance on human moral capacities is an expression of days in which we are "in the full and successful exercise of our moral energy," and "the life we feel tingling through us vouches sufficiently for itself." Monism, on the other hand, is too often rooted in days when we are "'all sicklied o'er' with the sense of weakness, of helplessness, failure and of fear."[69] Again, the "tough-minded" find materialism compelling, while the "tender-minded" find it unsatisfactory.

The influence of passion and need is not occasional or accidental. James clearly thinks that *every* world view is partially determined by it and that *no* world view seems compelling in its absence.[70]

The question, then, is not whether interests suffuse and shape our intellectual enterprises, for they clearly do. It is whether interests *should* do so – whether their influence *vitiates* inquiry and, in particular, whether the dominant role need and passion play in metaphysics makes metaphysical choices nonrational. James thinks it sometimes does not; metaphysical beliefs *are* sometimes rational. The question is, "Rational in what sense?"

"The Will to Believe" describes a set of circumstances in which people are justified in embracing beliefs that are not self-evident or adequately supported by "objective" evidence. One of the most important is that the issue "cannot by its nature be decided on intellectual grounds."[71] James is often interpreted as requiring that the objective evidence be equally balanced, but this is mistaken. James believed that, as a matter of fact, the objective evidence for and against the religious hypothesis, and for and against determinism, was more or less evenly balanced. The evidence for pluralism, on the other hand, seemed stronger to him than the evidence for monism. Even so, James thought that "subjective factors" were needed to decide the issue *conclusively*. This suggests that his only requirement is that the objective evidence not be "coercive."

James's language supports this interpretation. He says, for example, that the question is whether we should wait for "*coercive* evidence."[72] He announces his intention to defend "our right to adopt a believing attitude in religious matters in spite of the fact that our merely logical intellect may not have been *coerced*."[73] He attacks the "disdain for merely *possible* or *probable* truth" – the refusal, in other words, to countenance a believing attitude in the absence of proofs that "will convince men *universally*," compelling reasons that are "absolutely impersonal," "or *knockdown* proofs."[74]

In short, James's only requirement appears to be that the evidence should not *clearly* or *conclusively* point in one direction rather than another. Our passional nature can thus properly come into play not only in those cases in which the evidence is evenly balanced but also in cases in which the objective evidence *does* incline us to one belief rather than another but where, because of the evidence's quality, our inclination to believe is inhibited by doubts and hesitations.

James's discussions of metaphysical systems are instructive. Monism (absolute idealism), for example, provides "comfort" and permits "moral holidays." It is thus true "in so far forth." But monism also rests on an inadequate kind of logic[75] and "entangles one in metaphysical paradoxes."[76] Moreover, it cannot explain evil or the real existence of distinct centers of finite consciousness. Finally, monism is "fatalistic"; because all facts are necessary, freedom and contingency are illusory.

Pluralism, on the other hand, is confirmed by our experience of apparent disconnections between facts, and thus stays closer to "reality as perceptually experienced." It therefore claims less and so has a lighter burden of proof.[77] Pluralism is also more faithful to our moral experience. Because it allows for contingency and does not "derealize" the "only life we are at home in," it makes life "seem real and earnest."[78] It is true that monism provides more religious consolation. Nevertheless, pluralism, too, can accommodate our religious yearnings.

Reviewing these considerations, James concludes that monism should be rejected provided that its claim "that the absolute is no hypothesis but a presupposition implicated in all thinking"[79] can be shown to be unsound.

Or consider James's defense of the "religious hypothesis." The most general form of the hypothesis has three parts.

1. There is a "higher universe."
2. We are better off if we believe this and act accordingly.
3. Communion with the higher universe "is a process wherein work is really done," and effects are produced in the visible world.[80]

James also has a more specific proposal and this, too, has three parts.

1. "The conscious person is continuous with a wider self through which saving experiences come."[81]
2. "Our ideal impulses originate" in another "dimension of existence" – a dimension that is not "merely ideal, for it produces effects in this world."[82]
3. These effect are not limited to those "exerted on the personal centers of energy of the various subjects"; because the "higher universe" includes "a larger power friendly" to us and our "ideals," we have some assurance that the world's "tragedy is only provisional."[83]

James thought that these hypotheses are not capricious or ad hoc. To see why, consider his proposed "science of religions."

It must first "eliminate the local and accidental from" the characterizations by which "the spontaneous intellect of man always defines the divine." It must then confront these "spontaneous religious constructions with the results of natural science" so as to "eliminate doctrines that are now known to be scientifically absurd or incongruous." Successful performance of the first two tasks leaves a "residuum" of hypotheses that are at least possible. After examining this residuum to distinguish "between what is innocent over-belief and symbolism ... and what is to be taken literally," our hypotheses must finally be tested "in all manners, whether negative or positive, by which hypotheses are ever tested."[84]

James clearly thinks his hypotheses survive the first three tests. The first hypothesis is the common core of all religious creeds, and the second is the common core of popular religious faith. Neither hypothesis commits one to scientific absurdities, and both are to be taken literally. James also thinks his hypotheses survive the fourth test. The *objective* evidence is, admittedly, inconclusive. Apart from religious experience, the most essential fact is that "the last word everywhere, according to purely naturalistic science, is the word of Death, the death-sentence passed by Nature on ... everything she has made."[85] When we *include* religious experience, however, the balance shifts. Conversion (i.e., regeneration), saintliness, and mystical states "open out the possibility of other orders of truth" and "absolutely overthrow the pretension of non-mystical states to be the sole and ultimate dictators of what we may believe."[86]

But even though humanity's religious experience restores the balance, it does not tip it. Ultimately, "proofs" and "facts" are indecisive, or at least not "coercive." They only "corroborate our preexistent partialities," lending plausibility to "our passions or mystical intuitions."[87] Each of us, in the final analysis, must still make his or her "personal venture," and these ventures will express our individual attitudes, intuitions, and tendencies to believe.[88]

It is important to note, however, that these intuitions and tendencies are themselves subject to philosophical scrutiny. Many of us, for example, refuse to believe because our attitudes have been shaped by a science whose outlook is "materialistic" – systematically repudiating the "personal point of view." From this perspective, religion seems "an anachronism, a case of 'survival,' an atavistic relapse."[89]

This attitude is unreasonable. Science can only provide "ideal pictures of something whose existence we do not inwardly possess but only point at outwardly." "Full facts," facts "of the kind to which all realities whatsoever must belong," are found in concrete personal experiences. Only here do "we catch real fact in the making."[90] All conceptualizations, including scientific ones, are simply abstractions from the richness of concrete human experience. The "personal point of view" is thus essential. Moreover, religion's utility shows that it is not a "mere anachronism and survival."[91] Religious consciousness is highly useful because it is "dynamogenic." Religion "freshens our vital powers" and imparts "endurance[,] ... zest[,] ... meaning, [and], enchantment" to life.[92]

James concludes that the religious hypothesis "fits the facts so easily" that our "scientific logic" should "find no plausible pretext for vetoing [our] impulse to welcome it as true."[93] He adds that when *he* considers the claim that "the world of sensations and of scientific laws and objects ... [are]

all," the "inward monitor of which W. K. Clifford once wrote" whispers "the word 'bosh!' " "The total expression of human experience *as I view it objectively* invincibly urges me beyond the narrow 'scientific' bounds.... So my objective and my subjective conscience *both* hold me to the over-belief which I express."[94] In short, James claims that when he views the facts as honestly as he can, he finds himself so "impressed by the importance" of "the phenomena of religious life" that it seems to him most reasonable to "adopt the hypothesis which they so naturally suggest."[95] *Personal* idiosyncrasies (of temperament, passion, outlook, etc.) are not appealed to. "Subjectivity" enters the picture only insofar as, in assessing the whole drift of the total evidence, James refuses to stifle his (and what he also believes to be humanity's) natural religious proclivities.

Notice two things. The first is the way in which James weaves so-called "objective" and "subjective" considerations together in making his case for pluralism and religion. The second is James's clear belief that decisions to embrace pluralism and the religious hypothesis are reasonable – not only in the minimal sense that believing them is within our epistemic rights but also in the sense that we *should not* stifle the promptings of our passional nature, which incline us to believe them.[96] But rational in what way? What kind of rationality is involved in coming to these decisions?

The aim of epistemic rationality is to increase our stock of significant truths. James never disputes this goal's overriding importance. As he says, "the concrete man has but one interest – to be right."[97] The significant question is how we can best *achieve* this aim, and, in particular, whether we are more likely to achieve it if we suppress the promptings of our passional nature. James thinks we are not. Scientific method is useful when it helps us achieve our goal. But if "the means presumes to frustrate the end" and some other means will help, we should employ them. "In the total game of life, we stake our persons all the while; and if *in its theoretic part* our persons will help us to a conclusion, surely we should also stake them there."[98]

In James's opinion, the tendencies "in one's emotional life" can be "prophetic."[99] Our passional nature not only consists of desires and aversion, or hopes and fears. It also includes "concrete perceptions" and "insight giving passions"[100] – "instincts,"[101] "divinations," "a sort of dumb conviction that the truth must lie in one direction rather than anther,"[102] something in us that "whispers ... 'it *must* be true.' "[103] James clearly thinks that these "intuitions" or "dumb convictions" can be reliable indicators of "theoretic" (objective) truth. Determinism, for example, is a "theoretic" hypothesis about the (objective) structure of reality. James rejects it because it "violates" his "sense of moral reality," is a "corruption of our moral sanity," and runs afoul of "instinctive reactions," which he, "for one, will not tamper with."[104]

Why should we trust our passional nature? Human satisfactions are the pragmatic tests of truth or reality.[105] Because views that ignore or suppress our deepest needs and intimations are not satisfactory, they will not "ring true." So to construct a picture of the world that seems rational *and true* to us, we must respect the promptings of our passional as well as our theoretic nature.

Yet why think that our satisfactions are reliable indicators of reality or truth? James's answer seems to be this. Satisfactions and dissatisfactions are functions of a belief's ability to facilitate or hinder the exercise of the mind's vital powers. These powers, however, "are not irrelevant to" reality.[106] The "dumb region of the heart in which we dwell alone with our willingnesses and unwillingnesses, our faiths and fears," is "our deepest organ of communication with the nature of things."[107]

Is this at all plausible? It is *if* we can assume some sort of congruence between the mind's structure and the structure of reality. That James does assume this is clearly implied in at least one place. "Reflex Action and Theism" argues that the mind has three "departments." It receives sensations, reflects on them, and discharges itself in action. No view will seem rational that violates one of these "essential modes of activity" – that neglects facts, has "a lot of inconsistencies or unmediated transitions on its hands; or else, finally … has left some one or more of our fundamental active and emotional powers with no [adequate] object outside of themselves to react on or to live for."[108] The key to the significance of this passage occurs earlier in the essay, where James observes that a view that is not only rational (i.e., satisfying in the long run and on the whole) but also "really the living truth" must satisfy all three demands *if* "the structure of our mind … be in accordance with the nature of reality."[109] The whole drift of his discussion implies that James thinks it is.

A corollary of this thesis is that the passions and divinations that count are those that are universal and deep.

James's ultimate criterion is the normal human mind or, more accurately, what the normal human mind finds satisfactory in the long run and on the whole. This criterion imposes real constraints on the construction of world views. No philosophy will be acceptable, for example, "which utterly denies all fundamental ground for seriousness, for effort, for hope, which says that the nature of things is radically alien to human nature."[110] A "sympathetic" view of the universe is thus natural or "normal." "Cynics" or "materialists" hold their positions only because "they [wrongly] think the evidence of the facts impels them" to.[111] Monism is also unacceptable because it reflects a "morbid mind." Its denial of human freedom and of the ultimate reality of our individual centers of consciousness appeals to us only in "moments of discouragement … when we are sick of self and tired of vainly striving," moments when "our own life breaks down."[112]

Is this more than philosophical populism? I think it is. If the mind's congruence with reality explains why our passional nature is sometimes "prophetic," superficial desires, idiosyncratic needs, and eccentric "intuitions" should be viewed with suspicion and, perhaps, discounted. They are not universal and deep expressions of the (normal) human mind, and there is therefore no reason to trust them.

Hypotheses that satisfy deep and universal needs are, then, prima facie more rational. Is James abusing the concept of rationality? I submit that he is not.

The views James advocates (meliorism,[113] indeterminism, the religious hypothesis, and even pluralism) are not adequately grounded in epistemic reason *if* epistemic reasons are restricted to what philosophers have typically regarded as such. James, however, believes that the only *generic* concept of a good epistemic reason is the concept of a kind of consideration, that, when taken into account, tends to eliminate cognitive disturbance in the long run. Standard epistemic considerations[114] are likely to do so. But so are the sorts of subjective grounds to which James appeals. Hence, they too are good epistemic reasons.

The significance of this is not merely psychological. Taking such things as our need for significant action into account eliminates cognitive disturbance because it leads to a successful adjustment to the cosmos. Because this sort of success is the only criterion we have of being in touch with reality, the "sentiment of rationality" (the feeling we have when thought flows smoothly) is an indication that our thought has engaged "the nature of things." James's sense of "good epistemic reason" and the standard senses are materially equivalent. The considerations that, when we take them into account, tend to eliminate cognitive disturbance are those that, when taken into account put us in touch with reality. They are signs of *truth*, in other words, and not merely of utility.[115]

But suppose this is James's view. Is it at all plausible? The following argument lies just below the surface: (1) *Human* animals must not only adapt to their immediate environment, they must also adapt to the "cosmos in its totality." Intelligence evolved so that we might act successfully and enter into satisfactory relations with the world in general. The only views that will permanently satisfy intelligence, therefore, are those that make action possible and meaningful and enable us to adjust satisfactorily to the world *as a whole*. (2) The proper (normal) use of the intellectual and practical faculties by which we construct our views is shaped by our passional nature. Our faculties have evolved in such a way that passional factors infuse thinking. (3) Our faculties and powers have evolved as they have because they are adaptive. (4) The best, or most natural, explanation of the fact that these faculties and powers are adaptive is that the beliefs they produce when properly used "correspond" (in a rough and ready way) to reality.

James's argument is of course open to the following objection. He assumes that if (1) our mental faculties are the product of a long evolution, (2) they are adaptive, and that (3) they are adaptive if and only if the beliefs they lead to are for the most part true. He therefore concludes that (4) on the whole, our opinions are attuned to reality. The inference from 1 to 2 is suspect, however. For our mental capacities may be accidental evolutionary by-products of characteristics that are adaptive without those capacities themselves being adaptive.

This criticism has considerable force if evolution is identified with biological (i.e., Darwinian) evolution. But James construes it more broadly. For James (as for many other nineteenth-century intellectuals), evolution comprised psychological, social, cultural, and moral development as well as biological evolution. Its aim, moreover, was adaptation to one's environment in an inclusive sense, not just biological survival and reproduction or the transmission of one's genes. The human environment is the cosmos in its entirety, and the sorts of adaptation called for are psychological and moral as well as biological. If evolution is understood in this way, James's inference is more plausible. The broader evolutionary hypothesis is less firmly established, however, than the hypothesis of biological evolution.

James could also deploy two pragmatic arguments. The first is explicitly metaphysical. If the religious hypothesis is true, the world is "friendly" and so will not frustrate our deepest needs and yearnings or baffle our intellectual and practical powers. And this implies that our faculties are more or less reliable. But the religious hypothesis can be pragmatically justified; that is, it can be justified by using our intellectual and practical faculties in the manner James recommends. Pragmatism's account of rationality is thus self-certifying in the sense that (unlike foundationalism, for example[116]) it meets its own standards; that our faculties and powers are reliable is supported by a hypothesis that can be justified by using our faculties pragmatically.

The same result can be reached more directly. Trust in the reliability of our powers is itself a basic need, a demand of human nature. Hence, other things being equal, views that affirm the trustworthiness of our faculties are more satisfactory than views that do not. Therefore, in the absence of compelling reasons for *mis*trusting them, we should believe in their reliability. Pragmatism's account of rationality is thus again self-confirming. The application of its criteria supports the claim that our powers are trustworthy.

James's pragmatic justifications of the reliability of our passionally inflected epistemic faculties ultimately depend on the use of those faculties themselves. This, in itself, is hardly surprising. Justifications of the reliability of sense perception, or of deductive or inductive reasoning, typically rely on claims established by using those very procedures.

Are the self-certifying practices that James recommends subject to *special* difficulties? They may be, but what are they? Certainly not that the practices *countenance* inconsistency, obliviousness to obvious facts, wishful thinking, and rampant subjectivism, for they provide safeguards against these errors. Is the problem that different people can employ these methods and arrive at different and inconsistent conclusions? No doubt they can. But this objection, too, has little force since a similar complaint can be directed against any account of the type of reasoning involved in philosophy, literary and artistic criticism, and moral or political reflection. It is true that proponents of other methods often assure us that their proper use will resolve disagreement, but so too does James.[117] Are the promises made by advocates of more familiar procedures more reassuring or better grounded? I, for one at least, doubt it.

Wang Yangming

Positions such as those of James, Newman, or Edwards aren't confined to Westerners or to theists. For consider the following example from the iconoclastic Neo-Confucian, Wang Yangming: "The *liangzhi* is the innate ... faculty that enables one to know the *li* (... principle) of the mind and universe.... All things possess all the *li* of the universe within them," and, for Wang, "the mind is itself *li*: 'knowing is the conscious aspect of *li*.' "[118] The *liangzhi* or "complete and perfect mind,"[119] enables one to distinguish "naturally and spontaneously between right and wrong," and everyone possesses it.[120]

What then explains our bad choices? The obstructions of *qi* ("material force" or "lively matter"), which Wang primarily identifies with self-centered desires.[121] The most important point in the present context, however, is this: The *liangzhi* is at once a cognitive and an affective faculty. To truly know something, the mind must therefore be in the proper affective state. And, for Wang, the proper state is "the affective state of selflessness." Without this, "one's mere true belief" cannot be transformed "into what [he] calls 'real knowledge (*zhenzhi*)' or simply knowledge (*zhi*)." To accomplish this one must engage in the "rectification of thoughts" (*gewu*) and the "extension of knowledge" (*zhizhi*). One rectifies one's thoughts by attending to and eliminating one's self-centered thoughts, and one extends one's knowledge by engaging in the appropriate practical activity. (For example, one extends one's "knowledge" of [i.e., true belief about] one's filial duty by lovingly caring for one's parents.) The bottom line is that for Wang, as for Edwards, Newman, and James, right affections are a necessary condition of right knowing.

II. Objections

In spite of their attractiveness, the positions of Edwards, Newman, James, and Wang are controversial in a way in which more standard accounts of rationality are not. In particular, they seen open to charges of subjectivism and circularity.

Subjectivism

I will only briefly comment on the first. The objection is this. Allowing passion and feeling to influence our judgment opens the door to bias, distortion, and wishful thinking. Beliefs are made true by the states of affairs they represent. The concept of a true belief involves "the thought of a causal chain stretching back from the belief" to the state of affairs that makes it true. Passional believing, like wishful thinking, severs this connection. Once we learn that our beliefs are caused by passion and feeling, and not by the states of affairs they represent, we can no longer regard them as true.[122]

This objection rests upon a misunderstanding. Views such as Edwards's, Newman's, James's, or Wang's do not deny that beliefs are made true by the states of affairs they represent. Nor do they deny that justified true beliefs are causally connected to the states of affairs that make them true. On the contrary, the passions they privilege are believed to be correlated with the way things actually are. These passions are reflections of reality, causal or quasi-causal products of the states of affairs represented by the beliefs they generate. James, for example, thinks that our "willing nature" has evolved as it has because following its dictates has enabled us to adjust more successfully to reality. Behavior based on our passional nature wouldn't be so successful if it led us to egregiously misrepresent things as they are. Similarly, Edwards attempted to show that the "mechanism" underlying our renewed epistemic faculties, namely, true benevolence, "agrees" with reality. Reality's core is an infinite benevolence – the world's only true substance and its only true cause. The benevolence of the saints is grounded in this and mirrors it. Edwards concludes that benevolence isn't "arbitrary" but agrees "with the necessary nature of things." Likewise, if Wang's Neo-Confucian conception of ultimate reality as *li* is true, and his identification of our minds in their own nature with *li* is correct, then the beliefs that have been generated by a mind that has been purified of the obstructions of *qi* are probably true and probably warranted. Because charges of wishful thinking, rampant subjectivism, and the like presuppose that links of this kind don't exist, they beg the question against views of this type.[123]

Circularity

The more serious charge is circularity, and each of the four of the views we have discussed seems exposed to it. Edwards's arguments for the positive epistemic value of the saints' new use of their noetic faculties are based on scripture and theistic metaphysics. Newman's defense of the illative sense's reliability ultimately rests on an appeal to Divine Providence. James's arguments for the epistemic salience of our passional nature rest on his psychology, (what he believes to be) the facts of evolution, and his pragmatism. Wang's epistemology presupposes the truth of his Neo-Confucian world view. The premises of their arguments do not merely restate their conclusions, however, or immediately entail them in the trivial way a conjunction entails its conjuncts or "some S is P" entails its converse. Are they circular in some less obvious way? For the sake of simplicity, I will focus on Edwards.

In examining the question of circularity, it will be helpful to distinguish three things: (1) the conclusion that true benevolence and other holy dispositions are needed to use one's epistemic faculties rightly; (2) an implication of this conclusion, namely, that sincere theists are in a superior epistemic positions with respect to rational arguments about "divine things"; and (3) the theist's reliance on his or her own assessments of the evidence's force.

I shall argue that the conclusion is not presupposed. But theists *do* rely on their own assessments of the evidence's force, and this commits them to thinking that they are in a superior epistemic position with respect to its evaluation. I shall also argue, however, that *any* reliance on one's own assessments in matters of basic dispute involves similar assumptions. The kind of circularity that infects positions such as Edwards's affects all areas in which there are deep disagreements about the overall force of complicated bodies of evidence.

Let me begin by asking three questions raised by William Alston in another context.[124] Are theists such as Edwards implicitly assuming the truth of their conclusion? Could they be convinced of the truth of their premises (that is, of the propositions of theistic metaphysics that support it) if they doubted the conclusion or denied it? Must they appeal to the conclusion to justify retaining their confidence in the truth of their premises in the face of their critics' objections?

Are theists who employ premises that imply that true benevolence or other holy dispositions are epistemically necessary implicitly assuming the truth of the conclusion? Not clearly. Not only may the conclusion not previously have occurred to them, they may also initially (before they see where their premises are leading them) share the standard conception of rationality and simply accuse their critics of failing to appreciate the force of a body of evidence (the evidence for their brand of theism) that should convince anyone who employs normal epistemic procedures of the truth of their premises.

Could these theists be convinced of the truth of their premises if they doubted or denied the conclusion? For the reasons just given, I do not see why not. The evidence for premises such as, "An omnipotent benevolence is the only true substance and the only true cause," does not include the epistemic theory in question, and (as we have just seen) they may initially share their critics' conception of rationality.[125] But, if course, the challenge hasn't yet been pushed far enough.

For in trusting their own assessments of the evidence, aren't theists of this sort implicitly assuming that their judgments and those of others who make similar assessments are reliable while their critics' assessments are not? And if they are, and have their wits about them, can they help noticing that those who make assessments such as theirs are theists while most of those who do not are not? Are they not, then, implicitly assuming that theists are, by and large, better judges of the force of the evidence for theological conclusions – that is, that they are somehow in a superior epistemic position with respect to it? Are they not, in other words, implicitly assuming the truth of one of their conclusions' more controversial implications? If, as seems likely, the answer is "yes," we have uncovered our circle.[126]

What is not clear, though, is that this kind of circularity is vicious or should undermine the theist's confidence in her conclusion. For she *has* evidence that supports it and believes her conclusion because of it.

(It is important to note that the special perspective on the evidence furnished by her new holy dispositions is not functioning as a premise or as an inference rule in her argument. Nor is it part of her evidence for her premises. Treating true benevolence's assessment of the force of the evidence as a piece of evidence[127] is as misguided as treating an intellectually honest, critical, and fair-minded historian's assessment of the strength of her argument as one of her premises. One's evidence should be distinguished from one's take on it.[128])

Furthermore, she may *be* justified in trusting her assessment of the evidence's force (since, if the theory is true,[129] she is making it in the right way), even though (1) she has not justified her confidence and will not be in a position to do so until she has drawn her conclusion, and even though (2) she cannot justify every premise, inference rule, *and epistemic attitude or posture* involved in arriving at it without falling into a logical circle.[130] (Her justification would be logically circular since she would have to appeal to her conclusion to justify her special slant on the evidence.)

A point made by Michael Smith is also relevant.[131] Arguments whose conclusions appear among their premises are obviously circular. A more subtle kind of circularity occurs when principles of reasoning are supported by arguments that employ them. The circularity we have uncovered is a bit like the latter. (Assessing the force of certain sorts of evidence from the perspective of true benevolence bears some resemblance to using a principle of reason. Neither appears among the premises. Both are employed in deriving the conclusion.) Smith contends that arguments of the second type sometimes have explanatory value. (Edwards's theistic metaphysics, for example, explains why the truly benevolent are better judges of the relevant evidence.) Although arguments of this kind cannot provide "original justification," they can enhance the justification of the conclusion by making principles of reason and epistemic attitudes more reasonable than they would otherwise be; for the existence of a plausible explanation of an alleged fact can add to its probability.[132]

The important point, however, is this. The type of circularity we have uncovered infects history, archeology, paleontology, philosophy, literary and artistic criticism, and every other discipline in which apparently competent inquirers disagree about the overall force of complicated bodies of evidence. Philosophers or historians, for example, who think they have good arguments must implicitly assume that their assessments of the evidence's force are more reliable than those of their critics. They must therefore assume that the judgments of others who typically assess evidence of that kind as they do are more reliable than the judgments of those who assess it differently. But this implies that those who assess evidence of that sort as they do are in a superior epistemic position with respect to it.

And is this not, indeed, being tacitly presupposed? As Newman and others have pointed out, complicated assessments of historical and philosophical hypotheses (for instance) not only reflect a person's intelligence, education, and information, they also reflect that person's experience in dealing with issues of that kind, his or her imagination or lack of it, sensitivity to certain kinds of evidence, temperament, values, and a host of other tacit factors. If a good philosopher or historian is challenged to justify a controversial assessment of the evidence's overall force, doesn't she ultimately have to appeal to her critics' blindness to the importance of certain kinds of evidence, their failures of imagination, deficiencies in their experience, or something else of that sort?[133] And yet she surely knows that her critics would deny that such things as these are distorting their judgment. Can she sustain her charge against her critics without begging the question by arguing that their blindness to their deficiencies is partly caused by them? I, for one, doubt it.

But *are* the epistemic situations of the truly benevolent, on the one hand, and historians, philosophers, and so on, on the other, really parallel? William Rowe thinks they aren't since Edwards is implicitly using the conclusion of his argument in his assessments of the relevant evidence while proponents of controversial philosophical (or historical or literary critical or ...) positions typically are not. Incompatibilists, for example, believe that determinism precludes moral responsibility. My actions are free only if I possess a capacity (in some suitably robust sense) to act otherwise. If my choices are determined by causes beyond my control, I do not. And compatibilists, of course, disagree. But incompatibilists do not use their conclusion (that determinism is incompatible with moral responsibility) to show that they are in a superior position with respect to the relevant evidence. Edwards's argument is thus circular in a way in which the indeterminist's argument is not.[134]

I have two things to say about this objection. In the first place, similar circles *can* arise in debates between incompatibilists and compatibilists. For a reflective incompatibilist, for example, will undoubtedly wonder why her intuitions and those of her opponent differ. Suppose that she explains the compatibilist's failure to see what she sees by his overattention to the analogies between human and animal behavior and to routine human activity, and his insensitivity to the peculiarities of human moral behavior, especially in what James called "the lonely emergencies of life"[135] – by the absence, in other words, of the epistemic attitudes and postures that have led *her* to read the evidence rightly. If the compatibilist rejects this account of his intuitions (as he undoubtedly will), isn't the incompatibilist likely to explain the compatibilist's rejection of her explanation by citing the *same defects*? And if her original explanation is correct, isn't she right to do so? For the misdirected attention and insensitivity the incompatibilist alludes to will (if genuine) make it difficult for the compatibilist to recognize his own blindness.[136]

There is, of course, this difference between the incompatibilist's position and the theist's: the incompatibilist is not using the conclusion of her original argument (that determinism is incompatible with moral responsibility) to explain her opponent's blindness, whereas the theist is. Nonetheless, the cases are relevantly similar. For in drawing her conclusion, the incompatibilist contextually implies that *her* take on the evidence (and therefore the take of those who assess evidence of that sort as she does) is epistemically superior to the compatibilist's take on the evidence. The *act* of drawing her conclusion about determinism and human responsibility thus *contextually implies* something very much like the conclusion of Edward's (or Newman's, James's, or Wang's) argument. Furthermore, the same intuitions, hunches, proclivities, values, attentions, and sensitivities that determine the incompatibilist's take on her evidence are also likely to figure in her explanation of the compatibilist's blindness and of his resistance to her explanation of his blindness. (His attention is misdirected, for example, or he is insensitive to evidence to which she is sensitive.)

My second point is this: there may be a bad circle *if* the theist appeals to her possession of true benevolence or some other holy disposition to *justify* her initial acceptance of arguments for the conclusion that the possession of these dispositions place her in an epistemically superior position with respect to the evaluation of arguments to theological conclusions and her rejection of arguments to the contrary. For in that case, she has implicitly appealed to the conclusion whose truth is in dispute.[137] It does not follow, however, that the theist is involved in a bad circle if she only appeals to her holy dispositions and her opponent's lack of them to *explain* why she accepts arguments to the conclusion that these dispositions enable one to evaluate properly the force of arguments to theological conclusions while her opponents reject them. And an explanation may be needed.

Thinking that one's assessment of the evidence is right and one's critic's assessment is wrong doesn't *logically* commit one to a particular explanation of the disagreement, or even to the *existence* of an explanation. But it may *rationally* commit one to providing one. We are uncomfortable when we cannot explain the nature of the error committed by opponents who disagree with us and yet seem to be (and in many ways are) our epistemic peers. (They are as intelligent, highly trained, informed, and fair-minded as we are.) Furthermore, our discomfort is rational. For without an explanation, it isn't clear that we are entitled to think that our assessment of the evidence is correct while theirs is not. It isn't obvious that its provision involves us in a bad circle, however.

For the explanation isn't offered a justification for *adopting* a belief in my premises or my argument's validity but only as a justification for *retaining* my confidence in the face of disagreement. It functions in this respect like a "defeater defeater." My belief that it is raining outside may be based upon, and justified by, my just seeing that it is. A similarly well-placed observer's denial that it is raining can be defeated by my showing that his perceptual equipment is malfunctioning, that he is too drunk to be a reliable witness, or something else of the sort. My belief that it is raining outside isn't based on these claims, however, nor are they part of my justification for my belief that it is raining outside, though they may be needed for me to rationally retain it. It is thus not clear that the theist's appealing to her argument's conclusion (that holy dispositions are needed to assess properly the force of theological arguments) to defend her belief in the face of disagreement involves her in a bad epistemic circle.[138]

But be this as it may, the crucial point is that the kind of circularity that infects arguments such as Edwards's also infects reasoning in other disciplines, including philosophy and history.[139] Should one therefore conclude that one is not entitled to say that one knows, or is rationally confident of, propositions in contested areas like these? That one is not entitled, for example, to believe confidently in the truth of physicalism, incompatibilism, or anything else disputed by one's peers? Few philosophers would say, "yes."[140] If they would not, they are not in a position to cast the first stone.

That the type of circularity that infects accounts such as Edwards's is endemic to most disciplines, including philosophy, implies that the critic's only recourse is to provide special reasons for thinking that the theist's slant on the evidence is unreliable while his own is not. He must explain, for example, why true benevolence and other holy dispositions (Edwards) or a need for meaning and significant action (James) are likely to prove deceptive while inhibiting their influence is not. As we saw when discussing the charge of subjectivism earlier in this chapter, it will be difficult for the critic to do this without begging the question.

Neither side can avoid circularity. This is disturbing if a non-question-begging way of mutually resolving basic disagreements over the overall force of a body of evidence is a necessary condition of the possibility of being rational in these matters. If it is, theists aren't the only ones in deep trouble.

5

The Role of Rhetoric in Religious Argumentation

I. Philosophy's Quarrel with Rhetoric

Western philosophy has tended to drive a wedge between rational discourse and persuasion. Rational discourse is the domain of philosophy. Persuasion, on the other hand, is the domain of rhetoric, and rhetoric is epistemically and morally suspect. Thus, Plato argues that rhetoric isn't a species of knowledge, but rather a mere "knack" or "technique" (*empeiria*). The rhetorician has mastered the devices and stratagems that enable him to speak persuasively but lacks a theoretical understanding of their nature, of the psychological and social mechanisms that ensure that some techniques will be effective and others not. Furthermore, the rhetorician's aim is not to produce knowledge or true opinion but to convince his audience of the truth of his assertions, whether they are in fact true or not. And because the rhetorician's aim is persuasion, its mastery involves a command of those devices that *make* speakers persuasive. These include sound arguments. But they *also* include plausible but specious proofs, ad hominem attacks, appeals to one's hearers' baser emotions and prejudices, the creation of a favorable personal impression whether it is warranted or not, verbal style and ornament, and so on.[1] The rhetorician's means of persuasion are thus both rational and nonrational. And this is morally problematic. *Genuine* arts aim at the good of their subject matter. The aim of medicine, for example, is to produce health. By contrast, rhetoric is not concerned with the spiritual and moral well-being of its potential audiences but only with persuasion. The rhetorician *qua* rhetorician is indifferent to whether he produces knowledge or true opinion, on the one hand, or false opinion, on the other, and to whether he persuades us by employing reason and appealing to our nobler sentiments or convinces us by using specious arguments and pandering to our baser desires. The *philosopher* wishes to benefit the souls of her hearers and so employs *rational* means to produce knowledge or true belief. The rhetorician *as such* is not concerned with what would benefit us.

But of course, matters are not so simple. Plato himself concedes (in the *Phaedrus*) that the first defect could be remedied. The second cannot. But the force of his complaint is mitigated by at least three things. First, Plato himself is a master of rhetoric as he must surely have recognized. Second, while techniques don't *aim* at the good (as arts do), they can be used for people's benefit. The gourmet chef, for example, can make nutritious food tasty. Third, there is a place for a chastened rhetoric in Plato's ideal community. The use of "noble lies" is a notorious example. More significant, however, is the fact that the children are surrounded from infancy by "beautiful forms" (objects, practices, *and words*) in an attempt to induce harmony and order in both their bodies and souls. So Plato believes that there is a place for rhetoric after all, *but only when directed by philosophy.*[2]

Or consider Augustine. Rhetoric is useful when properly deployed. "While the faculty of eloquence … is of great value in urging either evil or injustice, [it] is itself indifferent." Why, then, "should it not be obtained for the uses of the good in the service of truth if the evil usurp it … in defense of iniquity and error?" And indeed, in certain contexts and for certain purposes, rhetoric is indispensable. "If those who hear are to be taught," clear and careful exposition is needed, and "in order that those things that are doubtful may be made certain they must be reasoned out with the use of evidence. But if [one's hearers] are to be *moved* rather than taught, so that they may not be sluggish in putting what they know into practice and so that they may *fully accept* those things which they acknowledge to be true, there is need for greater powers of speaking. Here entreaties and reproofs, exhortations and rebukes, and whatever other [rhetorical] devices are necessary to move minds must be used."[3]

Following Cicero, Augustine asserts that "he who is eloquent should speak in such a way that he teaches, delights, and moves." The first "resides in the things which we have to say, the other two in the manner in which we say it.… Just as the listener is to be delighted if he is to be retained as a listener, so also is he to be persuaded if he is to be moved to act." Even so, "instruction should [not only] come before persuasion," but may make persuasion unnecessary if one's hearers are "so moved by a knowledge" of things necessary "that it is not necessary to move them further by greater powers of eloquence." If, however, they are "taught and pleased and still [do not] consent," persuasion is needed. For "what use are" teaching and delight if consent "does not follow. But delight is not necessary either."[4]

The upshot is that while teaching is always necessary, persuasion is required only when teaching itself doesn't lead to action, and delight (being pleased with the speaker's manner of presentation) is of value only when needed to hold the hearer's attention and make him more receptive to the teaching of the speaker. The implication is that rhetoric has ancillary value only; it is subordinate to "teaching" (wisdom, or Christian philosophy) and should be directed by it.

This theme echoes and reechoes throughout the history of Western philosophy. Hobbes's, Locke's, and Hume's animadversions on metaphor and rhetoric are examples. Thus Hobbes thinks that one of language's most important functions is to communicate knowledge, and that this function is impeded whenever we "use words metaphorically; that is, in other sense than they are ordained for; *and thereby deceive others*."[5] "Metaphors, tropes, and other rhetoricall figures" can be used to decorate discourse or "in common speech … *yet in reckoning and seeking of truth*, such speeches are not to be admitted."[6] Or as Locke says:

All the art of rhetoric, besides order and clearness; all the artificial and figurative application of words eloquence hath invented, are for nothing else but to insinuate wrong ideas, move the passions and thereby mislead the judgment; and so indeed are perfect cheats: and therefore … they are certainly, in all discourses that pretend to inform or instruct, wholly to be avoided.… It is evident how much we love to deceive and be deceived, since rhetoric, that powerful instrument of error and deceit, has its established professors, is publicly taught, and has always been had in great reputation.[7]

And in a similar vein, Hume said, "Eloquence, when at its highest pitch, leaves little room for reason or reflection; but addressing itself entirely to the fancy or affections, captivates the willing hearers, and subdues their understanding."[8]

A less familiar and potentially more interesting example for the philosopher of religion is provided by the Puritans' attitude toward rhetoric. John Penry insisted that "the lord doth not ordinarily bestowe [full comprehension of the Word] upon any in our days, without the knowledge of the artes, especially the two handmaydes of all learninge, Rhetoricke and Logick.…"[9] Rhetoric "was the means by which the logical analysis of the Word was brought home to the congregation to spur repentance and conversion."[10] Indeed, "where there is one injunction to expound the will of God 'out of soundnesse of argument and plaine evidence' … there are a hundred that exclaim in more passionate accents 'O brethren let the fire burn clear; let there not be more smoke than fire.'" "It is not enough," said Thomas Hooker, "that we be stirring in the house and people be up, but we must knock at men's doors, bring a candle to their bedsides, and pinch the sluggard, and then if he have any life he will stir."[11]

Yet heat without light is equally undesirable. "The ministers of the gospel" are to "apply themselves … to Rational Men, who are to be led, not driven; who follow the conduct of Reason rather than force."[12] Thus Jonathan Edwards says, "When light and heat are … united in a minister of the gospel, it shows that each is genuine.… Divine light is attended with heat; and so, on the other hand, a truly divine and holy heat and ardour is ever accompanied with light."[13] It is true that in their reflections on the sermon, Puritan divines emphasized "application," and hence rhetoric. For as Edwards also asserts, "Though … clearness of distinction and illustration and strength of reason, and a good method, in the doctrinal handling of the truths of religion is in many ways needful and profitable, and not to be neglected … our people don't so much need to have their heads stored as their hearts touched."[14] Nevertheless, it is clearly assumed that the minister's use of rhetoric will be guided by his grasp of the truths of sacred science. The Puritan divines share Plato's view that, however necessary, rhetoric is a mere handmaid of right reason (philosophy, sacred science). Until recently, at least, this view has dominated Western philosophy and theology.

But the line between philosophy or theology and rhetoric isn't as clear-cut as Plato, Hobbes, Locke, Hume, and their followers imply. One of the most important and influential Western philosophers, for example, refused to draw such sharp lines between them.

II. Aristotle and Rhetoric

"Rhetoric," according to Aristotle, "is the counterpart of dialectic."[15] Dialectic, for Aristotle, was a mode of argument that "proceeds by question and answer," and "normally aims at refutation." Dialectical arguments are generally valid although they typically proceed from disputed premises. They are exemplified by Zeno's "arguments against motion and multiplicity" and by the arguments that Plato puts into the mouth of Socrates in his early and middle dialogues.[16]

As Paul Ricoeur astutely pointed out, rhetoric's associations with dialectic "keeps [it] under the sway of logic and, through logic, of philosophy as a whole." Even so, rhetoric differs from philosophy in at least two ways. First, it "comes into play in concrete situations – the deliberations of a political assembly, judgment by a tribunal, public orations that praise or censure" and, as a consequence, has "three genres ... deliberative, judicial, and epideictic." Second, "rhetoric can't be absorbed in a purely 'argumentative' or logical discipline because it is addressed 'to the hearer'."[17] Because "rhetoric is a phenomenon of the intersubjective and dialogical dimension of the public use of speech," the passions, beliefs, and habits of both speaker and hearer must be taken into account.[18] Since, as Aristotle says, "it is not enough to know what we ought to say, we must also say it as we ought." For "the way in which a thing is said" affects "its intelligibility," and hence its persuasiveness.[19]

Rhetoric's association with dialectic and logic emerges in another way as well. Jamie Dow has argued that, for Aristotle, "the only essential component of an expertise in rhetoric is an ability to produce proofs," where "proof (*pistis*)" comprises "giving an argument, presenting the speaker as trustworthy, and arousing the emotions of the audience." Everything else (style, tone of voice, personal appearance, figures of speech, and the like) is merely "an accessory to it," since persuasion or conviction "can take place without" them whereas it can't take place without a "proof."[20]

"The kind of proof appropriate to oratory," however, isn't "the necessary but the probable, because the human affairs over which tribunals and assemblies deliberate and decide are not subject to the sort of necessity, of intellectual constraint, that geometry and 'first philosophy' demand." Furthermore, the proofs in question typically appeal to widely accepted beliefs and attitudes, and draw on popular commonplaces, and familiar metaphors, proverbs, parables, and the like. Since these are often only implicitly alluded to rather than being clearly stated, the arguments in question are typically enthymatic. There is of course a danger that the beliefs and attitudes that are appealed to wouldn't survive critical scrutiny. Yet on the other hand, the rhetorician's arguments have the advantage of being developed "in the give and take of common opinion," and not "in some empty space of pure thought."[21]

The rhetorician, then, must not only be able to construct logically sound proofs for his conclusions, he must also be able to construct "the argument that – considering the beliefs of his audience – successfully persuades them." He must, in other words, "be able to suit his discourse to the occasion, even [sometimes] astutely choosing not to give the most rigorous, most truthful argument" if that would be less helpful.[22] (Compare his situation with another's. In teaching philosophy to introductory students, it is often better to present simplified [and therefore not entirely accurate] versions of the arguments of Descartes, say, or Berkeley by deliberately omitting a consideration of some of the less important and/or more technical issues surrounding them. While doing so may distort their positions to a certain extent, the alternative tends to leave one's students with little or no real understanding of these philosophers' arguments.)

Aristotle clearly believes that the practice of rhetoric can and should be virtuous. The successful rhetorician exercises "a range of intellectual abilities – understanding, cleverness, calculation, deliberation, good sense in artfully directed reasoning." But even though these "intellectual virtues can … be successfully exercised independently of the character virtues there is a norm for [them] to be used rightly as well as successfully exercised. As Aristotle puts it, virtue involves doing the right thing at the right time, in the right way, and for the right reason"; and "speaking, … rightly, and reasonably saying the right thing in the right way at the right time, is a central part of acting rightly. The *phronimos* – the man of practical wisdom – typically participates in public life. He engages in the deliberative activities of the Assembly; he serves on the Courts and his evaluative judgments [as expressed in public eulogies and condemnations] are models of praise and blame. In being a model of virtue, the *phronimos* is a model of all the skills that virtue requires, including those of finding the right words and arguments in the process of deliberation. Since the techniques of public deliberation provide the model for *all* forms of deliberation, the man of practical wisdom must [therefore] acquire the habits [and dispositions] that are involved in rhetorical persuasion."[23] Note that if this is correct, rhetorical skills and virtues are not only needed in politics but also in preaching, and in the practice and teaching of philosophy and theology – at least where deliberative and not merely "scientific" reasoning (in the Aristotelian sense) is at stake. And, that is, arguably, in all but the most technical aspects of these disciplines. (More on this later in this chapter.)

That the practice of rhetoric can be, and often is, virtuous is a direct consequence of other views of Aristotle. All skills, including rhetoric, have an end. Moreover, skills and their ends are "architectonically" arranged in such a way that the goal of the first is pursued for the sake of the second larger "skill or activity." Now rhetoric is a skill or "expertise which enables someone to perform well certain functions within a state – presenting arguments in court, advocating a course of action in political deliberation, recommending someone or something for public honor or censure." States, in turn, are designed to protect and further human flourishing. Aristotle's view of rhetoric is thus teleological: "rhetoric has a purpose which is ultimately to make a particular kind of contribution to the flourishing of the state and of the people." When the art of rhetoric is exercised as intended, its "proofs" will thus provide "*proper* sources of conviction," namely "proofs" that contribute to human flourishing.[24]

As Amelie Rorty points out, the differences between virtuous rhetoricians and philosophers can be exaggerated. Rhetoricians can, and sometimes do, offer "impeccable arguments and logical considerations," while Plato's "Socratic dialogues are full of analogies that carry the weight of argument." Both are concerned not merely with truth but with *persuading* their audiences. Again, "eulogists and litigants ... try to convince their audience of the truth of what they say," and if they are virtuous, are themselves convinced of its truth. And philosophers, too, often "try to realign and reform the desires and emotions of their interlocutors. The difference [between the two] lies in their ultimate aims, as these affect their relation to their audience." The rhetorician is typically "focused on particular contexts and situations: as a litigator, he is trying to win a case before a court; as a politician, he is trying to urge the adoption of a specific policy or law; as a eulogist, he is offering circumstantial homage and tributes. Other than gauging the plausibility of his arguments, however, the rhetorician, unlike the philosopher, is not committed to examining" the underlying assumptions of his arguments or their consistency, "let alone trying to lure his audiences to think critically and independently," following the argument wherever it leads.[25]

The first difference is doubtful. For why must the skills of a virtuous rhetorician be restricted to persuading oneself or others to adopt a *particular* action or stance? Why can't they be directed to the adoption of a *whole way of life*, or a significant portion of one, such as the life of a good soldier? If they can, and Pierre Hadot is more or less correct in thinking that philosophical systems are typically bound up with whole ways of life, then philosophers, too, must practice rhetoric.

The second difference to which Rorty calls our attention[26] is real and important. One of the most frequently alleged differences between rhetoric and philosophy is clearly specious, however – that the rhetorician appeals to the desires, emotions, and passions of his hearers while the philosopher does not.

III. Philosophy's De Facto Use of Rhetoric

Philosophical debates themselves are arguably structured on a forensic model.[27] In the Platonic dialogues, for example, opinions are broached and subjected to philosophical scrutiny in the hope that the truth will emerge through a process of questioning and answering. The medieval practice of examining philosophical and theological theses in public debates is reflected in the structure of Aquinas's *Summa Theologiae*. Modern philosophers proceed in the same fashion. Someone advances a thesis, offers arguments for it, and then responds to the criticism of other philosophers. The thesis that survives criticism is then regarded as the closest approximation to the truth currently available. It may therefore be significant that the medieval *disputatio,* in which "a specific problem [was] put to the speaker in the form of a question to which he had to formulate a satisfactory answer," bears a "strong resemblance ... to the *declamationes* of the Roman oratory schools. When rhetoric disappeared from public life at the end of the Republic ... and became a matter for the school, similar tasks were given to the pupils. Seutonius provides us with the following example." A group of young men and some fishermen agree that for a fixed price, the fishermen will let the young men have their catch. They haul in their nets, and, while there are no fish, there is a basket of gold. " 'The buyers claim that the catch belonged to them, while the fishermen said that the basket of gold was theirs.' The pupils had then to deliver a well-constructed speech to defend one of the two positions."[28] It is arguably significant that the debates of the late Roman oratory schools and hence the medieval *disputatio* were modeled on a judicial procedure, and that in the ancient world, rhetoric was principally prized as a tool for persuading others of the truth of one's assertions in the assembly and law courts. Rhetoric was highly valued, in other words, as the most effective means to power.

But precisely what follows from the fact that philosophical discussion follows a forensic model? Not that rational discourse and philosophical argumentation are no more than disguised expressions of the speaker's will to power, as Nietzsche, Foucault, and advocates of the "critical rhetoric" have claimed,[29] but, at most, that the lines between philosophy and rhetoric are less sharp than most philosophers have believed. And, indeed, it would be foolish to deny that philosophy itself has often been rather heavily "tainted" with rhetoric.

For example, some of the tools Berkeley freely employs in his *Alciphron* – ridicule, sarcasm, and the like[30] – are typically associated with rhetoric by rhetoric's philosophical critics. Yet, tellingly, they are just as often employed by philosophers themselves. More or less randomly selected examples include Daniel Dennet's critiques of religion or of mind-body dualism; Hume's critiques of religion; the opinions on rhetoric expressed in the quotations from Hobbes, Locke, and Hume cited earlier; and Plato's pictures of Thrasymachus, Callicles, and other opponents of Socrates.

A more interesting because slightly more subtle example is discussed by Matthew Sterenberg.[31] In the first sixty-odd years of the twentieth century, analytic philosophers deployed a rhetoric of revolution to defend the new movement. For example, they argued that analytic philosophy had overcome the obfuscation, imprecision, and untestability of the various forms of idealism that had dominated academic philosophy in the latter half of the nineteenth century and attempted to enhance analytic philosophy's prestige by aligning it with science. When they were attacked for analytic philosophy's alleged sterility, and for its inattention to the practical concerns and speculative questions that had traditionally preoccupied philosophy,[32] they responded in two ways. First, they constructed an essentially Whigish history of philosophy, arguing that Plato and Aristotle, the medievals, and early modern philosophers such as Descartes and Berkeley, when at their best, were essentially engaged in analysis and conceptual clarification, And second, they argued that analytic philosophy itself could be a tool for enhancing moral knowledge and advancing liberal values.[33]

IV. The Necessity of Philosophy's Use of Rhetoric

Analytic philosophers are highly likely to argue that deployments of rhetoric such as those discussed in the final two paragraphs of the preceding section are ancillary to their arguments; they are not essential to them. But while the *soundness* of their arguments[34] is independent of the employment of rhetoric,[35] they are clearly mistaken in thinking that the arguments *themselves* (when abstracted from context and other "extraneous" matter) are sufficient to sway all informed, fair-minded, properly trained, and intelligent hearers or readers. For one thing, those hearers or readers must be convinced that the analytic philosopher's approach to the problem is the most appropriate one to take to the kind of issues at stake, and it is unclear how the speaker can do this without employing rhetorical devices.[36] (The analytic philosopher might – and sometimes implicitly does – define "fully informed, fair-minded, properly trained, and intelligent hearers or readers" as those who are disposed to accept the kind of arguments that she and other analytic philosophers propose, but that would rather obviously be question begging.)

Rhetoric is essential in at least two interrelated ways. Chapter 4 called attention to seventeenth- and eighteenth-century Puritan and Anglican divines' insistence that not only the gospel but also the arguments of natural theology can obtain "a free admission into the assent of the understanding" only when they "bring a passport from a rightly disposed will." We saw that Plato, too, thought that "neither quickness of learning nor a good memory can make a man see [the Good] when his nature is not akin to the object." In his view, reason has its own loves and desires[37] that must be carefully nurtured if it is to function as it ought. Then too, as Ernesto Grassi has pointed out, "in several of his dialogues Plato connects the philosophical process with *eros*, which would lead to the conclusion that he attributes a decisive role to the [emotions] even in philosophy."[38] Finally, Plato's mature account of moral failure explains why rhetoric is still needed. Moral failure is rooted in either of two causes. The first is reason's failure to discern the good. The second is a failure in the lower parts of the soul that prevents them from concurring in reason's judgment (sensuality or avarice, for example, which are failures of appetite, or cowardice or arrogance, which are failures of "spirit" [*thymos*]). The function of rhetoric in the ideal state is to induce "friendship" (Plato's term) or psychic harmony in the soul so that appetite and *thymos* willingly concur in the judgment of reason. So rhetoric is necessary for the production of virtue, and virtue is in turn needed for a full understanding or appreciation of the Good. And Augustine says something similar. Reason should not be discarded once faith has been achieved. For "God forbid that He should hate in us that faculty [reason] by which He has made us superior to all other living beings. Therefore, we must refuse so to believe as not to seek a reason for our beliefs." Nevertheless, faith (*which includes appropriate motions of the will and heart*) is a precondition of the success of this enterprise. For some things must first be believed to be understood. "Therefore the prophet said with reason: 'if you will not believe, you will not understand.'"[39]

Plato and Augustine's official view is that even when it is properly employed, rhetorical persuasion is second best, a mere substitute for rational persuasion. I have argued, though, that, *in their own view*, certain affective and conative states are needed to achieve knowledge. If this is correct, then rhetoric isn't a more or less dispensable tool that reason employs to induce acceptance of its dictates; a properly deployed rhetoric is, instead, an essential *part* of rational discourse. Rational persuasion *includes* rhetorical persuasion, the arousal of the passions desires, and emotional states needed for the sort of knowledge in question – a love of justice in the case of ethical knowledge, perhaps, or (if Jonathan Edwards or Pascal are correct) "true benevolence" or a hunger for God, or (if Wang Yangming is right) selflessness.[40]

Note that rhetorical tools are already uncontroversially employed in *teaching* philosophy. We employ them to inculcate such standard intellectual virtues as fair-mindedness, honesty in the handling of evidence, openness to criticism, or the elimination of "unjust" prejudice or bias.[41] The practice of philosophy involves cherishing, exemplifying, and advocating such values. Commitment to them is *intrinsic*, not extrinsic, to it. Teaching philosophy involves inducting students into a rational practice that involves possessing and exercising these intellectual virtues; their acquisition is *part* of what is involved in becoming a good reasoner. Yet if I am correct about the role our passional nature plays in good reasoning about ethical and religious matters and, more generally, in good reasoning about any value saturated subject matter,[42] then the same is true of certain virtues of the heart. Example, praise and dispraise, imaginative and emotional appeals[43] – rhetoric, in short – play an essential role in the practice of philosophy and theology because they are needed to inculcate and reinforce the intellectual, ethical, and spiritual values that suffuse good reasoning.

In commenting on Aristotle, Arash Abizadeh notes that the "phonetic rhetorician can, when faced with an unvirtuous crowd, use the power of rhetoric itself to attempt to persuade the audience by appealing not to the virtues that the crowd actually has but to an ideal virtuous image of the crowd which the orator rhetorically paints and inspires the crowd to emulate." Similarly, the speaker, "in order to deploy the *pistis* ['proof'] of *ethos* ['character']" must "represent himself in his speech as virtuous – a creative representation which in turn can inspire the good-willed speaker [a speaker who wishes well to his audience] to rise up to his own rhetorical model." The resources of rhetoric can thus be deployed "to instill virtue in both the speaker and the crowd to a degree not previously realized."[44]

I believe that these remarks can also be applied to the phronetic reasoner. Because the deliberator *qua* persuader wishes well to the deliberator *qua* persaudee, she will appeal to an ideal image of herself, not just to the emotions and character traits she actually has. Similarly, in constructing and deploying her arguments she will represent herself (play the role of) a virtuous phronetic deliberator, thus inspiring herself to "rise up to [her] own rhetorical model." This has important implications for the sort of reasoning appropriate in ethical and religious matters. One's reasoning in these areas should not only be informed by the epistemically relevant emotions and character traits one in fact has but also (or rather?) by those one thinks one *should* have. This may involve role playing. But role playing can be morally and epistemically virtuous. For example, one should morally deliberate *as if* one were a morally good agent, and one should reason *as if* one possessed the standard epistemic virtues. (Suppose, for instance, that one tends to be intolerant of criticism. One can attempt to reason *as if* one weren't intolerant so that, while one doesn't presently find the conclusion that would be reached by a virtuous epistemic agent fully persuasive, one may, by continued exercises of this sort, come to *be* a virtuous epistemic agent and, as a consequence, end up wholeheartedly endorsing those conclusions.) Moreover, when the epistemically relevant virtuous dispositions are also morally and spiritually virtuous (as many of those in moral and religious reasoning are), then the case for epistemic role playing becomes even more compelling.

Rhetoric is also essential in a second way. Ernesto Grassi argues that reason's function is to derive conclusions from antecedent premises. But because our first principles or ultimate starting points can't be derived from anything more basic, they can't themselves be established by reasons.[45] They instead rest on poetry and imagination. They can't be proved but can sometimes be "shown" by "figurative" or "imaginative" language – that is, by the deployment of rhetoric."[46]

Nicholas Rescher's position is in many ways similar. Rescher distinguishes between "discursive philosophy," or argumentation, and "evocative philosophizing," or rhetoric. The first proceeds inferentially by deriving one proposition from another, and "pivots on inferential expressions such as 'because,' 'since,' 'therefore,' 'has the consequence that,' 'and so cannot,' etc." The chain of reasons must end, however, and, when it does, its first premises can only be supported "by representing certain contentions in a favorable light, seeking to elicit their acceptance, through noting their intrinsically appealing features," that is, by rhetoric. Evocative philosophizing "bristles with adjectives of appro-bation or derogation – 'evident,' 'untenable,' 'absurd,' 'inappropriate,' and the like." The rhetorician "seeks to secure the reader's (or auditor's) assent by an appeal to values and appraisals – and above all by appeals to fittingness and consonance within the overall scheme of things." The "rhetorical evocative mode of" philosophizing, in short, is "preoccupied with forming or reforming our sensibilities with respect to ... value and, above all, with shaping or influ-encing one's priorities and evaluations. It is bound up with a view of philoso-phy that sees the discipline in axiological terms ... it exerts its impetus directly upon the cognitive values and sympathies that we have fixed on the basis of our experience of the world's ways." The rhetorical mode of procedure's "impact upon [our cognitive] beliefs," is indirect, however, and occurs "only in so far as our beliefs and opinions are shaped by and reflective of our values."[47]

Rescher's account is both broader and narrower than Grassi's. It is broader because it doesn't restrict itself to a consideration of the "root metaphors" of comprehensive philosophical systems but extends to any argument's ultimate presuppositions or starting points. It narrows Grassi's view by implying that rhetoric's effect on cognitive beliefs is only indirect. But this, I believe, is a mis-take. For (like our beliefs in simple modal or logical propositions) evaluations, too, are, arguably, cognitive beliefs. If they are, then they are candidates for supportive or critical *argumentation*, as well as for appeals to intuition and to what just "seems right" to us, that is, for rhetorical support.[48]

Metaphor and tropes have historically been regarded as belonging to rheto-ric. Yet if Grassi and Rescher are right, as I believe they are, then philosophy, too, is saturated with metaphor. Philosophers such as Plato, Plotinus, and Bergson are obvious examples. But, arguably, most if not all metaphysical schemes are structured by metaphors (the world as mechanism or organism, for instance, or as spirit or force). Nor is it clear that these metaphors are dispensable, that the insights they express could be as adequately conveyed without them. Aristotle thought there was an important connection between metaphor and resemblances, claiming that to metaphorize well "is a sign of genius, since a good metaphor implies an intuitive perception of the similar-ity in dissimilars."[49] The poet, he says, is one who "perceives similarity," and in the *Rhetoric* adds that "in philosophy also, an acute mind will perceive resemblances even in things far apart."[50] Pace Hobbes, Locke, and Hume, the deployment of metaphors (and hence rhetoric) is deeply embedded in philoso-phy itself.

But is it *essential*? Although Paul Thagard and Craig Beam agree that the deployment of metaphor is a *common* feature of philosophical discourse, they don't appear to regard it as essential. In their view, philosophy's use of meta-phor is more closely akin to metaphor's use in science than to its use in poetry and rhetoric. Metaphors and analogies are employed in both disciplines in the "discovery, development, evaluation, and exposition of theories,"[51] but in nei-ther case is the point of their use primarily to delight or to persuade regardless of the truth or adequacy of the discourse in which they are utilized. Yet they tellingly admit that because "there is not much empirical evidence directly relevant to the assessment of theories of knowledge [or to other philosophical theories for that matter], ... metaphors and analogies carry much more of the evaluative burden [in philosophy] than is the case in science."[52] In other words, metaphors and analogies play a much larger role in *justifying* the theories (in persuading oneself and others of their rational superiority) than they do in science. Now as already noted, metaphor has traditionally been part of the theory of rhetoric. So if the deployment of metaphors is indispensable to philosophy, *rhetoric* (as traditionally understood) is indispensable to it. If Thagard and Beam are right, then, while metaphor is indispensable to the discovery, development, and exposition of scientific theories, it plays at most a comparatively minor role in both their articulation (which is typically mathematized) and evaluation. But neither is true of philosophical theories. Hence, metaphor and analogy (and thus rhetoric) are essential to philosophy in a way in which they are not essential to science.

Note that even if one rejects my account of the essential epistemic role played by passion in good reasoning about value-laden subject matter and by the central role images and metaphors play in the articulation and evaluation of philosophical and theological theories, rhetoric may still be epistemically relevant. John Wisdom, Ian Ramsey, John Hick, and others have argued that religious discovery involves seeing one thing as another (nature as God's handiwork, for example, or the saints as manifestations of Reality itself). If they are right, then rhetoric may be needed to effect the necessary gestalt shift. If the gestalt shift is *appropriate* – involves a richer, truer, more satisfying (including rationally more satisfying in James's sense) view of reality, then rhetoric has performed a valuable *epistemic* role. Rhetoric (preaching, spiritual literature, the admonitions of a spiritual director, and the like) may also help effect religious perceptions (cognitively valid religious experiences). In both cases, there is an analogy with the tools and/or training one needs to make the subtle discriminations of wine tasters, good judges of music or art, or the observations of experienced trackers or sailors. If the discriminations or observations are epistemically virtuous, then so too are the tools or training needed to make them.

V. An Example: The *Confessions* of Augustine

Cicero's rhetorical teachings focused on "deliberative and forensic oratory," and presupposed the centrality and viability of "the legal and political institutions of republican Rome." But as we have seen, when those institutions decayed under the empire, the "traditional rhetorical program" devolved into meaningless "contests of declamation" that aimed at applause and prizes, and a "schoolroom emphasis on style, delivery and performance."[53] The rhetoric Augustine learned and taught as a young man was thus essentially "an art of display," a "means of coming off better in the debate," the end of which was applause and earning "what passes for wealth in this world."[54]

But while Augustine "taught his students the 'tricks of pleading,'" he professes to have "'had no evil intent,' and 'never meant them to be used to get the innocent condemned but, if the occasion arose, to save the lives of the guilty.'" Even so, he says, "'I sold the services of my tongue,'" and taught my "students to learn 'lies and the insane warfare of the courts,' ... [and] it is with a palpable sense of regret, ... that he recalls ... 'preparing a speech in praise of the emperor' [in which he] shamelessly composed 'a great many lies which would certainly be applauded by an audience who knew well enough how far from the truth they were.'"[55]

He came to see that the primary flaw of the rhetoric he taught and practiced was its cavalier attitude toward truth. And when (before he was a Christian) he compared the public discourses of the Manichaean Faustus and Ambrose, what most impressed him was the latter's concern with truth. Both men were eloquent and both had a "'charming delivery' but in Ambrose's case, he 'could not keep' the manner of delivery 'apart ... from the truth of what he said.'"[56]

While *On Christian Doctrine*[57] exhibits a "close affinity with Cicero," there are also clear differences. The most important are these: (1) The Christian orator's efforts are grounded in the Truth (that is, in God who *is* the Truth). (2) They are aimed at the hearer's eternal, and not merely her temporal, welfare. (3) They are thus expressions of the speaker's charity, her loving concern for the souls of her audience. In Augustine's view, the "art of eloquence" shouldn't be rejected out of hand because it is tainted with paganism, but employed in the service of truth and for the good of one's hearers.[58]

Plato thought that philosophy, unlike rhetoric, is essentially (and not merely incidentally or accidentally) directed toward truth. In *this* respect, *Christian* rhetoric, as understood by Augustine, is indistinguishable from philosophy. As the *Gorgias* makes clear, however, Socrates' critique is directed not only toward the *end* of rhetoric but also toward its *means* (appeals to the emotions and other nonrational sources of belief). Yet as I have argued, some emotions are truth-directed, and Plato himself implicitly recognized this. Augustine explicitly does so. Faith (belief with its attendant affects) is directed toward *understanding*.

While it contains many dialectical passages, James Farrell argues that the *Confessions* as a whole is a paradigmatic exercise in Christian rhetoric. To whom, though, was it directed?

A number of answers have been given: to "Manicheans, skeptics, and also Christians," and to "God Himself," for example, or to a "loosely affiliated network of highly educated laymen, nuns, priests and bishops spread throughout the Roman Empire." Yet in Book X, Augustine imagines his audience to be, more generally, his "true brother," that is, "those who rejoice for me in their hearts when they find good in me, and grieve for me when they find sin," and those also who share God's kingdom, and "accompany me on this pilgrimage, whether they have gone before me or are still to come or are with me as I make my way through life." "Augustine's audience," in short, "consists of Christians of all ages. He writes for the communion of saints." The *Confessions* thus presupposes and creates a Christian sensibility or at the very least a receptiveness toward it.[59] What, though, is the *Confessions'* rhetorical message?

"The main action of the text is self-disclosure," although *not* "self-disclosure for its own sake." "By recounting his own great sins, by giving his life fully to his readers, Augustine … shows his own powerlessness over sin, and consequently acknowledges God's saving action in his life." *On Christian Doctrine* defines a "sign [as] a thing which causes us to think of something beyond the impression the thing itself makes upon the senses." The sacraments are, in this sense, "outward and visible signs of an inward and invisible grace." In the same sense, Augustine's life is a sign pointing the reader to the redemptive action of God, whose workings are exhibited in that life. "When they hear what I have to tell, all who adore you will exclaim 'Blessed be the Lord in heaven and on earth. Great and wonderful is his name.' "[60]

"How," finally, should "*we* respond to the work?" Borrowing from Cicero, Augustine tells us (in *On Christian Doctrine*) that "he who is eloquent should speak in such a way that he teaches, delights, and moves." "The last is the most important. 'The truth of what is said is acknowledged in vain and the eloquence of discourse pleases in vain unless that which is learned is implemented in action.' " And "the action of which Augustine speaks is repentance and conversion," and it is "this action that he [depicts and] enacts in the narrative of the *Confessions*." As he says in Book IV of *On Christian Doctrine*, "I did not think I had done anything when I heard [my] congregation applauding but when I saw them weeping." "The effect of rhetoric is to be seen, not in the approval" of one's hearers, "but rather through their groans, sometimes even through tears, and finally through a change in their way of life."[61]

VI. Three Objections

I shall conclude the chapter by examining three objections to the claim that the deployment of rhetoric is intrinsically bound up with good philosophical reasoning about religious or other matters. The first two purport to demonstrate that philosophy and rhetoric are essentially opposed. The third attempts to show that even if some uses of rhetoric are inseparable from the practice of philosophy, appeals to our passional nature should play no part in it.

Objection 1
Kant thinks that poetry is an expression of our freedom, of the pure play of the imagination. Poetry "*plays* with illusion," however; it doesn't use it "to deceive us … it does not seek to sneak up on the understanding and ensnare it by a sensible exhibition."[62] Rhetoric or the art of persuasion, on the other hand, "is a violent threat" to its audience's autonomy, depriving its hearers of

their "freedom to think, decide and judge for" themselves.[63] Rhetoric "move[s] people like machines to a judgment that must lose all its weight with them when they meditate about it calmly … [O]ratory …, the art of using people's weaknesses for one's own aims (no matter how good these may be in intention or even in fact), is unworthy of any respect whatsoever."[64] For "the motto of enlightenment" is "have courage to use your own reason."[65] By substituting his own judgment for ours, the successful orator keeps us in "tutelage," and thereby prevents us from achieving our full humanity.

But Kant's polemic is successful only if (a) what we most essentially are is pure reason, and (b) the emotions, feelings, and passions *as such* play no role in good reasoning. If these presuppositions are correct, then appeals to our emotions, feelings, and "prejudices"[66] are attacks on our autonomy. Yet both claims are suspect. Our subjectivity (Kierkegaard) or passional nature (James) helps to *define* who we are; it is as much a constituent of our being as our reason is. The second presupposition is equally dubious. If the epistemological position I defended in Chapter 4 is correct, our emotions, passions, and feelings play an essential role in good reasoning about value-laden subject matters.[67]

Moreover, pace Kant, poetry often *does* seek to engage our understanding. Coleridge's distinction between "fancy" and "imagination" seems to me to be on target. The former "is no other than a mode of memory emancipated from the order of time and space … modified by [arbitrary] choice." Imagination, on the other hand, is "essentially vital"; in "creating," "idealizing," and "unifying," it "answers to something in reality itself."[68]

How does it do so? Aristotle's account of tragic poetry provides one example. In discussing metaphor in the twenty-second chapter of the *Poetics*, Aristotle says that the dramatic poet must be a "master of metaphor." The creation of fresh metaphors is a sign of genius; it can't be learned from others. For a good metaphor rests on an intuitive "perception of similarity in dissimilaties." The remark is significant, for Aristotle thinks that perceiving and grasping likenesses is equally important for philosophers, and in the *Topics* "discusses its relevance to a range of types of philosophical argument."[69] Again, in the *Poetics'* ninth chapter, Aristotle says that poetry is more philosophical than history "since its statements are rather of the nature of universals, whereas those of history are singulars," and adds that "by a universal statement I mean one as to what such or such a kind of man will probably or necessarily do." Even though it may not be entirely clear just what Aristotle has in mind, it *is* clear that he thinks that the fictions of tragedy (and comedy) teach us something important about life ("action") that a mere chronicle of events (or a newspaper) couldn't teach us. History is just "one damned thing happening after another." But because poetry represents action as a unified whole, with a beginning, middle, and end, it enables us to *see* it "as a unified whole, with an intelligible shape."[70]

Stephen Halliwell suggests that the effect of tragedy is to refine our values. To understand and appropriately respond to tragedy at all, one must approach it with an understanding of human life, which is already quasi-universal – some grasp of what it is to be a human agent, a sense of what is and isn't important in life, an ability to "distinguish degrees of innocence, responsibility and guilt; to know in a mature way what merits pity and fear; to have a grasp of [what constitutes] human successes and failures," and so on. But tragedy doesn't simply "confirm or codify our experience … it provides us with imaginative opportunities to test, refine, extend, and perhaps even question the ideas and values" that we bring to tragedy and that help us to understand it.[71] The idea, in short, is that by refining and extending our understanding of what is pitiful, fearful, and the like, the emotions of pity, fear, and so on will be "purified" or "clarified." Can we be more specific?

In some cases, tragedies "teach specific lessons. For example, *The Trojan Women* reminds an audience who had voted for the slaughter of the Mytilenians, [and] the enslavement of their women and children[72] … exactly what it is to lose one's male relations, to be enslaved, and turned out of one's home. Forgetfulness, ignorance, self-preoccupation, military passion[73]… are 'cleared up' by the sharp experience of pity and fear." But more generally, tragedy teaches us something about the limitations of human life and the fragility of happiness (*eudaimonia*) – that not only external fortune, but also "ethical success, acting and living well," depend not only on human effort but "on things beyond our control."[74] – A realization that is highly useful in combating a vice that Aristotle greatly feared, namely, *hubris* ("vaunting oneself because of one's success," excessive pride or arrogance or self-confidence).[75]

Plato thought that poetry harms character. Aristotle thinks that by purifying or "clarifying" the painful and pleasurable emotions (i.e., through *katharsis*[76]) poetry's effect on character is beneficial. Plato's primary concern, however, was arguably the poet's pretensions to ethical knowledge – knowledge of how to live. Plato denies that poets have this knowledge because they often depict their protagonists behaving in ethically inappropriate ways, because many of the ethical opinions expressed in their works are false, and because they can't give a reasoned account of the true ethical opinions their work may happen to convey. By contrast, Aristotle believes that poetry does have something important to teach us about life that (at least by implication) can't be as effectively conveyed in any other way. Poetry brings truths home to us (about the fragility of *eudaimonia*, for example) in a way in which straightforwardly didactic accounts cannot.[77]

Objection 2

Henry W. Johnstone, Jr., too, thinks that rhetoric and philosophy are essentially opposed. The devices of the rhetorician are effective only when they are concealed from his audience since "it is impossible to be persuaded by a technical device [of rhetoric] at the same time that one sees it as *merely* a device." By contrast, not only are the "devices" (namely, rational arguments) of the philosopher ideally transparent to those to whom they are addressed, their endorsement by the latter is essential to securing the *kind* of agreement she aims at (namely, *rational* agreement). Moreover, the very enterprise in which the philosopher is engaged includes making her "tools" available to her audience to criticize her own assertions.

Another difference between the philosopher and the rhetorician is that the latter needn't share the beliefs, attitudes, or prejudices to which he appeals in order to be effective nor privately endorse the views he is advocating. Yet this would be totally inappropriate for the philosopher. Because philosophy is a search for truth, the philosopher undercuts her enterprise if she employs premises she regards as false or dubious, or attempts to persuade her audience of the truth of opinions she believes to be false.[78]

The most that Johnstone has shown, however, is that philosophy and a certain *kind* of rhetoric are opposed. He has not shown that the sort of rhetorical appeal I am defending can't play a legitimate role in philosophical argumentation. Note first that the rhetorician's devices don't always lose their effectiveness when his audience becomes aware of them. Appeals to the audience's emotions, for example, don't lose their effectiveness when the audience is convinced that the emotions the speaker is evoking are relevant or appropriate. Sermons, or an impassioned discourse designed to arouse one's compassion for the less fortunate, are examples. In such cases, the hearer may be fully aware of what the speaker is doing and yet legitimately endorse and be moved by it because he rightly regards the emotions in question as epistemically relevant to the discernment of spiritual or moral truth. Moreover, where both speaker and hearer agree that the emotion to which the speaker is appealing belongs to a *class* of emotions that are epistemically relevant, the hearer can appeal to other members of that class to criticize and/or refine the speaker's own assertions.[79] Nor does Johnstone's last point militate against the use of rhetoric I am advocating. For, in the cases I am envisaging, the speaker shares and prizes the emotions she appeals to or is attempting to elicit, and endorses the conclusions she is advocating. (Cf. our attempts to elicit a commitment to the appropriate epistemic virtues in our philosophy students.)

But the most important point is this. The underlying assumption of Plato's, Locke's, Kant's, or Johnstone's dismissal of rhetoric is that appeals to emotion and "prejudice" are not just epistemically irrelevant but undermine the search for truth. If my argument in Chapter 4 is correct, this assumption is false. When the emotions and "prejudices" in question are of the right sort, they may be needed to discern it.

Objection 3

The third objection to my defense of the use of rhetoric in argumentation may be more serious. Even if there are accidental connections between particular cultures or historical periods and good reasoning,[80] the connection isn't essential. Similarly, if the universalist pretensions of the world religions are legitimate, then neither the acceptance of their claims nor the experiences of conversion or enlightenment they foster should be dependent upon the adoption of a particular culture. Now, if I am right, our passional nature plays a role in good reasoning. Our passional nature is shaped by our personal histories, however, and these, in turn, by our culture. The following example is illustrative. William James appeals to hopes and fears, interests and sentiments, which he believes are universal, and, in particular, to humanity's alleged horror of meaninglessness and its need for significant action. Yet is the latter really universal? Or is the need for significant action, instead, rooted in Western (and especially American) society as that took shape in the second half of the nineteenth century? Would a Buddhist or Taoist, for instance, acknowledge its power or (more significantly) agree that any satisfactory world view must satisfy it? Since the Buddhist believes that ignorance (*avidya*) and craving (*trisna*) are the source of suffering (*duhkha*), it is pretty clear that he, at least, would not. There are potential tensions, then, between classical ideals of rationality, and the world religions' universalist pretentions, on the one hand, and appeals to our passional nature, on the other.

Insofar as philosophy and philosophical theology share these ideals and make claims on universal assent, their use of rhetoric must be sensitive to the distinction between aspects of our passional nature that are culturally specific or personally idiosyncratic and those that are not. If reason and truth *are* universal, then *even if* good reasoning in religion is passional reasoning, appeals to the culturally specific or personally idiosyncratic should at best play no more than an ancillary role in philosophical and theological discourse. (It should be noted, however, that states of the heart can be culturally nonspecific and nonidiosyncratic without being universally shared. Fairness to one's intellectual opponents, for example, may be rare but isn't *essentially* tied to particular cultures.[81])

Whether the classical ideal of rationality is consistent with my account of the role of passion and rhetoric in reasoning and speaking about religious and other value-laden topics may ultimately stand or fall on the outcome of a research project in comparative philosophy and theology. The project involves three elements. First is an examination of, say, Christian or Buddhist theories of rhetoric as well as of logic, and Buddhist and Christian accounts of the relation between them. Second is an examination of Christian or Buddhist rhetorical practices, for example, in contexts in which arguments are offered, examined, and rebutted. And third is an examination of the passions and virtues valued in, for example, Christian or Buddhist inquiry, and the extent to which these passions and virtues are culturally or temperamentally specific.

An examination of Chinese philosophy may prove especially illuminating in the present connection since "rhetoric has always been an integral aspect of philosophizing in the Chinese tradition without it ever having been bifurcated off [from philosophy] as a separate tradition."[82] For example, in many Confucian texts, rhetorical appeals are seamlessly interwoven with structured argumentation and systematic reflection. Of course, the latter *can* be abstracted from the former. The price of doing so, however, is to partially undermine the rational (and not merely emotional) force of the text.[83]

While these investigations remain incomplete, I am reasonably confident that they will continue to show that rhetorical strategies are essentially connected with rational inquiry into religious and other value-laden matters in all the major religious traditions. I also believe that they will continue to support the hypothesis that even though some of the passions and virtues intrinsically connected with practices of rational inquiry are essentially tied to specific *world views*,[84] they are *not* essentially bound to particular *cultures* such as that of ancient China or the Western Middle Ages or medieval India,[85] or to particular temperaments or psychological types.

6

Reason, Revelation, and Religious Argumentation

The anti-Pelagian arguments of Augustine discussed in Chapter 1 rely heavily on appeals to Christian scriptures. They are not the only proofs discussed in that chapter that do so, however. Peter Geach thinks that being omnipotent (being able to *do* all things) should be distinguished from being almighty (having power *over* all things), and claims that although the former is arguably incoherent, being almighty must be ascribed to God to ensure that the powers of darkness will ultimately be defeated. He concedes, though, that while a belief in God's ultimate triumph is essential to traditional Christian belief, its truth can be established only by an appeal to revelation – not by philosophical argumentation. Again, one of Ramanuja's objections to Advaita Vedanta is that their denial of the reality of distinctions undercuts Advaita's appeal to the Vedas, which both he and the Advaitins believe to be an inerrant revealed text.

Chapter 3 argued that religious reading inflects the construction and appreciation of religious arguments in the major religious traditions. For their influence to be epistemically benign, however, the relevant texts must be truthful. Now many if not most of the texts in which the religious intellectuals of these traditions are immersed are thought to be *revealed* texts.[1] If they really are revealed, then presumably they are truthful. Yet *are* the alleged revelations authentic?

The question of revelation comes up in Chapter 5 as well. The unstated but implicitly assumed presuppositions of the religious rhetorician's enthymatic arguments are often allegedly revealed truths. So if the rhetorician's arguments are to carry their full weight, the revelations must be authentic.[2]

Do the appeals to reason in these cases therefore have a limit? Or can the appeal to revelation itself be rational?

I. Vedantin and Christian Views of Revelation

Orthodox Hindus regard the Vedas as revealed texts. Vedanta believes that the Vedas are eternal. "Two kinds of eternity are distinguished.... A thing is *kutastha nityata* [immutably eternal] if is unchanged forever. A thing is *pravaharupa nityata* [mutably eternal]" if it exists for ever, changing incessantly but always according to the same pattern. (If the movements of our solar system were everlasting, they would therefore be said to be mutably eternal.) Shankara appears to have thought that the Vedas are mutably eternal, produced anew at the beginning of each world cycle according to the same unchanging pattern. Thus, the content of the Vedas[3] that are in use in this world period is identical to the content of the Vedas that are produced at the beginning of each past and future world cycle. The Vivarana school of Advaita Vedanta, on the other hand, believed that the Vedas are immutably eternal. The everlasting, unchanging Vedas are *manifested* at the beginning of each world cycle and are *concealed* at each cycle's end but do not themselves undergo change.[4]

But why think that the Vedas are eternal? For at least three reasons. First, because the dharma (the rules for right conduct) and the Brahman are unchanging and eternal, the scripture "which contains knowledge of them" must also be unchanging and eternal.[5] Second, current Vedic study is guided by the memory of past Vedic study. Moreover, we find that no matter how far back we go, Vedic study at any given time is governed by the memory of past Vedic study. When we couple this with the fact that no one is known to be the author of the Vedas, it is only reasonable to infer that they are beginningless. Third, "the Veda declares itself to be eternal."[6]

But even though the Vedas are eternal, Vedantins believe the Brahman is in some sense their cause. Advaita Vedanta thinks that the Brahman underlies the Vedas in the same way that it underlies the space-time world. Ultimately, though, both are illusory. Theistic Vedantins such as Ramanuja and Madhva regard Brahman (Vishnu) as the Vedas promulgator. He isn't their *author*, however. God (Brahman or Vishnu) causes the Vedas in somewhat the same way in which I cause the words I quote. I bring these words into being, but I am not their author. My words don't express my own thoughts but simply repeat the words of another. Similarly, the Vedas that are re-created or manifested by Brahman at the beginning of a world cycle are only echoes of the Vedas that were created or manifested at the beginning of each preceding world cycle. There is no time at which their contents were *originated* by the Brahman.[7]

At least one theistic Hindu school believes that God is their author, however: the Nyaya. Jayanta, for example, argues that "only an omniscient being could know what is good and what is bad, which action is right and which is not." Since the Vedas provide such knowledge, we must conclude that they are the work of omniscience. Because it is simpler to suppose that the Vedas are the work of only one omniscient being rather than several, however, and because it is difficult to conceive of a *finite* omniscient being, we may conclude that *God* is their author.[8] Again, "about half of the arguments proffered by Udayana [for God's existence] concern God as the author or 'speaker' of the Vedic scriptures."[9] Nyaya's conception of revelation is thus similar in this respect to that of Jews, Christians, and Muslims.

Christians, for example, have interpreted the concept of revelation in three ways. Some have used the term "revelation" for moments of religious discovery and insight. The "bearers of revelation" are those who "perceive something new and introduce it into man's religious outlook."[10] Others have applied the term to encounters in which God actively thrusts his mind and purposes into ours. According to this view, God doesn't reveal the truth of scriptural or dogmatic propositions but, rather, reveals *himself*. Classical Christian theists disagree. In their opinion, revelation consists in God's communicating truths about himself and the world. Some of these truths can be confirmed by reason. Others cannot. In either case, one should believe them because the person who communicates them is necessarily truthful.

The first view is clearly stated by C. H. Dodd. Dodd compares scriptural authority to authority in science or art. The authority of the prophets and saints who speak to us through scripture is that "which belongs intrinsically to genius." Newton's authority is based on his superior scientific insight. Tolstoy's is based on his deep understanding of human nature. Similarly, the prophets' and saints' authority is based on an experience of divine reality that is "fuller, deeper and more compelling than" our own.

Authorities see more deeply than we do. Even so, their insights are mixed with error. Hence, while they provide "stimulus, support and direction," they don't absolve us of responsibility for our own judgment. The prophets' apprehension of the "thought of God," for example, was mediated through their historically conditioned and morally imperfect personalities. We should not, therefore, "submit to them blindly, or expect them to be infallible," but follow their guidance to see whether what they say can be confirmed by our own experience.[11]

Traditional Christian theologians fault this conception. In their view, the content of revelation isn't *discovered* but disclosed by God himself. Revealed knowledge exceeds human capacities – even the capacities of genius. In equating revelation with scientific or artistic discovery, Dodd neglects God's active role in the process of revelation and thus empties the concept of most of its content.

The second conception is more traditional. Divine revelation is analogous to situations in which people reveal themselves to others, not to those in which they disclose information. H. H. Farmer, for example, characterizes revelation as a personal relationship in which God approaches men and women in their immediate situations as an "active personal will" that poses an "absolute demand" and offers "final succor." God takes the initiative, "thrusting" his mind and will into ours, his "values and purposes among" ours. The "essential content of revelation" is thus "God himself, and not general truths about

God" – although Farmer does admit that truths about God "are implicit in the divine self-giving," and will be articulated once one begins to reflect on one's encounter. "The proper response to revelation ... is faith, which is not an intellectual assent to general truths, but the decisive commitment of the whole person in obedience to, and quiet trust in, the divine will." Faith cannot be created at will. It "must be evoked by the other presenting itself as trustworthy. Hence," while faith is "man's deed," "it sees in God its giver."[12]

Farmer's view is similar to Karl Barth's: revelation is a free and gracious act of divine sovereignty addressed to individual human beings. Neither scripture nor the proclamation based on scripture can be *identified* with revelation, however. Scripture and its proclamation *becomes* revelation when God speaks to us *through* them, and we succeed in seeing and hearing what (e.g.) John or Paul saw and heard. Through God's grace, their human words become God's word, a word that can be grasped only in faith.[13]

The first two accounts have a common feature. In both views, scripture and the theology based on it are essentially *human* products. If they are, then the world views they express should presumably be assessed in the same way we assess any world view.

Newton's theory was revolutionary. Nevertheless, it was assessed by the same scientific standards used to evaluate other scientific theories. Although Tolstoy's novels introduced new perspectives on human nature, they were subject to the same critical norms as any other work of literature.[14] The discovery of a religious world view may also be an act of genius. But if it is only that, its adequacy should be judged by the appropriate human criteria.

The second account has similar implications. In this view, God doesn't communicate general truths, but reveals himself. The words of scripture and theology are human attempts to articulate these encounters and their implications for human life. Jewish or Christian world views differ from systems of belief that aren't based on revelation because their primary data are the events through which God has allegedly revealed himself. Interpretations of the history of the Jews or of the life of Jesus provide the key for interpreting reality as a whole. But even though God may encounter us in the historical events recounted in the Hebrew Bible or in the life of Christ, scriptural and theological *interpretations* of the depicted facts are human and fallible. We should consequently assess them by the same standards we use to assess other historical interpretations and explanations.

Suppose, though, that God reveals not only himself but also truths about himself. After all, people usually reveal themselves to others by telling them about themselves. Perhaps, then, God not only reveals himself but also guides the process of interpretation. This, of course, is the traditional Judeo-Christian view. The biblical God, for example, not only encounters Moses but also informs him of his plans and purposes.

However, it is important to note that the ultimate object of faith on this view is *not* propositions, as critics sometimes allege. Aquinas, for example, believes that faith is a complex act that includes believing *that* there is a God, *believing* God, and believing *in* God. That is, the faithful (1) believe that God exists; (2) believe certain propositions (the creeds, for instance) because God has promulgated them; and (3) do so because they see that it is good to believe – an insight that involves a movement of the will toward God as one's end or good.[15] So even though propositions are faith's *immediate* objects, on Aquinas's view, faith's *ultimate* object is God himself (that is, what those propositions are *about*). Faith "grasps" (is directed toward) God *through* revealed propositions: "the act of the believer terminates in the reality not in the propositions. For we formulate propositions only in order to know things by means of them."[16]

Why, though, is revelation necessary? For several reasons. Some important religious truths can't be made out by reason at all. The triunity of God and God's Incarnation are often offered as examples. And while other central truths about God can, in principle, be established by reason, faith is needed in practice. Because many of these truths can't be made out without extensive study and hard thought, *none* of us would arrive at these truths until comparatively late in our lives. And because of "dullness of mind," or "laziness in learning," or the press of worldly business, and the like, many of us would *never* arrive at these important truths if we were to employ reason alone. Moreover, because the investigations of reason are uncertain at best, it is easy to be led astray. The upshot is that faith is needed if a person is to be guided throughout his or her life by a firm belief in God and his requirements.[17]

Almost five hundred years later, and in a very different cultural and intellectual environment, Samuel Clarke, too, concluded that the failures and uncertainties of reason make revelation and faith necessary. Even though reason can, in principle, discover many of the most central truths about God and his requirements, it functions imperfectly in practice. In the first place, "through supine negligence and want of attention," men and women "let their reason ... sleep ... minding only the things that are before their eyes." Reason's vision is also obscured by "early prejudices" and "vain and foolish notions" produced by an "evil education."[18] Moreover, we are so captivated and distracted by the "business and the pleasures of the world" that we are "unapt to employ [our] reason and fix [our] attention upon moral [and divine] matters, and still more backward to apply [ourselves] to the practice of them." Finally, we are prone to idolatry – worshiping the creature (nature, for example, worldly success, the nation, and the like) rather than the creator. Idolatry of this sort infects and corrupts reason, making it more difficult for us to discern divine truths by "that light of nature in [our] own minds."

Revelation helps correct these defects, however. It does so by (1) by raising and stirring up our "attention, to move [us] to shake off [our] habitual carelessness" (that is, it brings truths to our attention that might otherwise be overlooked or ignored); and (2) by confronting us with the truth, it cuts through the cloud of prejudice, custom, and superstition which surrounds and infects our reason. It also helps us (3) by impressing truths that we only dimly discern upon our souls with "great weight and authority" so that they come home to us.

Yet if we were to restrict ourselves to these considerations alone, we would probably conclude that while revelation may be necessary for most of us, it wouldn't be needed if reason were to function as it should. To meet this point, Clarke argues that, *even at its best*, reason is inadequate. He invites us to consider the "heathen" philosophers who employed their reason in an attempt to think rationally about divine matters. First, very few of them discerned much of the truth or even wished to, since, for most, philosophy was "an exercise of wit and subtlety and an instrument of vainglory" (though Clarke admits that Plato, Socrates, and "some others of that rank" were notable exceptions). Second, some of the things we need to know can't be made out by reason alone. Exactly how God should be worshiped is an example. Even the best philosophers, such as Socrates, usually recommended conformity to local custom and practice even though these practices involved idolatry and superstition. Again, reason can't determine how atonement should be made for sin, that is, how those "who have erred … and offended God may yet again restore themselves to the favor of God." Although repentance "be the most probable and only means that nature suggests," reason cannot discern "whether this will be alone sufficient or whether God will not require something further for the vindication of his justice." Hence, "there arises … from nature no sufficient comfort to sinners but anxious and endless solicitude about the means of appeasing the deity."

Third, even at its best, reason can't produce certainty – a conviction free from all "hesitancy and unsteadiness." Thus even after having offered "excellent arguments" for the immortality of the soul, Plato concluded by saying that "we ought not to be overconfident of it." Fourth, even the best heathen philosophers failed to grasp all of the relevant truths. "The truths they taught were single and scattered … and hit upon by chance rather than by any knowledge of the whole true state of things," and Clarke quotes Lactantius, who said, "The philosophers did indeed discover all the particular doctrines of true religion … but this was done by different men, and at different times and in different manners," and none was "able to collect into one whole and entire scheme the things which they were all sure were true singly."

Moreover, fifth, because the reasoning of the philosophers was "abstract and subtle," few could follow it. "None but men of parts and learning, of study and liberal education, have been able to profit by the sublime doctrine of Plato or by the subtle disputations of other philosophers." And finally, sixth, the doctrine of the best philosophers failed to have the weight it should have had because they lacked authority. Their teaching, "however evidently reasonable and fit to be obeyed seems still to want weight and to be but the precepts of men."

Clarke concludes that in "speculation indeed it may seem possible" that the truth be discovered and men's lives be reformed by reason. "But in experience and practice it hath on the contrary appeared to be altogether impossible for philosophy and bare reason to reform mankind effectually without the assistance of some higher principle." In practice, reason is not a sufficient guide to life.[19]

But granted that revelation alone can provide a sure guide to life, *which* alleged revelation (if any) should we accept?

II. Can Reasons Be Given for Subscribing to an Alleged Revelation?

Some Vedantins argued that the Vedas should be accepted because (1) the Veda declares itself to be reliable; (2) the testimony of the *Code of Manu* and other sacred books vouches for its authority; and (3) the authority of the Vedas is universally accepted. But Vedantins such as Sayana clearly recognized that these arguments aren't probative. The first is circular. The conclusion (the Vedas are reliable) follows from the premise (the Vedas declare themselves to be reliable) only on the assumption that the Vedas are reliable, and this is precisely what is at issue. The second argument begs the question, since whatever authority secondary scriptures such as the Code of Manu possess is derived from the authority of the primary scriptures (the Vedas) on which their own authority is based. And the third argument also fails because "many false ideas ... are universally entertained."

Vacaspati[20] argued that the Vedas are shown to be reliable because they are accepted by all great and good people. The Vivarana school of Advaita rejected this, however, pointing out that while many great and good persons accept Buddhist scriptures, Buddhist scriptures are not reliable.

The general Vedantin view was that the Vedas are to be accepted because (1) they teach us "about things which are highly useful" (namely, about what is right and wrong and how to obtain salvation); (2) which "are not known otherwise" (that is by reason or perception alone); and (3) which are uncontradicted by other sources of knowledge (that is by reason or perception).

In the last analysis, however, attempts to establish the reliability of the Vedas by independent argument are beside the point. For "the Veda is its own witness and proof"; it is self-luminous and therefore "intrinsically reliable." Just as the sun not only establishes other things but is seen in its own light, so the Veda "establishes its own reliability as well as the reliability of other things."[21]

Can reason certify the credentials of revelation? Many Christian theists have thought so. John Locke, for example, believed that propositions shouldn't be accepted as divinely revealed in the absence of sufficient evidence that God has revealed them. Reason must test revelation. A person who stifles reason to make room for revelation is like someone who blinds herself "the better to receive the light of an invisible star by a telescope." Christianity is credible – but only because it is confirmed by miracles. (Moses not only "heard" a voice, he saw a burning bush.) Reason is also needed to interpret revelation.[22] In Locke's view, revelation is simply "natural reason enlarged."[23]

Locke is making two claims: that the rational evidence for a particular revelation (Christianity) is sufficient and that, if it weren't, it would be wrong to believe it. We will deal with the first claim first.

Locke's appeal to miracles is hardly unusual. But he is comparatively unique in placing most of the weight of his argument upon them. For in addition to the miracles that allegedly accompanied the promulgation of the gospel, Christians have typically appealed to the trustworthiness of the biblical witnesses, the gospel's apparent fulfillment of Old Testament prophecies, and the growth of the church. They have further claimed that the gospel contains nothing that is contradictory or clearly erroneous, and point to its beneficial effect on people's lives as well as to its "power to meet even the highest aspirations" of humanity. Christians have also appealed to "the internal conviction felt by the soul as to the truth of the doctrine" – a sense of its splendor and appropriateness to the human situation.[24] Whether these appeals are sufficient to establish the divine origin of Christian revelation is controversial, however.

Such criteria specify the features that a divine revelation would allegedly have. They presuppose certain conceptions of ultimate reality and the human situation, and are reasonable if those conceptions are reasonable. For example, that a revealed doctrine would improve people's lives and be free from error presupposes ultimate reality's goodness and truth. The appeal to miracles presupposes that God can perform them and would attest to the truth of his communications by doing so. A revelation's "intrinsic luminosity" or the "soul's internal conviction of its truth" is relevant only if a genuine revelation would be likely to exhibit this quality or have this effect.

The criteria for assessing revelations thus rest on conceptions of ultimate reality and its relation to human life. Hence, if appeals to the criteria aren't to be circular, these conceptions must be independently plausible. For example, the major religious traditions agree that ultimate reality is the Good and the True. They therefore agree that a divine revelation must be beneficial and truthful. Hence, a Christian who is arguing with an Advaitin, or an Advaitin who is arguing with a Christian, can appeal to these criteria without begging the question in favor of his or her own system. If one can independently justify the claim that ultimate reality is personal, one can also employ criteria shaped by a theistic understanding of the transcendent without falling into circularity.[25]

But what sort of justification of the claim that ultimate reality is good and true, or personal, is possible? One answer is arguments such as those discussed in Chapter 1. But whether these are sufficient may be doubted. Revelations such as the Bible, the Vedas, or the Quran incorporate or presuppose world views. Reason may be capable of provisionally eliminating some alternatives, and there may be better reasons for some world views than for others. If the third argument discussed in Chapter 1 is sound, for example, there are better reasons for endorsing a theistic world view than for endorsing nontheistic world views such as Theravada Buddhism or Advaita Vedanta. But even if reason manages to *reduce* the number of relevant alternatives, it may fail to eliminate all but one. It may be unable to discover decisive reasons for preferring one theistic revelation to another, for example. And even if reason *should* find a (slight?) probability in favor of one alternative, the evidence is, arguably, too complex and ambiguous to compel assent.

If this is correct, reason can't fully resolve the problem of choosing between world views. To embrace a religion with firm conviction, one may ultimately have to venture beyond the evidence or rely on one's immediate impression that, for example, the Gospels, the Vedas, or the teachings of the Buddha contain the "words of eternal life." This decision or impression may have a theological explanation. It might be explained as an expression of one's ontological kinship with the Brahman, for instance, or by the indwelling of the Holy Spirit. These doctrines may make the decision or impression intelligible and also provide a kind of retrospective warrant for it. Still, one can't use them to justify one's adoption of the system of teachings in which they are embedded without falling into circularity.

The evidence may, then, support (some) religious beliefs. But it doesn't seem strong enough to justify a firm and steady commitment to a religious tradition. If it isn't that strong, then faith's certainty must at least partly rest on other foundations.

The major religious traditions have usually recognized this. Advaita, for example, believes that reason supports the authority of the Vedas but can't establish it. If one is to grasp their truth, one's eyes must be opened to their intrinsic luminosity. John Calvin said, "Profane men ... desire to have it proved by reason that Moses and the prophets were divinely inspired. But I answer ... these words will not obtain full credit in the hearts of men until they are sealed by the inward testimony of the Spirit. The same spirit ... who spoke by the mouths of the prophets, must penetrate our hearts, in order to convince us that they faithfully delivered the message with which they were divinely entrusted."[26] Similarly, while Thomas Aquinas thought there was good evidence for the divine origin of Christian teaching, he did not think that it was sufficient to compel assent. "Of those who see the same miracle, or ... hear the same sermon, some believe and some do not. Hence, we must assert another internal cause, which moves men inwardly to assent to matters of faith." This cause is a movement of the will that embraces the truths proposed for belief because it seems "good or fitting" or "useful" to believe.[27] The will, though, must be moved by God through grace. The free act by which one embraces revealed truths is thus grounded in a "supernatural principle."[28]

Locke would presumably reject appeals to the "light of faith" or to the "inner testimony of the Holy Spirit" for the same reason that he rejects the pretensions of the "enthusiasts" who claimed to be the recipients of special illuminations and divine communications. So-called enthusiasts claim to see God or feel him, but "stripped of the metaphor," all that this amounts to is that "they are sure because they are sure, and their persuasions are right because they are strong in them." The inner light that supposedly attests to the fact that a given proposition is revealed is "but a strong ungrounded persuasion of their own minds that it is a truth." Appeals to an inner light and the like are unpersuasive because the strength of one's beliefs isn't a reason for them. Subjective certainty is not a sign of truth.[29]

(Calvin and Aquinas would object to reducing the "light of faith" or the "interior testimony of the spirit" to a mere feeling of assurance. The "light of faith" or "inner testimony of the spirit" are arguably more like the feeling of self-evidence one has when contemplating modus ponens or the obviousness of "There's a table before me" when I am looking at one two feet in front of me. Both the feeling of self-evidence and the obviousness of the perceptual claim are phenomenologically distinct from an unsupported conviction that [e.g.] a certain horse will win the afternoon race.[30] There is also an epistemic difference. That p seems self-evident and that I seem to see a table in front of me are good reasons for p and "There is a table in front of me," respectively, while a bare conviction is evidence for nothing.)

Are firm and steady religious beliefs improper when one's evidence isn't fully compelling? Locke thought so. The strength of a person's belief should be proportioned to the strength of his or her evidence. But Locke was an evidentialist, and evidentialism is controversial. Its plausibility largely depends on what one means by "evidence." Evidentialists typically identify it with publicly accessible evidence and assume that the evidence's objective weight or force is the strength that would be assigned to it by impartial and disinterested reasoners who have abstracted from their desires and predilections. Chapter 4 has argued that if "evidence" is construed in this sense, evidentialism is false. There is also another consideration.

To suppose that the strength of one's belief should never exceed the strength of one's evidence may beg the question against theism and other religious outlooks. For the following might be true: (1) Human beings are capable of sharing in God's life or in some other way participating in divine reality. (2) One can't adopt the proper attitude toward the divine, however, if one doubts its reality or is ignorant of its nature. A firm belief in its reality, goodness, and so on is necessary if one is to share in it. Finally, (3) our intellectual faculties are instruments for acquiring as many important truths as possible, and the most important truths are about the transcendent and our relation to it.

Suppose these claims are true. Knowing divine truths might be better than merely believing them. (Aquinas thought so.) Disbelief might be better than irrational belief – that is, a belief for which one has *no* good reasons, or is such that one has (or should have) good reasons for thinking it false. But is it improper to hold firmly a *true* religious belief that isn't *fully* supported by the evidence at one's disposal? It isn't obvious that it is. If the belief happens to be true, one securely holds correct beliefs about the most important matters and has met a necessary condition for sharing in an overwhelming good. If it happens to be true and one doesn't believe it, however, one has failed to hold correct beliefs about the most important matters and has thus failed to meet a necessary condition for sharing in that overwhelming good.

But suppose that Locke was right, and that nothing should be believed that can't be fully certified by reason. Suppose further that traditional arguments for the reliability of Christian, say, or Hindu scriptures aren't rationally compelling. Does either agnosticism or atheism follow? Does religion, in other words, presuppose the truth of (some) revelation? It does not.

III. Deism, Bayle's Skeptical Fideism, and Revelation

Deists such as Charles Blount asserted that "that rule which is necessary for our future happiness ought to be generally made known to all men.... Therefore, no revealed religion," with its attendant mysteries, "is necessary for human happiness."[31] John Toland and other deists thought that, because God's perfection entails his "justice and reasonableness," "nothing in true Christianity ... is either contrary to or above reason.... Nothing in true Christianity," therefore, "can be a mystery – a proposition or notion impenetrable to ordinary human intellectual capacities."[32]

According to Matthew Tindal, natural religion comprises two things. First is a knowledge "that there is a God; or in other words, a being absolutely perfect and infinitely happy in himself who is the source of all other beings," and whatever perfections they may happen to have. Second is a knowledge of our duty toward ourselves and others. Both are evident by "the light of nature." Since God is perfectly happy in himself, we can do nothing to add to his happiness. Since he is "all-wise,"

he could not demand anything of his creatures "to no end or purpose." Since he is "all-good," he cannot command "anything but for their good" – namely, that (1) they regulate their "natural appetites" in such a way "as will conduce most to the [proper] exercise of [their] reason, the health of [their bodies], and the pleasure of their senses," and that (2) their relations with others be governed by their recognition that (a) their "common parent" (that is, God) wills the good of all his creatures, and that (b) they cannot "subsist without the assistance of others, who have it in their power to retaliate the usage" they give them.

True religion consists in the practice of duties such as these that result from the relation we stand in to God and our neighbors, and are fully accessible to reason. "Since God is unchangeable, ... [and] human nature" is always the same, and people "at all times stand in the same relation to one another, ... our duty both to God and man must, from the beginning of the world to the end, remain unalterable." Since the Gospel is merely a "republication of the religion of nature," Christianity is as old as creation.[33]

A few deists such as Toland allowed that revelation might be a "source" of true propositions, although he insisted that "once such truths come to [our] notice by revelation," they must pass the bar of human reason, that is, we must be able to make out their truth for ourselves on the basis of publicly available evidence. More radical questioners of revealed religion refused to grant "even this limited role" to tradition since doing so would preclude some people from salvation (namely, those who lived before the truth in question had been revealed).³⁴ *All* deists, however, agreed with Locke that we should only believe propositions that can be fully certified by reason.

At the opposite extreme from the deists lies Pierre Bayle. Bayle professed faith in the Christian mysteries but insisted on their contrarationality. The doctrine of the Trinity, for example, contradicts the self-evident principle that if x = y and y = z, then x = z, for any x, y, and z. And more generally, "there is a clear incompatibility between accepting the Cartesian standard of clarity and distinctness," which Bayle believed to be appropriate in philosophy, "and accepting the Christian doctrine[s].... Mysteries ... are necessarily non-evident."³⁵ Hence, while faith "produces a perfect certitude ... its object will never be evident. Knowledge, on the other hand, produces together both complete evidence of the object and full certainty of conviction." So "if a Christian ... undertakes to maintain the mystery of the Trinity," for example, "against a philosopher, he would oppose a non-evident object to evident objections."³⁶

Bayle claims that skeptical arguments drive us to faith. "It is through a lively awareness" of "the difficulties that surround the doctrines of the Christian religion ... that one learns the excellence of faith and the blessing of heaven. In the same way, one learns the necessity of mistrusting reason and having recourse to grace." "It has pleased the Father, and the Son, and the Holy Ghost, Christians ought to say, to lead us by the path of faith, and not by the path of knowledge and disputation.... We cannot lose our way with such guides. And *reason itself commands us to prefer them to its direction.*"³⁷

Yet *can* one "assert doctrines while simultaneously holding that they contradict self-evident principles"?³⁸ Bayle thinks that one can. For in doing so, one is not inconsistently "believing and not believing the same [proposition] at the same time." Rather, one consistently believes that "(1) the light of reason teaches me that [the doctrine] is false; [yet] (2) I believe it nonetheless because I am convinced that this light is not infallible and because I prefer to submit ... to the Word of God, than to a metaphysical demonstration."³⁹ Is this coherent? Penelhum thinks that it isn't. For in spite of Bayle's explicit disclaimer, he *does* believe two inconsistent things at the same time. Through faith, Bayle believes the doctrine of the Trinity, for example, and yet at the same time believes that the doctrine's falsity is entailed by self-evident principles. But because one can't believe that a proposition, *p* is entailed by self-evident principles without believing *p*, Bayle must also believe that the doctrine of the Trinity is false.⁴⁰

I do not find this objection compelling. Granted, one can't both *find* a set of principles self-evident and *find* that they self-evidently entail *p*, and not believe *p*. To rest on this, though, seems to miss Bayle's point, namely, that his radical skepticism has led him to *doubt* so-called self-evident principles. Since he no longer finds them self-evident, he no longer finds the propositions they entail evident either, and so does *not* inconsistently believe the doctrine of the Trinity, for instance, while simultaneously believing its denial.

Whether Bayle can escape *all* charges of incoherence is more doubtful. For if *all* principles of reason are called into question, it is difficult to see how Bayle can be justified in asserting that reason itself directs us to set reason aside. As far as I can tell, Bayle has only two recourses. The first is to restrict his skepticism to only some of reason's self-evident principles. This seems to me a nonstarter, however, for if his doubt extends to self-evident logical and mathematical principles, as his animadversions on the doctrine of the Trinity imply, it is difficult to see how he can retain his confidence in *any* principle of reason. The second is less obviously incoherent, and this is to regard the apparent bankruptcy of reason as a *cause of*, rather than a *reason for*, the flight to faith. Bayle's procedure would then bear some resemblance to that of the Buddhist Madhyamikas, who employ reason to show the incoherency of reason, thereby, in their view, clearing a space for the occurrence of the nondual, nonconceptual intuition of the Suchness of things.

There may be another problem. John Toland characterizes views such as Bayle's as follows. Doctrines such as the Trinity "cannot in themselves be contradictory to the principles" of reason; yet, because "of our corrupt and limited understandings," they may *seem* to us to contradict them. On "the authority of divine revelation," however, "we are bound to believe … in them," and "*to adore what we cannot comprehend.*"[41]

Toland has two responses to this position, the second of which is more telling,[42] namely, that we cannot understand what is or seems to be contradictory and cannot believe what we don't understand (although "a man may give his *verbal* assent to he knows not what out of fear, superstition, … interest, and the like … motives"): "For what I don't conceive, can no more give me right notions of God, or influence my actions, than a prayer delivered in an unknown tongue can excite my devotion." Of course, strictly speaking, Toland is mistaken because we can and do understand contradictions. Indeed, it is just *because* we understand them that we know they are necessarily false. In a larger sense, though, Toland is right. Because contradictions entail everything, in believing a contradiction I am implicitly committed to believing that God both is and is not evil, that we both should and shouldn't worship him, and the like, and it is difficult to see how a belief of this sort could give me right notions of God or guide my behavior. Moreover, this is true even if the doctrines proposed for our belief, while not contradictory, are wholly impenetrable by our understanding. The divine mysteries, then, cannot be contradictions and they cannot be totally opaque to finite intellects.

The fact that the divine mysteries can't *be* contradictory, however, does not entail that they can't *seem* to me to be contradictory. Can we rationally believe a proposition that seems to us to be contradictory? Toland thinks not. ("A seeming contradiction is *to us* as good as a real one."[43]) Yet, pace Toland, we *can* do so if we have good reason to trust the words of someone who assures us that the proposition in question is true (and therefore *not* contradictory). Thus Jonathan Edwards points out that it is reasonable for us to accept "the reasonings and conclusions of the best metaphysicians and mathematicians concerning infinities" in spite of the fact that they are "attended with paradoxes and seeming inconsistencies."[44] (Hilbert's hotel is an example.[45]) Again, in discussing some of the implications of a Berkeley-like idealism (which he thinks is not only coherent but true), Edwards asserts that we "have got so far beyond those things for which language was chiefly contrived, that unless we use extreme caution, we cannot speak, except we speak exceedingly unintelligibly, without literally contradicting ourselves."[46]

Yet be that as it may, Toland believes that "the very supposition, that reason might authorize one thing, and the Spirit of God [scripture] another, throws us into inevitable skepticism." For if propositions that seem to reason to be self-contradictory can be true, then the authority of reason itself is called into question. And if the authority of reason is called into question, then so too is scripture's authority, since the latter rests on the former. "We believe the Scripture to be divine, not upon its own bare assertion [or upon an inner impulse or intuition, or the so-called testimony of the Holy Spirit], but from a real testimony consisting in the evidence of the thing contained therein; from undoubted effect, and not from words and letters."[47] We believe scripture, in other words, because what it tells us – that God exists, that we are immortal, that the best offering we can give God is a moral life – is intrinsically evident to reason. However inadequate this account of the authority of scripture may be,[48] Toland has put his finger on a real problem. For calling reason's authority into question undercuts any attempt to offer rational arguments for relying on scripture, including not only traditional appeals to miracles, fulfilled prophecy, and so on, but existential or pragmatic arguments such as Bayle's. The problem is even more general than this, however. For "to suppose anything in revelation [is] inconsistent with [the apparent dictates of human] reason" is to suppose implicitly that human reason is an unreliable guide in religion, and thus not only undermines our reasons for believing the alleged revelation to be genuine, but even our reasons for believing that there *is* a God.[49]

For Toland, Tindall, and the other deists, reason is not only the de jure, but also the de facto authority in matters of religion. For "what can be a fuller evidence of the sovereignty of reason than that all men, when there is any thing in their traditional religion, which in its literal sense can't be defended by reason, have recourse to any method of interpretation, though ever so forced, in order to make it appear reasonable."[50]

If theism is defined as the belief in the existence of an omnipotent, omniscient, all good creator and ruler of everything in heaven and earth, then Judaism, Christianity, Islam, Vaishnavism, and other traditional monotheisms entail theism. They also include much more. Christianity, for example, includes a belief in God's triunity, incarnation in Jesus of Nazareth, and redemption through the latter's death and resurrection. The Shri Vaisnavas believe that Vishnu is one with his divine consort, Shri, and has descended to the space-time world in various forms, the most important of which are Rama and Krishna. Shri Vaishnavism and Christianity as well as other monotheistic religions do share a common core,[51] of course, which is now sometimes referred to as "bare theism."

Christians and other traditional theists have never believed that bare theism was sufficient. The seventeenth- and eighteenth-century deists thought that it was. In their opinion, true religion is "natural religion," a body of truths about God and our duty that can be discovered by natural reason, and which they identified with bare theism. In their view, religious traditions such as Christianity, Islam, or Vaishnavism originated in a mixture of credulity, political tyranny, and priest craft that corrupted reason and overlaid natural religion with numerous impurities. All were convinced that Christian doctrines, in particular, offend reason.

In spite of their protestations, however, it is by no means obvious that bare theism is significantly more successful in passing the bar of reason than Christianity. Atheists and agnostics, in any case, clearly think that it isn't. There are deeper problems than this, however.

IV. Deism's Religious Inadequacy

From the point of view of Christianity, bare theism seems religiously inadequate. It may do a poorer joy of handling the problem of evil, for example. The quantity and kinds of evil that exist are not what we would antecedently expect given the hypothesis of bare theism alone.[52] Indeed, the antecedent probability of existing evils on the deistic hypothesis would seem to be either low or inscrutable. (The probability would be inscrutable if, given God's transcendence and our limitations, it is highly unlikely that we would know God's reasons for permitting many of the evils we encounter even if he had good reasons for permitting them.) By contrast, great evils are not only probable on the Christian hypothesis, they are certain. For the Christian hypothesis includes the atonement and redemption, and the atonement and redemption presuppose the existence of horrendous sin and suffering. In short, the existence of evil would seem to be less of a problem for Christian theism than for bare theism since the former includes a great good that entails it and the latter does not.

Of course, it is also true that the antecedent probability of Christianity is lower than the antecedent probability of bare theism since it is more complex or includes more doctrinal propositions. Even so, the probability of Christian theism on the *total* evidence (including evil) may still be higher than the probability of bare theism[53] on the same body of evidence. Furthermore, Christian theism may provide resources for making *existential* sense of the evils we experience that aren't available to deists. Marilyn Adams, for example, has argued that Christian theodicists should explore the implications of such goods as Christian martyrdom and Christ's passion. Suffering may be a means of participating in Christ, thereby providing the sufferer with insight into, and communion with, God's own inner life.[54]

Another reason for doubting deism's religious adequacy is the suspicion that it fails an important existential test. To be adequate, a comprehensive religious or other world view must not only meet formal criteria and possess explanatory power, it should also satisfy a pragmatic criterion. Paul Tillich thought that philosophical theories should be partly judged by "their efficacy in the life process of mankind."[55] According to Frederick Ferré, a comprehensive metaphysical system is adequate only if it is "capable of 'coming to life' for individuals," enabling them to cope with their "total environment." It must have a "capacity for ringing true with respect to" those who use it, enabling them "to cope successfully with the challenges of life."[56] William James made a similar point: metaphysical schemes must meet practical as well as intellectual demands.

The question is, does bare theism do so, that is, can one obtain the good that religion promises "if good there be" by embracing bare theism or some other alleged religious common denominator while rejecting, or suspending judgment about, the points on which the religions differ? Not clearly. Consider James's generic religious hypothesis, for example: Religion's first affirmation is that "the best things are the more eternal things ... the things in the universe that throw the last stone, so to speak, and say the final word.... The second affirmation of religion is that we are better off even now if we believe her first affirmation to be true."[57] Religious hypotheses like these are arguably too thin to guide life or to provide it with depth and meaning. In order to *embrace* or *existentially appropriate* one of these hypotheses by acting in accordance with it and shaping one's life by it, one must adopt it in some concrete form or other. One strongly suspects that men and women who practice their religion but believe they are only embracing abstract or generic religious hypotheses such as bare theism unwittingly flesh them out with currently fashionable opinions, private philosophical speculations, and their own imaginative constructs, that is, their theism is in fact not "bare" at all. And one may reasonably wonder whether their "do it yourself" versions of religion, with their own private embellishments, are as likely to be true as those forms of religion that have stood the test of time and satisfied the intellectual and existential demands of countless thousands. (There are degrees here. The beliefs of many professed deists seem to have had little visible impact on their lives and actions.[58] Except for the difference in professed beliefs, the intellectual, affective, and moral lives of deists such as Thomas Jefferson or Thomas Paine seem no different from those of contemporary agnostics and atheists such as David Hume and Denis Diderot. Where deism has been institutionalized, however, as in the case of nineteenth-century New England Unitarians, the differences between deism and more long-standing religious traditions are less sharp.)

V. Bare Theism and Idolatry

A potentially deeper problem from the Christian's point of view may be this. The seventeenth-century Puritan divine, John Owen, conceded that when functioning at its best, natural reason can arrive at both the knowledge of "the goodness, the amiableness ... the all sufficient satisfactoriness of the infinite perfections of the divine nature," and the conviction that human blessedness consists "in the soul's full satisfaction in the goodness and beauty of" that nature.

"Scripture gives us another notion of heaven and glory," however, "not contrary unto [that of the philosophers, nor] inconsistent with it, but more suited unto the faith and experience of Believers" and to God's gracious dispensation. "The infinite incomprehensible excellences of the divine nature" that the philosophers speak of "are not proposed in scripture as the immediate object of our faith here," or of our "sight in heaven." That object is rather "the manifestation of the glory of the infinite wisdom, grace, love, kindness and power of God in Christ." A person who is unacquainted with the glory of God in Christ can't have "any other heaven in his aim but what is erected in his own [febrile] imagination," and is thus an idol.[59] How could this be?

Note that a description of something can be misleading, present a false picture, even if every statement included in that description is true. It can do this by omitting important truths, including truths that would modify the contextual implications of truths that *are* included in the description if they too were included in it. The deistic picture of God is arguably false or misleading (idolatrous) in just this way. By omitting to mention that God exhibits his power chiefly in showing pity and mercy, for example, by making it easy to construe God's goodness as utility maximization, and especially by refusing to recognize that God's glory is primarily revealed "in the face of Jesus Christ" (2 *Corinthians* 4:6), the Christian believes that the deist's portrait of God as the God of bare theism is an impoverished and potentially misleading simulacrum of the real thing.

Yet how can this be if Christian theism *entails* bare theism, and "the God of Abraham, Isaac, and Jacob" and "the God of the philosophers" refer to or pick out the same thing? The answer, I believe, is this.

Although Christianity entails theism, it modifies theism's contextual and pragmatic meaning. Deists identify a rational faith with (an existentially appropriated?) belief in bare theism. In their view, Christian doctrines such as the Incarnation or Trinity are irrational, or at least nonrational, accretions that have been tacked on to it by priest craft, superstition, ignorance, and the like.

But this is misleading at best. In the first place, the deist's claim is historically false. Humans don't *begin* with bare theism and then add things to it. Far from Christianity and other revealed religions being parasitic upon a primitive deism that they have overlaid with absurdities, the converse is closer to the truth. Deism didn't arise spontaneously but only in reaction to the alleged absurdities and irrationalities of revealed religion in general and of Christianity in particular. Historically, at least, deism is parasitic on Christianity, not Christianity on deism.

More importantly, in living theistic religions like Christianity, theses of bare theism such as God's omnipotence or perfect goodness are intimately interwoven with other theses that by articulating them help to determine the meaning they have for the tradition in question. Christians articulate the doctrine of God's goodness, for example, by deploying the Christian story of redemption, and in so doing inflect or qualify its meaning. Christianity's insistence on God's mystery provides another example of the way in which its doctrines can inflect the theses of bare theism. Thus if God is simple[60] and/or his essence can't be grasped, then the only literally true statements we can make about him are negations and analogies (that is, statements of the form "God has a property, P, which is related to him as (e.g.) power or knowledge is related to us," or, "God has a property, P, which is more perfect than, and the causal ground of, (e.g.) creaturely power or knowledge"). But in that case, God's power, knowledge, or goodness, for instance, has a dimension or depth that exceeds our conceptual grasp – and taking this into account affects those concepts' wider meanings.

Attacks on theism whose ultimate target is Christianity or some other revealed religion can misfire because by focusing on bare theism, they mistake a fragment for the whole or an abstraction for the rich reality from which that abstraction is drawn. An attack on God's goodness that ignores the Christian's understanding of that goodness, for example, can be largely beside the point. (I do not mean to suggest that *all* agnostic or atheistic arguments against God's goodness, for example, make this mistake. I do mean to suggest that too many do.)

VI. Deistic and Christian Conceptions of Sound Reason

The most philosophically problematic feature of deism, however, is that its conception of "sound reason" is, arguably, flawed:

(1) If we restrict the deliverances of sound reason to propositions that are self-evident or can be established by arguments which would convince every intelligent, fair-minded, and adequately informed person, as the deists appear to do, then no interesting claim about God, immortality, morality, or any other fundamental issue rests on sound reason – *including those made by deists*. For it is by no means difficult to find intelligent, fair-minded, and adequately informed persons who think that theism is false or that Christianity is true.

(2) Nor is it clear (as deists seem to think) that the only relevant evidence is *public* evidence or evidence that can be reproduced on demand. Restricting evidence in this way rules out in advance someone's taking her mystical experiences or other apparent perceptions of God as evidence since her *experiences* (as distinguished from their *report*) are private and not reproducible on

demand. And this seems as unreasonable as not taking one's sense experiences as prima facie[61] evidence for the existence of their apparent objects. Again, as John Henry Newman pointed out, even when our convictions *do* ultimately rest on public evidence, we cannot always reproduce that evidence on demand. For example, a historian of the Middle Ages may assert that the *Aeneid* could not be a thirteenth-century forgery. Her conviction is partly based on her knowledge of the capacities of the medieval mind. This knowledge in turn depends on a lifetime of reading and study. Many of the considerations that have contributed to it have been forgotten, however, and others have merged into a general impression of what the medieval mind could and could not do. Her knowledge is nonetheless quite real.[62]

(3) Part of the deist's problem with revealed religion lies in his insistence that to be credible, truths of scripture must be capable of being established without recourse to it. Thus Toland says, "revelation [is] not a necessitating motive of assent, but [at most] a means of information. We should not confound the way whereby we come to the knowledge of a thing with the grounds we have to believe it. A man may inform me concerning a thousand matters I never heard of before, and of which I should not as much as think if I were not told; yet I [should] believe nothing purely upon his word without evidence in the things themselves."[63] And Tindal makes a similar point: The "light of nature" (reason) is "the standing rule by which we must judge of the truth of all those doctrines contained in the scriptures. So that scripture can only be a secondary rule as far as it is found agreeable to" reason. One can no "more discern the objects of his own understanding, and their relations, by the faculties of another than he can see with another man's eyes, or than one ship can be guided by the helm of another."[64] But this is problematic.

That a credible epistemic faculty or tool or rule can be used to assess the credentials of another epistemic faculty or tool or rule does not imply that opinions formed by a reason that does not employ that faculty or tool or rule can be used to determine the truth or falsity of opinions established *by* its means. The naked eye, for example, "determines the goodness and sufficiency" of the optic glass, yet it would be absurd for a person to "credit no representation made by the glass, wherein the glass differs from his eye," and to refuse to believe "that the blood consists partly of red particles and partly of limpid liquor because it all appears red to the naked eye."[65] It would be equally absurd to reject truths that can be established by a reason that employs the rule "memories are generally reliable" on the grounds that the reliability of a memory can't be established by a reason that does not employ that rule. Jonathan Edwards argues that it is equally unreasonable to discount what can be discovered by a reason that employs the rule that scripture is credible on the grounds that truths learned in this way cannot be established by a reason that rejects it.

Deists will of course respond that they have good reasons for rejecting the authority of scripture, and hence the rule in question. A large part of their reason for doing so, however, is the supposed absurdity of its teachings (about God's triunity, Incarnation, and the like). But because this alleged absurdity is established by assessing the truth of the propositions in question without employing the relevant epistemic tool (scripture) or rule ("Consult scripture") that their Christian opponents claim is needed to do so correctly, their method of proceeding begs the question.

A second deistic response isn't open to this objection, however. The goodness of the optic glass is established by the naked eye and hence without using it. By contrast, one may wonder whether the authority of scripture can be established without appeal to it. Of course, Edwards and many other seventeenth- and eighteenth-century Christians thought that it could. In their view, scripture's authority is certified by miracles, fulfilled prophecies, the harmony between revealed and natural religion, scripture's beneficial effects on morality, and so on – that is, on things they believed could be established by naked reason. Considerations of this sort lost a good deal of their persuasiveness in the following centuries, however, and no longer seem convincing even to many Christians. It is therefore important to note that Edwards himself thought that considerations of this kind were often insufficient in practice. The *strongest* evidence for scripture's divine authority, in his opinion, is its spiritual beauty – a feature that cannot be detected by unaided natural faculties. Only those with converted hearts can "perceive," "taste," and "relish" the stamp of divine splendor on scripture and thus be *certain* of its teachings. As we have seen, both Aquinas and Calvin said something similar. In the view of all three, what is too often lacking in assessing the credentials of scripture, or the truth of other existentially significant claims, is not adequate evidence for them but the dispositions needed to read that evidence correctly.[66] And this takes us to perhaps the most fundamental issue dividing classical deists and their modern followers, on the one hand, from traditional Christians and the adherents of other religious traditions, on the other.

(4) Most Christian theologians, at least, have thought that reason can establish many important truths about God and what he demands of us. The reason in question must be what seventeenth-century English Christians called "right reason," however. For example, Cambridge Platonists such as John Smith claimed that reason is "a light flowing from the foundation and father of lights," given "to enable man to work out of himself all those notions of God which are the true ground-work of love and obedience to God, and conformity to him."[67] Reason is more than a faculty of calculation or ratiocination, however. Henry More spoke for all the Cambridge Platonists when he said, "The oracle of God [reason] is not to be heard but in his holy temple – that is to say in a good and holy man, thoroughly sanctified in spirit, soul, and body."[68] What is needed, in short, is a proper orientation of one's hopes and fears, desires and affections, feelings and emotions, that is, of one's affective or willing nature.

The deists' conception of sound reason, on the other hand, excludes what Pascal called "reasons of the heart" and William James referred to as the promptings of our "passional nature." Reason in their view is only "objective" or "truth-oriented" when it is unaffected by our wants, interests, sentiments, and desires. Yet as Chapter 4 argued, a restriction of this sort is utterly implausible when applied to reasoning about ethics or any other value-laden matter.[69]

VII. Traditional Christian Attitudes toward Philosophy (Reason) and Revelation

Christianity's attitude toward philosophy has been ambivalent. One strand of the tradition is openly hostile. Its seminal figure is Tertullian.

Tertullian did not deny that the writings of the philosophers contain truths. Nor did he deny that God can be (imperfectly) grasped without the aid of revelation. For he can be known from his works and by the interior witness of our souls. Philosophy is nevertheless repudiated. "What indeed has Athens to do with Jerusalem? The Academy and the Church? What concord is there between heretics and Christians? Our instruction comes from the porch of Solomon, who had himself taught that the Lord should be sought in simplicity of heart. Away with attempts to produce a mottled Christianity of Stoic, Platonic, and dialectical [Aristotelian] composition. We want no curious disputation after possessing Christ, no inquisition after enjoying the gospel."[70] Tertullian's objection is threefold. First, the introduction of philosophy among Christians has resulted in heresy. Second, whereas schools of philosophy have human founders, the school of the gospel is founded by God. Christianity is a *revealed* doctrine that demands obedience and submission. Philosophy, on the other hand, relies on *human* understanding, and is an expression of self-seeking and of a fallible and corrupt reason.

Finally (and most profoundly), the mysteries of faith *repel* reason. "The Son of God died; it is by all means to be believed because it is absurd. And he was buried, and rose again; the fact is certain because it is impossible."[71]

Tertullian is by no means alone. In the Christian Middle Ages, Bernard of Clairvaux claimed that those who "called themselves philosophers should rather be called the slaves of curiosity and pride." The true teacher is the Holy Spirit, and those who have been instructed by him can "say with the Psalmist (Psalm 119: 199): *I have understood more than all my teachers*." Commenting on the text, Bernard exclaims: "Wherefore, O my brother, dost thou make such a boast? Is it because ... thou hast understood or endeavored to understand the reasonings of Plato and the subtleties of Aristotle? God forbid! thou answerest. It is because I have sought thy commandments, O Lord."[72]

This attitude persists and was especially prominent in some of the Protestant reformers and among the skeptical fideists of the sixteenth and seventeenth centuries.

An equally important and ultimately more widespread attitude toward philosophy, however, was expressed by Justin Martyr, Clement of Alexandria, and Origen. Philosophy is a preparation for the gospel. According to Clement, for example, it was "a schoolmaster to bring the Hellenic mind, as the Law, the Hebrews, to Christ."[73] This positive attitude toward philosophy was supported in two ways. The first was the "loan" hypothesis: the truths in the philosophers were ultimately plagiarized from Moses and the prophets. The second was the Logos theory: all human beings participate in the Logos – God's eternal word or wisdom who became incarnate in Jesus Christ. The Greek writers were thus, as Justin said, "able to see realities darkly through the sowing of the implanted word that was in them." Since "Christ ... is the Word of whom every race of men were partakers, ... those who lived reasonably are Christians, even though they have been thought atheists; as among the Greeks, Socrates and Heraclitus, and men like them."[74]

It is important to note, however, that while these doctrines make a positive evaluation of Greek philosophy and "unbaptized" reason possible, they also imply philosophy's or naked reason's inferiority to revelation. The loan hypothesis implies that the truths found in philosophy are fragmented and mixed with error. Whatever authority they have depends on their origin. Only in scripture can truth be found whole and undistorted. The Logos theory implies that Christians are better off than the philosophers. For, as Justin says, Christians "live not according to a part only of the word diffused [among humans] but by the knowledge and contemplation of the whole Word, which is Christ."[75]

Even so, philosophy isn't just a preparation for the Gospel. Both Clement and Origen believed that our blessedness consists in knowing or understanding the Good, and that philosophy can be employed to deepen our understanding of the truths of scripture in which that Good reveals itself. The attitudes of Justin, Clement, and Origen toward philosophy are echoed by Augustine and Anselm and dominate the Christian Middle Ages. Modern Christian attitudes toward philosophy are, on the whole, variants of those seminally expressed by Tertullian and the early Greek fathers.

Closer inspection reveals that the two views are not always as sharply opposed as at first appears, however. Consider, for example, the attitudes toward reason expressed by sixteenth- and seventeenth-century Puritan divines, on the one hand, and by the Cambridge Platonists, who opposed their so-called "dogmatism" and "narrow sectarianism," on the other.

As good Calvinists, Puritans believed that even though reason was competent in "civill and humane things," it was not competent in divine things. Because of the fall, "the whole speculative power of the higher and nobler part of the Soule, which wee call the understanding ... is naturally and originally corrupted, and utterly destitute of divine light."[76] Francis Quarles therefore recommends: "In the Meditation of divine Mysteries, keep thy heart humble, and thy thoughts holy: Let Philosophy not be asham'd to be confuted, nor Logic blush to be confounded.... The best way to see day-light is to put out thy Candle [reason]."[77] The great Puritan divine, William Perkins, thought that one should "reject his owne naturall reason, and stoppe up the eyes of his naturall minde, like a blinde man, and suffer himselfe wholly to be guided by God's spirit in the things of God." Similarly, the Puritan mystic, Francis Rous, commended those who "have … quenched their own naturall lamps, that they might get them kindled above by the Father of Lights."[78]

The Cambridge Platonists sounded a very different note. According to Benjamin Whichcote, "Reason is the Divine governor of man's life; it is the very voice of God."[79] And as we saw, John Smith asserted that reason is "a Light flowing from the Foundation and Father of Lights." It was given "to enable Man to work out of himself all those Notions of God which are the true Ground-work of Love and Obedience to God, and conformity to him." Scripture simply reinforces and clarifies what a properly functioning reason discerns.

Neither position was as extreme as this suggests, however. Puritan diatribes against reason are often expressions of their emphasis on experience and not of a belief that reason's "notional" understanding of religion is invariably false. As Arthur Dent said, "The knowledge of the reprobate is like the knowledge which a mathematicall geographer hath of the earth and all the places in it, which is but a generall notion, and a speculative comprehension of them. But the knowledge of the elect is like the knowledge of a traveler who can speake of experience and feeling, and hath beene there and seene."[80] Or as Richard Baxter asserted,

I do … neither despise evidence as unnecessary, nor trust to it alone as the sufficient total cause of my belief; for if God's grace do not open my eyes, and come down in power upon my will, and insinuate into it a sweet acquaintance with the things unseen, and taste of their goodness to delight my soul, no reason will serve to stablish and comfort me, however undeniable soever; the way to have the firmest belief of the Christian faith, is to draw near and taste, and try it, and lay bare the heart to receive the impression of it, and then, by the sense of the admirable effects, we shall know that which bare speculation could not discover.[81]

It should also be noted that Puritans insisted that God's word is *intrinsically* rational. "The Sunne is ever cleere" although we are prevented from seeing it because "wee want eyes to behold it" or because it is "so be-clowded, that our sight is thereby hindered."[82] Furthermore, grace can cure our blindness and remove the clouds. Regenerate reason can unfold scripture and defend the faith. Puritan divines were therefore prepared to ascribe a high instrumental value to reason and humane learning in practice. As John Rainolds said, "It may be lawfull for Christians to use Philosophers, and books of Secular Learning … with this condition, that whatsoever they finde in them, that is profitable and usefull, they convert it to Christian doctrine and so, as it were shave off … all superfluous stuffe."[83] Even a radical Puritan such as John Penry could insist that "the Lord doth not ordinarily bestowe [full comprehension of the Word] ... without the knowledge of the artes," especially rhetoric and logic, and Hebrew and Greek.[84] Logic was indeed so important that the missionary John Eliot translated a treatise on it into Algonquin "to initiate the Indians in the knowledge of the Rule of Reason," so that they might learn to read their Bibles properly.[85]

In spite of their recognition of the necessity and value of learning, however, Puritan divines believed that it was fraught with dangers. For one thing, it could infect and distort one's study of scripture and sacred theology. William Pemble warned against the

prophane studie of sacred things, to know onely, not to doe, to satisfy curiositie or give contentment to an all searching and comprehending wit; [to] study Divinitie as [one] would doe other arts, looking for no further aide than Nature's ability, ... [to] read the Scriptures, as wee doe morall authors, collecting what pleaseth [our] fancy ..., but no whit for sanctification of the heart.[86]

A still greater danger, though, was that learning "would become an end in itself, the focus of the scholar's endeavour, not subordinated to godly utility."[87]

These fears are reflected in the Puritan's desire to minimize the appeal to nonscriptural authorities in preaching. Richard Rogers, for example, pointed out that it was the "sound plaine, and powerful preaching of the Gospell" that God had chosen to reach both the educated and the uneducated alike, and he criticized preachers who "stuffe their sermons with authorities of men." And while the learned Thomas Adams didn't utterly reject the employment of "the morall Sayes [sayings] of a Poet, or a Philosopher, or perhaps some golden sentence of a Father," in a sermon, he insisted that preachers not "make ... the Pulpit a Philosophy, Logicke, [or] Poetry-Schoole."[88]

There were at least two reasons for this. The first was the fear of vanity. John Udall, for instance, condemned the "painted eloquence" of some ministers who made "preaching little else, but an ostentation of wit and reading," thereby putting the "Sword of the Spirit into a velvet scabbard," so that "it cannot pricke and wound the heart, cannot worke, by working death first." The second was the fear that the preachers' hearers would infer that scripture alone wasn't sufficient. According to Bartimeus Andrewes, for example, preachers seem to too often

think Christe too base to bee preached simply in him self ... and thinke that Christe commeth nakedly, unlesse cloathed with vaine ostentation of wordes. Others esteeme him too homely, simple and unlearned, unlesse he bee beautified and blazed over with store of Greeke or Laten sentences in the pulpits ... or els he must be glosed out and printed with the frooth of Philosophi, Poetry or such like.[89]

But the final thing to note is that more often than not the Puritan's view was that revelation *transcends*, rather than conflicts with, or opposes, reason. Cotton Mather, for example, said that "the more of the *Gospel* there is in our *Preaching*, the more of Reason there is in it. Scripture is *reason in its highest elevation.*"⁹⁰ And according to John Preston, "faith is but the lifting up of the understanding, by adding a new light" to scriptural truths and to the human mind, "even as a new light in the night discovers to us that which we did not see before, and as a perspective glasse reveales to the eye, that which we could not see before, and by its owne power the eye could not reach unto."⁹¹

The Cambridge Platonists exaltation of reason must be similarly qualified. Because of the fall, reason "is but an old MS., with some broken periods, some letters worn out," a picture "which has lost its gloss and beauty, the oriency of its colours, ... the comeliness of its proportions."⁹² As a consequence, divine assistance is now needed and God has provided it. Not only is there "an outward revelation of God's will to man [namely, scripture], there is an inward impression of it on their minds and spirits ... we cannot see divine things but in a divine light."⁹³ "Right reason" is indeed sufficient to discern the things of God, but right reason is *sanctified* reason. Thus Smith says

were I to define divinity, I should rather call it a divine life than a divine science.... Every thing is best known by that which bears a just resemblance and analogy with it, and therefore the scripture is inclined to set forth a good life as the ... fundamental principle of divine science.... The reason why, notwithstanding all our acute reasons and subtle disputes, truth prevails not more in the world is that we so often disjoin truth and true goodness, which in themselves can never be disunited – they grow from the same root and live in one another.... Some men have too bad hearts to have good heads; they cannot be good at theory who have been bad at practice.⁹⁴

A good life and a good head aren't sufficient, however, for the Cambridge Platonists believed that revelation is also needed. Thus Nathaniel Culverwel says that "created intellectuals depend upon the brightness of God's beams, and are subordinate to them. Angelical starlight ... borrows and derives its glory from a more vast and majestic light. As they differ from one another in glory, so all of them infinitely differ from the sun in glory. Yet [this "aristocratic light"] is far above the ['democratic light'] ... which appears to the sons of men.... If God should shut all the windows of heaven and spread out nothing but clouds and curtains, and allow it nothing but the light of a candle," the world would appear to be nothing more than "a nethermost dungeon, a capacious grave. Yet this were a more grateful shade, a pleasanter and more comely darkness, than for a soul to be condemned to the solitary light of its own lamp, so as not to have any supernatural irradiations from its God."⁹⁵ This does not mean that reason and revelation are opposed, however.

A candle neither can nor will put out the sun ... The light of reason does no more prejudice the light of faith than the light of a candle does extinguish the light of a star.... Did you never observe an eye using a prospective glass for the discovering and amplifying and approximating some remote yet desirable object? And did you perceive any opposition between the eye and the glass? Was there not rather a loving correspondence and communion between them? Why should there be any greater strife between faith and reason seeing they are brothers?⁹⁶

Yet even though faith and revelation don't conflict with reason, they immeasurably transcend it. As Culverwel says:

Man ... cannot expect that God should now communicate himself ... in such glorious manifestations of himself, as he means to give hereafter.... Nature and reason are not sufficiently proportioned to such [sights].... There are such depths ... such oceans of all perfections in a Deity, as do infinitely exceed all intellectual capacity but its own. The most that a man's reason can do is fill the understanding to the brim, but faith throws the soul into the ocean, and lets it roll and bathe itself in the vastness and fullness of a Deity.... Should angels and men have united and concentrated all their reason, yet they would never have been able to spy out such profound and mysterious excellencies as faith beholds in one twinkling of her eye.... Revealed truths shine with their own beams; they do not borrow their primitive and original luster from this "candle of the Lord," but from the purer light with which God has clothed and dressed them as with a garment. God clothes his own revelations with his own beams. The "candle of the Lord" does not discover them; it does not oppose them; it cannot eclipse them. They are no sparks of reason's striking, but they are flaming darts of heaven's shooting.[97]

And indeed, if (*per impossibile*) all divine truths could be established by unaided human reason, then, as Peter Sterry said, they "would become 'no more Divine, but human truths.' Heavenly things would lose their majesty" and luster, "and 'grow weak and contemptible,' becoming 'apish, mimicall imitations' of themselves like the 'Mistresse in her Cook-maid's clothes.' "[98]

    In spite of their many differences, then, sixteenth- and seventeenth-century Puritan divines and the Cambridge Platonists agree that scripture contains mysteries that reason can't fully penetrate. We will explore the relation between reason and mystery in the next and final chapter.

7

Theology and Mystery

Christianity's critics have often accused it of mystery mongering. Hume, for example, says that "all popular theology, especially the scholastic, has a kind of appetite for absurdity and contradiction. If that theology went not beyond reason and common sense, her doctrines would appear too easy and familiar. Amazement must of necessity be raised: Mystery affected: Darkness and obscurity sought after: And a foundation of merit afforded to the devout votaries, who desire an opportunity of subduing their rebellious reason, by the belief of the most unintelligible sophisms."[1] And John Toland asserts that Christian theologians and priests have gone even further than the heirophants of the ancient mystery cults. The latter swore their initiates to secrecy but their mysteries were intelligible in themselves. Only Christians dared maintain that their doctrines were mysterious in a more radical sense, "that is, inconceivable in themselves, however clearly revealed."[2]

Hume's and Toland's explanations of this phenomenon differ.[3] But whatever one thinks of their explanations, there is little doubt that the appeal to, and adoration of, mystery is a characteristic feature of much Christian thought and practice. The Pseudo Dionysius, for example, begins his *Mystical Theology* by asking the Trinity to guide him to the "most exalted" and hidden secrets of scripture "which exceedeth light and more than exceedeth knowledge, where ... the mysteries of heavenly truth lie hidden in the dazzling obscurity of the secret silence, outshining all brilliance with the intensity of their darkness," and exhorts his disciple "to leave the senses and the activities of the intellect" and their objects behind, and "strain ... toward him whom neither being nor understanding can contain."[4]

Nor are themes like these peculiar to Christian mystics and mystical theologians. They are commonplace in the church fathers and in a number of later Christian theologians. Two examples will suffice to illustrate my point. Consider first John Chrysostom. St. Paul said:

"The Lord ... dwells in unapproachable light." And pay heed to the accuracy with which Paul speaks.... He does not say: "Who dwells in incomprehensible light," but: "in unapproachable light," and this is much stronger than "incomprehensible." A thing is said to be "incomprehensible" when those who seek after it fail to comprehend it, even after they have searched and sought to understand it, but does not elude all inquiry and questioning. A thing is unapproachable which, from the start, cannot be investigated nor can anyone come near to it. We call the sea incomprehensible because, even when divers lower themselves into its waters and go down to a great depth, they cannot find the bottom. We call that thing unapproachable which, from the start, cannot be searched out or investigated.[5]

Yet, suppose ... we forget Paul and the prophets for the moment," and "mount up to the heavens.... Do you think that the angels in heaven talk over and ask each other questions about the divine essence? By no means! What are the angels doing? They give glory to God, they adore him, they chant without ceasing their triumphal and mystical hymns with a deep feeling of religious awe. Some sing: 'Glory to God in the highest;' the seraphim chant: 'Holy, holy, holy,' and they turn away their eyes because they cannot endure God's presence as he comes down to adapt himself to them in condescension."[6]

My second example is from Jonathan Edwards, who concludes a philosophically sophisticated explication of the Trinity by saying: "I don't pretend fully to explain how these things are, and I am sensible a hundred other objections may be made, and puzzling doubts and questions raised, that I can't solve. I am far from pretending to explain the Trinity so as to render it no longer a mystery," or "asserting that [my account of the Trinity is] any explication of this mystery that unfolds and removes the mysteriousness and incomprehensibleness of it: for I am sensible that however, by what has been said, some difficulties are lessened, others that are new appear; and the number of those things that appear mysterious, wonderful, and incomprehensible are increased by it."[7]

As these examples illustrate, both Christians themselves and their critics have historically thought that the concept of mystery is central to Christian reflection and Christian worship.[8] It is initially surprising, then, to find that the indices of six important recent reference works contain few if any references to mystery. None are found in the index to Philip Quinn and Charles Taliaferro's *A Companion to the Philosophy of Religion*, for example, or in the index to Taliaferro and Chad Meister's *Cambridge Companion to Philosophical Theology*. And the indices to my *The Handbook of Philosophy of Religion* and to William Mann's *The Blackwell Guide to the Philosophy of Religion* contain only one each. What is perhaps even more surprising is that the only reference to mystery in Peter Byrne and Leslie Houlden's massive *Companion Encyclopedia of Theology* is to a discussion of Rudolf Otto's numinous experience in my article on "Religious Experience and Language" in that volume, and that the index of Charles Taliaferro, Victoria S. Harrison, and Stewart Goetz's seven hundred–plus–page *Routledge Companion to Theism* contains only two references to mystery, the first to a page in my article on "Christianity" and the second to a paragraph comparing scientific and religious mysteries in Michael Ruse's article on the "Natural Sciences." What explains this?

Partly, I think, a not unreasonable fear of obfuscation – a suspicion that appeals to mystery can be an excuse for avoiding hard thought and a justification for obscurantism and superstition. Part of the explanation may also be a suspicion[9] that the aphophatic tradition that fuels much classical discussion of mystery isn't really Christian or is not Christian enough, although this I believe, is a mistake. Even "Dionysius is not without a sense of personal devotion to the God-man, as when he prays that his discourse may be guided 'by Christ, by my Christ,' at the beginning of [the] *Celestial Hierarchy*." Christ also plays an important role in Dionysius's understanding of mystical union. For God reveals and communicates himself through the celestial and ecclesiastical hierarchies, and Christ is the head and inner power of both. "The highest hierarchy of angels," for example, "is said to be contemplative precisely because they have entered 'into communion with Jesus ... by truly coming close to him in a primary participation.'" Again, the sacraments of baptism, Eucharist, and anointing, which are the heart of the ecclesiastical hierarchy, work by effecting "participation in Jesus and his saving work." Finally, Dionysius "again and again ... insists on the Incarnation as a work of divine love."[10]

The centrality of Christ is, if anything, even clearer in Dionysius's first major Western disciple. For John the Scot, the end of creation as a whole is the Word of God. "The beginning and the end of the world are in the Word of God, indeed, to speak more plainly, they are the Word itself, for It is manifold end without end and beginning without beginning, ... save for the Father."[11] Moreover, only the Word *made flesh* makes the return of all things to God possible. "God's Word cried out in the most remote solitude of divine Goodness.... He cried out invisibly before the world came to be in order to have it come to be; he cried out visibly when he came into the world in order to save it."[12]

Dionysius's and John's Platonism differs from that of Plotinus and other pagan Neo-Platonists in three important ways. Dionysius, for instance, does not accept Plotinus's doctrine of emanation. In his view, God creates out of nothing. "We do not receive our being from creatures higher than us in the hierarchies" who, in turn, "receive their being from creatures at a still higher level." Dionysius appears to think that, on the contrary, an implication of the doctrine of creation *ex nihilo* is that each creature is *immediately* created by God. "Emanation," for Dionysius, is "ultimately a matter of light, illumination and revelation, not of being." The higher levels mediate light or illuminating and purifying knowledge to the lower levels but they do not mediate being.[13] In the second place, there are rather clear indications that Dionysius believes that salvation is ultimately a consequence of grace. The sensible symbols (baptism, Eucharist, and anointing) that the Christian initiate uses to purify herself and begin her ascent to God owe their power to divine institution or decision, not to inherent fitness or natural sympathy, as they do for the pagan

Neo-Platonic theurgists. Furthermore, in the ascent's final stage the Christian's soul is essentially passive, doing little or nothing other than holding herself open to the action of the divine energies. Plotinus's ontological system, on the other hand, can't accommodate the concept of grace; for grace is an undeserved gift bestowed upon one person by another. But in the first place, his One is not a person.[14] And in the second, union, for Plotinus, isn't an unmerited gift but a "natural" occurrence. It is not a consequence of supernatural intervention but of the soul's own efforts and the ontological structure of reality that makes union possible.[15]

Finally, and perhaps most important, the Dionysian contemplative experiences God's love for her as well as her love for God. The soul unites with God in an ecstasy that is not an "abandonment of will and intellect but an extension of their capacities beyond their nature."[16] The ecstasy in question is an ecstasy of love (*eros*) that Dionysius defines as a power "to effect a unity, and an alliance, and a particular commingling in the Beautiful and the Good." The experience is ecstatic because one who is possessed by this love "belongs not to self but to the beloved."

Thus "the great Paul, swept along by his yearning for God, and seized of its ecstatic power," said, "It is no longer I who live, but Christ who lives in me." He "was truly a lover ... and beside himself for God, possessing not his own life but the life of the One for whom he yearned." Similar language can be found in Plotinus. But what is inconceivable in Plotinus or any pagan Neo-Platonist is that, in ecstasy, the soul encounters the divine power which comes to meet it. The soul's ecstatic love is met by the ecstatic love of God. For "it must be said too that the very cause of the universe in the beautiful, good superabundance of his benign yearning for all is also carried outside of himself in the loving care he has for all. He is, as it were, beguiled by goodness, by love, and by yearning and is enticed away from his transcendent dwelling place and comes to abide within all things, and he does so by virtue of his supernatural and ecstatic capacity to remain, nevertheless, within himself."[17] Plotinus, on the other hand, explicitly denies that the One has any love or care for what proceeds from it. While love (a kind of "drunken" loving ecstasy) does appear to be a feature of the pagan Neo-Platonic mystic's experience of union, the love in question is the love *of the mystic* for the One; there is no indication that the mystic has a sense of being loved *by* the One.

And indeed, in the Western spiritual tradition at least, Dionysian apophatism was combined with an intense love mysticism. Dionysius's *Celestial Hierarchy* "had ... noted that ... 'seraphim' means 'fire makers or carriers of warmth' while 'cherubim' means 'fullness of knowledge or carriers of wisdom' but he never identified the seraphic fire as the fire *of love*." Both John the Scot[18] and Hugh of St. Victor did. While John doesn't add "any references to charity or love" to his translation of the *Celestial Hierarchy*, his *commentary* on it "explains warmth as the warmth of charity, and fire as the ardor of love." The motion of the Seraphim around the One is "'super-burning' because the first hierarch of celestial powers burn above all who come after them in the love of the highest good," and Hugh of St. Victor agrees.[19]

Hugh's most important contribution to the Western affective Dionysian tradition, however, is his association of seraphic love with the bridal imagery of the *Song of Songs*. According to Hugh, the beloved of the *Song* "is loved more than understood…. Love (*dilectio*) surpasses knowledge and is greater than intelligence." In the divine bridal chamber, humans and angels "surround by desire what they do not penetrate by intellect" (Hugh). Because "the bridal chamber of love is beyond the realm of knowing … later authors [such as Bonaventure] can associate it with the darkness of unknowing, whether this be the cloud of Mt. Sinai or the dark night of the lovers' embrace."[20]

The anonymous author of the enormously influential *Cloud of Unknowing*,[21] for example, says that "by passing beyond yourself … you shall be carried up in your affection, and above your understanding, to the substance beyond all substance, the radiance of the divine darkness," and he exhorts the reader to "enter by affection into the darkness" that Moses entered through "exercising his affection alone."[22] Similarly, "the last of the great Victorines," Thomas Gallus, claimed that Moses "was united to the intellectually unknown God through a union of love, which is affective or true cognition, a much better cognition than intellectual cognition." But, "for Gallus, while Dionysius offered a *theoretical* account of the soul's ascent to God," Solomon (in the *Song of Songs*) "gives us the practice of the same mystical theology." The "ecstatic climax" of the soul's ascent merges "the love-sick night" of the *Song of Songs*, "and the apophatic darkness of Dionysius' Moses."[23]

This affective Dionysian tradition not only infused the thought and practice of the Victorines and the great Rhineland mystics such as Suso, Tauler, and Ruysbroek but also deeply influenced Teresa of Avila, John of the Cross, and sixteenth-century Spanish mysticism more generally,[24] as well as many later Roman Catholic mystics. What is less commonly noted is the deep impact these currents have had on Protestant spiritual traditions. Luther was a great admirer of the *Theologica Germanica*,[25] for example. Johann Arndt was deeply influenced by Tauler, and Miguel de Molinos and Madame de Guyon were widely read by Pietists and other Protestants who emphasized the centrality of the interior life.[26]

The most important reason for the recent neglect of mystery, however, may be this. William Alston began his recent "Two Cheers for Mystery" by observing that "contemporary Anglo-American analytic philosophy of religion" exhibits "a considerable degree of confidence in" its ability "to determine what God is like; how to construe his basic attributes; and what his purposes, plans, standards, values and so on are." No one "thinks we can attain a *comprehensive* knowledge of God's nature and doings. But on many crucial points, there seems to be a widespread confidence in our ability to determine exactly how things are with God."[27] And, of course, the more confident one is, the less need one will see for according the concept of mystery a central place in one's reflections on God. But what if failing to do so distorts these reflections? The burden of this chapter is that it does.

I. Senses of Mystery

What precisely is meant by "mystery"? In its ordinary sense, the word refers to a question or problem whose answer or solution is unknown to us (although perhaps not to everyone) or to everyone at a given time. For example, one might say, "I've searched to find the cause of the squeak in my automobile, but it is still a mystery to me," or, "The nature of consciousness is currently a mystery." The term itself derives from the Greek mystery cults where the initiates who had undertaken "vows of secrecy not to disclose the contents of the rites" were referred to as *mystoi*. It could also be used in a more extended sense, however. Thus Plato used the language of the mystery rites to refer to an intellectual and moral process that culminated in a vision of the Good: outward rites, purifications, and the like are employed as symbols or metaphors for intellectual and spiritual purification, and the sacred objects that the hierophant[28] displayed to the initiates are treated as symbols or metaphors of the forms. Yet, significantly, there was no suggestion that the secrets of the mystery cults that *should* not be revealed *could* not be revealed, nor does Plato think that the Good cannot be understood by all who are properly qualified to do so. By contrast, Christians came to use the term for certain truths about God's nature and deeds (the Trinity, Incarnation, atonement, and the like), which can't be fully penetrated by finite intellects.[29]

The latter notion has roots in the Bible, and here I follow Michael Foster's excellent discussion in *Mystery and Philosophy*. The God of the Bible is hidden, and his hiddenness derives from a holiness which "belongs to him alone." Other things can be holy – the ark, the temple, priests and kings, and the like – but their holiness is conferred on them from outside; it is derived from, and wholly dependent on, God. The holiness of God "makes man repent," and, "indeed, … cannot be recognized without repentance." (Think in this connection of Isaiah's vision in the temple or Job's confession [Isaiah 6; Job 42: 1–6].) For, as Jonathan Edwards pointed out, one can't appreciate the splendor of holiness without at the same time appreciating the horror and ugliness of sin and consequently recognizing one's own deformity and guilt. And yet "for the Bible, the intellect is *part* of the 'flesh' " that Paul speaks of. "When [it] is faced with God, it must [therefore] be seized with a conviction of intellectual inadequacy parallel to the [consciousness of] moral inadequacy with which we commonly identify the sense of sin."[30]

The God of the Bible does not make "himself known" except "by an act of will or grace: it is not his nature to be unhidden." (And this helps explain what might otherwise seem puzzling. Initiates in the Greek mysteries were warned not to reveal their secrets to outsiders. Christians, by contrast, are told to preach the Gospel and proclaim the Christian mysteries to all nations.

What may at least partly account for this difference is that the decision "to reveal or not to reveal is not held to be in the [Christian's] power, but in God's. Only those *can* hear whose ears God opens, i.e., whom God has *chosen* to initiate.")[31] Moreover, even if God does reveal himself, he "is hidden in his very revelation of himself."[32] Why? Because in revealing himself to us, God necessarily accommodates himself to our capacities with the result that "the revelation of God is at the same time ... a veiling of God. The Incarnation," for example, is, "as Kierkegaard said, ... the assumption of an incognito, which obscures the person of the Incarnate, and lays it open to misinterpretation."[33] Or as Karl Barth says, the God of the Bible is "a God who reveals himself *as* mystery, who makes himself known *as* the One who is Unknowable."[34] Can we be more specific?

II. Christian Uses of "Mystery"

First, a sense of mystery can refer to wonder, surprise, or astonishment at something the human mind did not expect and could not have anticipated. For example, "things beyond our seeing, things beyond our hearing, things beyond our imagining, prepared by God for those who love him" (I Corinthians 9). Mysteries in this sense, however, are not (though they may be) things we can't know or understand once they have occurred or been revealed to us (the resurrection, for example, or the new life in Christ).

Second, "mysteries" may refer to doctrines that are either incongruent or formally inconsistent with "common notions." Jonathan Edwards uses "mystery" in this sense when he says that we should expect a revelation of "spiritual" or "invisible" things to be attended with much mystery and difficulty since they are remote from "the nature of things that language is chiefly formed to express – viz. things pertaining to the common affairs and vulgar business of life, things obvious to sense and men's direct view ... and of an exceeding different nature from the things of this world, ... and not agreeable to such notions, imaginations, and ways of thinking that grow up with us and are connatural to us."[35] Thus Edwards argues that without a love of holiness and its consequent horror of sin, the doctrine of hell will seem absurd (unfair, unjust, and, in that sense, irrational) since one fails to appreciate what makes infinite punishment appropriate.

Again, a common pagan reaction to the "scandal" of the cross was that it was not "God-befitting." It is often assumed that what troubled reflective or philosophically minded pagans was the doctrine of a crucified God's seeming inconsistency with God's impassibility. Paul Gavrilyuk has convincingly shown, however, that, for the most part, pagan theologians did *not* think that the divine's impassibility precluded emotions (love or benevolence, for example) or an involvement in human affairs. What troubled them, rather, was the attribution of *suffering* to God, and the *kind* of involvement implied by the doctrine of the crucifixion. "A slave's death on the cross was unanimously regarded as shameful and degrading." Docetic forms of Christian Gnosticism were at least partly motivated by a desire to defuse this scandal. Thus, "a Basilidean account of the crucifixion … puts the following confession into the mouth of Christ … 'I did not die in reality but in appearance, lest I be put to *shame* by them.…'" Similarly, "in the docetic segment of the apocryphal *Acts of John*," Christ reveals himself to John on the Mount of Olives at the very moment at which the crucifixion is taking place at Golgotha as the cosmic being he really is, but says that others (namely orthodox Christians) "'will call me something else, which is vile and not worthy of me.'"[36]

Third, a doctrine or truth may seem absurd, unbelievable, or, at the very least, mysterious because we are deprived of relevant information. Suppose, for example, that it is true that God exists and that every evil is necessary for a greater good, and consider William Rowe's example of a fawn who dies slowly and painfully in a raging forest fire. Even if we believe that because God exists, the fawn's horrid death is necessary for a good that outweighs it, *how* it does so may well seem mysterious. But, the *reason* it seems mysterious is, arguably, that we are ignorant of certain relevant facts. Finite intellects or, in any case, finite intellects *in via* cannot grasp all of the relevant logical connections between goods and evils, and are unavoidably ignorant of some of the relevant goods and evils (either because they don't know what these goods and evils are or, if they do, fail to fully appreciate their goodness or badness). The truths in question are not *intrinsically* mysterious, however, since the mystery would be dispelled if we were to come into possession of the relevant information – through a special revelation, perhaps, or at the eschaton. Thus, Edwards thinks that some central doctrines are "very mysterious," and "have difficulties in them, inexplicable by us." The doctrine of predestination, for example, is "very difficult to reconcile with the justice of God." Nevertheless, "the time is coming when these mysteries will all be unfolded, and the perplexing difficulties that have attended them will all be perfectly vanished away, as the shades of night before the sun in a serene hemisphere."[37]

In other cases, however, the mystery may be uneliminable by any addition of information or strengthening of our intellectual powers. In cases of this sort, the mystery is irreducible because its object is intrinsically mysterious. These are mysteries in Gabriel Marcel's sense. Marcel distinguished "problems" from "mysteries." Problems[38] – a chess problem or mathematical problem, for instance, or the puzzles brought to Sherlock Holmes – have solutions, although these solutions may never be discovered. If and when the solutions are discovered, however, the problems disappear. A mystery, on the other hand, *has* no solution. No matter how much we may come to learn about it, it remains as mysterious as it was before.[39] A mystery in Marcel's sense is more or less the same as what Rudolf Otto called the "*mysterium.*" That which is mysterious "in the religious sense" is "the 'wholly other' … that which is quite beyond the sphere of the usual, the intelligible, and the familiar, which therefore falls quite outside the limits of the 'canny' [of what is 'within our ken'], and is contrasted with it, filling the mind with blank wonder and astonishment."[40] The concept of mystery, like the concept of transcendence, is formally negative. "On the side of the feeling-content," however, "it is otherwise; that *is* in very truth positive in the highest degree, though ... it cannot be rendered explicit in conceptual terms."[41]

Mysteries in this fourth sense are, arguably, the subject of the passages from the Pseudo-Dionysius, John Chrysostom, and Jonathan Edwards which I quoted at the beginning of this chapter. They are also my primary concern in what follows.

III. Reasons for the Divine Mystery Thesis

Alston offers four reasons for what he calls the "Divine Mystery Thesis," namely, that "God is inevitably so *mysterious* to us, to our rational capacities ... that nothing we can think, believe, or say about him is *strictly* true of God as he is in himself." These reasons include the doctrine of simplicity to which I shall turn in a moment, and the experiences of the great Christian mystics, which were briefly discussed earlier in this chapter. John of the Cross, for example, or the anonymous author of the *Cloud of Unknowing* claim to have enjoyed "a taste of what it is like to know God as he knows himself," and to have undergone "a fundamental transformation in which" they became "united to God as much as is possible in this life." Christian mystics such as these invariably claim that the knowledge they have acquired is "something radically different from any knowledge we can capture in our concepts and modes of thinking and speech." It is a sight "without seeing," a knowledge "without knowing, ... for in contemplation we know by 'unknowing,' Or, better, we know *beyond* all knowing or 'unknowing'.... The closer we get to God, the less is our faith diluted with the half-light of created images and concepts ... [for] it is then that our minds are most truly liberated from the weak, created lights that are darkness in comparison to him; it is then that we are filled with his infinite light which seems pure darkness to our reason."[42]

The other reasons for the mystery thesis are, first, "the puzzles, paradoxes, and insoluble problems which theological thought [about the Trinity, for example] seems so frequently to lead"; and, second, our limited capacities. "If we think about the relation of human cognitive powers to the absolutely infinite source of all that is other than itself, it seems reasonable to suppose that the former would not be in a position to get an account of the latter that is exactly correct, even in certain abstract respects."[43] Or as Edwards argues: "A very great superiority, even in beings of the same nature as ourselves," makes many of their actions, intentions, and assertions "incomprehensible and attended with inexplicable intricacies." Witness the relation that "little children" bear to "adult persons," for example, or the "vulgar" to "learned men [or] great philosophers and mathematicians." God "is *infinitely* diverse from and above all in his nature," however. So if God vouchsafes a revelation of himself (of his triune nature, say) "which is entirely diverse [not only] from anything we do now experience in our present state, but from anything that we can be conscious or immediately sensible of in any state whatsoever that our nature can be in, then especially may mysteries be expected in such a revelation."[44]

Or consider Aquinas. In Part Four of the *Summa Contra Gentiles*, Aquinas argues that because "the human intellect" must "derive its knowledge from sensible things, [it] is not able through itself to reach the vision of the divine substance in itself, which is above all sensible things and, indeed, improportionately above *all* other things." Yet "man's perfect good is that he somehow know God." Therefore, because "it was [but] a feeble knowledge of God that man could reach" by unassisted reason, "God revealed certain things about himself that transcend the human intellect.... These things [the doctrine of the Trinity, for example] are revealed to man as ... not to be understood but only to be believed as heard, for the human intellect in this state ... is connected with things sensible [and] cannot be elevated entirely to gaze upon things which exceed every proportion of sense," although "when it shall have been freed from the connection with sensibles, then it will be elevated to gaze upon the things which are revealed."[45] Although the general thrust of this passage is clear enough, it does raise an important question to which we will return later. For if God "improportionately" transcends *all* finite things, as Aquinas says, why think that freedom from connection with sensibles will be sufficient to remove the mystery or darkness that surrounds God's nature?

The arguments I have discussed so far focus on the relation between our necessarily limited intellects, on the one hand, and the divine, on the other. Others focus more directly on God's own being.

According to John the Scot, for example, God knows *himself* but does not know *what* he is. John's reasons for this are essentially these. To know what God is one would have to grasp God's essence. God "is not essence," though, "but More than Essence and the infinite Cause of all essences, and not only infinite but the Infinity of all infinite essence, and More than infinity." God is beyond essence because essences are the sorts of thing that can be captured or expressed in definitions, and definitions proceed by marking out a thing's boundaries. God has no boundaries, however, since he is infinite or limitless. Not even God, then, can know what God is. But this does not imply that God is ignorant (because "He does not understand of Himself what He is"), nor does it imply that God is impotent (because "He is unable to define His Substance"). For God *has* no what.[46] Nor does it imply that "God does not know himself," or know himself *as* infinite, and as indeed "above every finite thing and every infinite thing and beyond finitude and infinity."[47]

John's case for the claim that God has no essence or "what" depends on the following subargument. If a definition is to succeed in distinguishing its definiendum from other things, it must *exclude* the item being defined *from* other things. An "absolutely infinite" God would exclude *nothing*, however, since if it did exclude something, it would have limits and thus not be "*absolutely*" infinite (or limitless).

This subargument has a certain (specious) plausibility if "absolutely infinite" is construed in arithmetical or geometrical terms. The series of natural numbers excludes no natural numbers, for example, and an infinite line excludes none of its segments. Yet why should we construe "absolutely infinite" in this fashion? Why not, instead, construe it as "absolutely perfect"? If we were to do so, however, the subargument wouldn't go through because absolute perfection *does* exclude things, for it excludes *im*perfections, such as ignorance and injustice, and *mixed* perfections,[48] such as repentance.[49] Let us turn, then, to another (and I believe more successful) attempt to show that God's nature is such that he transcends what can be thought of him.

In *Proslogion* xv, Anselm exclaims: "Lord, not only are you that than which a greater cannot be thought, but you are also something greater than can be thought. For since it is possible to think that there is such a one, if you were not this same being something greater than you could be thought – which cannot be."[50] Commenting on this passage, M. J. Charlesworth observes that Anselm is reminding us that "even if we understand God to be 'that than which nothing greater can be thought,' we do not thereby have a *positive* or *determinate* knowledge of God";[51] and refers us to the reply to Gaunilo, where Anselm says that just as one can think or understand "the ineffable" though one can't "specify [or describe] what is said to be ineffable; and just as one can think of [or understand] the inconceivable – although one cannot think [or conceive] of what 'inconceivable' applies to – so also 'that than which a greater cannot be thought' ... can be thought of and understood even though the thing itself cannot be thought and understood."[52] But granting this, one may still wonder why Anselm thinks that a being *greater* than can be thought is greater or more perfect than one lacking this property.

Being such that one cannot think it is not *itself* a perfection, if for no other reason than because our inability to think something (adequately capture it in concepts) may be a function of its *im*perfection. Plato's Receptacle or Aristotle's or Plotinus's *hyle* are examples,[53] Again, a thing might be too complicated or too hidden for our intellects to comprehend it. The true nature of the physical universe might be an example. It doesn't follow that its impenetrability to finite intellects is a good-making feature of it.

Being too *perfect* for us to conceive, on the other hand, might be a *second-order* perfection, that is, a perfection parasitic on a thing's other perfections. And perhaps God has this second-order property. Yet why think he does? Perhaps because while we know that God's joy, for instance, or his knowledge are perfect we don't have a good conceptual grasp of either of them. In the case of a degreed property such as joy, which lacks an upper limit, this might be because the bliss that God enjoys is incommensurable with any finite analogue of it.[54] Or in the case of a degreed property such as knowledge, which *has* an intrinsic maximum, finite intellects may know *that* God knows all truths, and yet not know *how* he knows them or just what his knowledge of them is like. Moreover, if God is simple, as much of the tradition maintains, then *no* positive characterization of God is strictly true of him since "all our proposi- tional thought and speech is necessarily carried on by making distinctions."[55] Or perhaps Karl Rahner is right, and mystery in Marcel's or Otto's sense is an intrinsic positive feature of the Godhead. (More on this later.)

But suppose we agree that being greater than can be thought is a conse- quence of (some of?) God's first-order perfections, of the relation between them (that is, of his simplicity),[56] or of the fact that mystery is an intrinsic fea- ture of the divine essence.[57] Does it straightforwardly follow that being greater than can be thought is not only a divine property but also a *divine perfection*? Only if we assume that any property entailed by a perfection is itself a perfec- tion. And this assumption is false. Repentance entails a prior sin, and while the former is a perfection, the latter is not. Again, intelligence trivially entails two plus two equaling four, but two and two summing to four is not a perfection. Even so, since being greater than can be thought is arguably entailed by God's first-order perfections, if God were not greater than can be thought, he would necessarily lack one or more of those perfections and so would not be God, a being greater than which none can be thought.

There is reason to think, then, that God necessarily transcends what can be said and thought of him. Just *how* mysterious is he, though? We will turn to this question in the next section.

IV. The Nature and Extent of God's Unknowability

Thomas Aquinas claimed that some important truths about God exceed "the power of human reason." In a paper published in 1988, George Mavrodes suggested that we gloss the phrase "exceeds the power of human reason" as follows: "A truth exceeds the ability of all human reason if and only if it is not possible to prove that truth demonstratively." Why think that, in this sense, the doctrine of the Trinity, say, exceeds the power of human reason? Perhaps because, as Aquinas suggests, there are only two ways of demonstrating a truth about something: by deducing it from our "understanding of the substance [or essence] of the thing which is the subject of that knowledge" or from the thing's causal effects.[58] Truths about things like the Trinity can't be demonstrated in this way, however. For we can't (prior to the beatific vision at least) grasp God's essence. And Aquinas assumes that "the creative power of God is *common* to the whole Trinity, and hence ... belongs to the *unity* of the essence, and *not* to the distinction of the persons." So while "by natural reason we can know what belongs to the *unity of the essence*" from God's casual effects, we *cannot* know "what belongs to the distinction of the persons" from them.[59]

Mavrodes's principal objection to this line of thought is that there are dif- ferent but no less reasonable interpretations of "demonstration." For exam- ple, following Plantinga and others, we might identify a demonstration with a sound, noncircular deductive or inductive argument from universally (or nearly universally) accepted premises. Or, following Mavrodes and Penelhum, we might identify a demonstration with a sound, noncircular argument from premises that its proponent or recipient knows to be true or has strong reasons to believe are true. Although it is unlikely that one can provide demonstrations of the doctrine of the Trinity in the first sense (or of any other interesting philosophical or theological truth, for that matter), the prospects of doing so in the second may be brighter. And, in fact, Richard of St. Victor, Jonathan Edwards, and Richard Swinburne claim to have provided demonstrations of the doctrine of the Trinity in the sense in question.[60]

The tradition does more or less unanimously attest that God's essence is unknown or unknowable by finite creatures.[61] The fact that a thing's substance or essence is unknown or unknowable does not entail that we can't rationally establish many truths about it, however. Locke thought that the substances or essences of physical objects were currently unknown but did not think that there were no well-grounded truths about them. Again, many truths about water were known before it was discovered that water is H_2O. Nor would matters obviously have been different if we had not discovered that water is H_2O or even if, for some reason, humans never *could* have discovered this.

Yet if God's essence or inner being is unknown or unknowable, what *can* we know about God? One of the most common answers hinges on a distinction between knowing *that* a proposition is true and knowing or understanding *how* it can be true. As Edwards observes in "The Mind" 71, "it is not impossible to believe or know the truth of mysteries, or propositions that we cannot comprehend, or see the manner how the several ideas that belong to the proposition are united ... we may perceive *that* they are united and know *that* they belong one to another, though we do not know the manner *how* they are tied together."[62] In view of remarks that Edwards makes elsewhere, it is clear that he is not only referring to propositions that we know to be true because their truth is attested by reliable authority but also to propositions that we can prove or demonstrate without fully comprehending them. In a late entry, for example, Edwards asserts that "Tis not necessary that persons should have clear ideas of things that are the subject of a proposition, in order to being rationally convinced of the truth of the proposition," and cites "many truths of which mathematicians are convinced by strict demonstration ... concerning which they have no clear ideas," such as propositions about "surd quantities and fluxions."[63] It is in this sense, presumably, that after having given his rational account of just why God must be triune, Edwards exclaimed "I don't pretend fully to explain how these things are ... I am far from pretending to explaining the Trinity so as to render it no longer a mystery."[64]

In what sense, though, can propositions that we know to be true elude our comprehension? In some cases, we may observe, and hence know, that an event has occurred without understanding how it *could* have occurred, or be cognizant of a phenomenon such as lightning or combustion yet be utterly baffled by it. In such cases, what is lacking is a grasp of the occurrence's causes or of the mechanisms or internal structures underlying the phenomenon that puzzles us. Something like this may be involved in our understanding of God's providence, for example.

As James Kellenberger observes in discussing Job's faith, one can believe or even know *that* God exists, is good and merciful, and the like without understanding *how* God is good and merciful, since "his *ways* of goodness, mercy," and so on, "are beyond our conceiving….This source of mystery – the inconceivability of God's ways – would remain just as it is if it were *known that* there is a God, *that* he is good and *that* he is merciful."[65] What Job lacks, in short, is an understanding of the *mechanisms* of divine providence. The extent to which divine providence is a mystery in this sense is a matter of debate, of course. Job confesses that he has "obscured [God's] designs with [his] empty-headed words, … holding forth on matters [he] cannot understand, on marvels beyond [him] and [his] knowledge" (Job 42: 3). Edwards, on the other hand, preached an entire sermon series explicating the wondrous "machine," composed of wheels within wheels, which underlies and constitutes the history of redemption.

Edwards's "Discourse on the Trinity" suggests a somewhat different sense of "incomprehensibility." He compares the Christian inquirer to a student of nature. When the latter "looks on a plant" or an animal, say, "or any other works of nature, at a great distance, [he] may see something in it wonderful and beyond his comprehension," and so desire to view it more closely. And if he does, he "indeed understands more about them …; and yet the number of things that are wonderful and mysterious in them that appear to him are much more than before. And if he views them with a microscope, the number of the wonders that he sees will be much increased still. But yet the microscope gives him more of a true knowledge concerning them."[66] What this comparison suggests is that even though Christian divines' investigations of the Christian mysteries are progressive in the sense that more and more facets of these mysteries are revealed, more questions answered, and more puzzles removed, the knowledge that is gained only leads to new questions and new puzzles: "However … some difficulties are lessened, others that are new appear; and the number of those things that appear mysterious, wonderful and incomprehensible are increased by it."[67] Edwards's point in this passage, I think, is not that some questions about the Trinity, for instance, are unanswerable (although they may be), but rather that any answers we may discover simply lead to more questions. The problem the passage isolates is thus quantitative rather than qualitative. Yet unlike some of the more optimistic estimates of the possibility of progress in science, Edwards seems to think that our mounting success in answering questions about the Christian mysteries takes us no closer to the goal of answering all questions about them.

Yet another sense of "incomprehensibility" is suggested by "Miscellany 839." Divine mysteries "are not only so above human comprehension that men can't easily apprehend all that is to be understood concerning them, but [they] are difficult to the understanding in that sense, that they are difficult to be received by the judgement or belief."[68] Why is this the case? At least partly because the Christian mysteries are attended with "paradoxes" and "seeming contradictions." Now as we saw in Chapter 6, difficulties of this sort aren't peculiar to divinity. "The reasonings and conclusions of the best metaphysicians and mathematicians concerning infinities," for instance, are also "attended with paradoxes and seeming inconsistencies."[69] (Hilbert's hotel was offered as an example.) The problem is partly due to the limitations of language. As Edwards observes in "Miscellany 83," "The things of Christianity are so spiritual, so refined, so high and abstracted, and so much above the things we ordinarily converse with and our common affairs, to which we adapt our words," that "we are forced to use words ... analogically ... and therefore [does] religion [abound] with so many paradoxes and seeming contradictions."[70] Yet if I understand Edwards, the problem is not just with our language but also with our imagination or sense of grasp.[71] Our analogies and metaphors are ultimately inadequate. We lack an adequate model or, perhaps more accurately, an adequate *unified* model of the deep things of God. Edwards sometimes employs an Augustinian psychological model of the Trinity, for example, while at other times employing patristic social models. He makes no attempt to unify them, however – presumably because he sees no way of doing so.[72]

V. Is the Mystery Removable?

Suppose that we grant that the veil between God and ourselves cannot be removed in this life. Will we – indeed, can we – behold God unveiled in the next? Some texts suggest that we will. Paul, for example, asserts that while "we now see only puzzling reflections in a mirror, we shall then see face to face." Our "knowledge now is partial," but "then it will be whole, like God's knowledge of me" (I Corinthians 13: 12). Does the beatific vision, then, include an unclouded vision of God's essence? Some Christian theologians, at least, have thought not.[73]

Thus, Aquinas says that "since our mind is not proportionate to the divine substance, that which is the substance of God remains beyond our intellect and so is unknown to us. Hence the supreme knowledge which man has of God is to know that he does not know God, in so far as he knows that what God is surpasses all that we can understand of him."[74] Rahner seems to me to be correct in arguing that, because "the reason for saying" that knowing God involves knowing that one does not know God[75] "holds good for the beatific vision" as well as for the veiled glimpses of God we have in this mortal life, "there is no reason for not applying [it] to the knowledge of God in the beatific vision."[76]

Some of the things that Edwards says have similar implications. Edwards believes that while many of the difficulties and perplexities surrounding

Christian doctrines will be cleared up in the "future appointed time of joy and glory to the church [on earth], ... the perfect and full explication of these mysteries is part of the last and eternal state of the church [in heaven], to heighten the joy and praises of the wedding day of Christ and his church."[77] For just as we may find it difficult to locate what we are looking for in the dark by feeling, or in a dim light by seeing, yet find it easily when "a clear light comes to shine into the place, and we discern it by a better faculty, viz. of sight, or the same faculty in a clearer manner, so ... many truths will hereafter appear plain, when we come to look on them by the bright light of heaven, that now are involved in mystery and darkness."[78] It doesn't follow that *all* mystery will be dispelled, however, and at least some things that Edwards says suggest that it won't. Thus, as we have seen, in "Miscellany 1340," Edwards asserts that because God "is infinitely diverse from and above all others in his nature," any revelation he chooses to vouchsafe of his intrinsic nature (of his triunity, say) will be so "entirely diverse [not only] from anything that we do now experience in our present state, but from anything that we can be conscious or immediately sensible of *in any state whatsoever that our nature can be in*," that many "mysteries may be expected in such a revelation."[79] The clear implication is that even the light of heaven won't, and indeed cannot, dispel all mystery.

One of the most powerful statements of this view is that of John Chrysostom, who exclaims: "let us call upon him, then, as the ineffable God who is beyond our intelligence, invisible, incomprehensible.... Let us call on him as the God who is inscrutable to the angels, unseen by the Seraphim, inconceivable to the Cherubim, invisible to the principalities, to the powers, and to the virtues, in fact to *all* creatures without qualification, because he is known *only* by the Son and the Spirit."[80] Why do the seraphim "stretch forth their wings and cover their faces? For what other reason than that they cannot endure the sparkling flashes nor the lightning which shines from the throne? Yet they did not see the pure light itself nor the pure essence itself. What they saw was a condescension accommodated to their natures."[81] So unless the beatified see God more clearly than the angels do, they do not grasp God's essence. The mystery of God is thus ineluctable.

And, indeed, it is possible that it is ineluctable in an even stronger sense. For there may be a sense in which even God's own knowledge of himself does not dispel the mystery. Karl Rahner points out that in postmedieval scholastic theology (and, I would add, in much if not most contemporary analytic philosophy of religion), mystery is a property that statements have when they exceed our reason or cannot be fully understood. This conception of mystery has three noteworthy features. First, while it is admitted that the mystery of doctrinal statements is rooted in features of their object, the *focus* of scholastic theology's discussion of mystery is on the statements, rather than on what those statements are about. Second, mystery is regarded as a function of the relation of the propositions in question to human reason. Third, reason is construed in its modern sense as ratiocination or "calculation," and thus sharply distinguished from the will and affections. Rahner thinks that each of these features reflects a mistake. In the first place, mystery is primarily a characteristic of the deep things of God – not of the doctrinal statements that express them. In the second, mystery is not (in the first instance, at least) a function of the relation between certain propositions about God and finite intellects, but instead an intrinsic property of God himself. Finally, we can only cognize mystery by faith, and faith is an expression of our will and affections as well as of our intellect. To recognize mystery is not just to acknowledge that certain propositions exceed our grasp; it is to prostrate ourselves in loving wonder before something that can't be comprehended by any sort of propositional cognition.

In short, as Rahner says, if God's incomprehensibility "is the very substance of our vision and the very object of our blissful love," then "vision must mean grasping and being grasped by the mystery, and the supreme act of knowledge is not the abolition or diminution of the mystery, but its final assertion."[82] The beatific "vision of God face to face" does remove many mysteries, "but this only means that *what* [the mysteries] express is manifested in its own being and substance, is experienced therefore in itself and must no longer rely for its manifestation on the [authoritative] word that does duty for it[83] … Nonetheless, these mysteries [that is, what one now directly beholds] remain mysterious and incomprehensible."[84] The Greek fathers are thus right when they speak of "the highest stage of life and knowledge" as entering "into the darkness in which God is" (Pseudo-Dionysius) or a not-knowing that is "the supra-rational knowledge" (Maximus the Confessor), or tell us that "to enter the holy of holies is to be encompassed by the divine darkness" (Gregory of Nyssa).[85]

But all this, if correct, has a potentially startling consequence. For if mystery is not, in the first instance, a function of the relation between God and finite intellects, but rather an intrinsic property of God's own nature, then God's complete and perfect knowledge of himself must include a recognition of it. "The absolutely clear self-awareness of" God may thus include "something positive which does not appertain to the [propositional] intellect[86] but to the mystery in contradistinction from such an intellect." If this is so, then mystery "appertains to God's knowledge [of himself], essentially, in a preeminent and analogous sense."[87] There may thus be a sense in which God himself can't comprehend his own essence[88] but must enter into the "divine darkness," knowing himself, or aspects of himself, through a "not-knowing" that is at one and the same time a supreme "supra-rational knowledge" of the deep things of his own being.

To see why this suggestion isn't outrageous, we need to say a bit more about the kind of knowledge involved in apprehending a mystery in Marcel's or Rahner's sense.

An awareness of mystery in the sense in question is perhaps best construed as a species of appreciation or knowledge by acquaintance.[89] Other examples of this sort of knowledge are my knowledge of what strawberries taste like or silk feels like, my awareness of a thunderstorm's sublimity or the beauty of a Bach fugue, or my knowing what it is like to suffer or to love. Notice that these forms of knowledge by acquaintance are related analogically, and vary with their objects. Our appreciation of beauty, for instance, is importantly different from our acquaintance with sense modalities such as the taste of strawberries or the feel of silk, and both different significantly from a firsthand knowledge of the horror of war or what Kierkegaard calls "first love."

Instances of knowledge by acquaintance aren't just differentiated by their objects, however. Consider the wonder over her own beauty that Semele expresses in an aria in Handel's opera of the same name; the Greeks' wonder at the world (the fact of its being);[90] or the Christian's, Muslim's, or Shri Vaishnava's wonder at the glory of God. These instances of wonder differ not only in object but in phenomenological quality or feel. Semele's wonder, for example, is qualitatively different from the Greeks' wonder at the world, and both differ qualitatively from the theists' wonder at the glory of God.[91]

The object of a sense of mystery in Marcel's or Rahner's sense is God's own being or nature, and the best description of its phenomenological character is probably Otto's – "blank wonder, an astonishment that strikes us dumb, amazement absolute," occasioned by coming "upon something inherently 'wholly other,' whose kind and character are incommensurable with our own, and before which we therefore recoil in a wonder that strikes us chill and numb," yet whose "feeling-content" is nonetheless "positive in the highest degree."[92]

Does a sense of mystery in this sense entail lack of understanding or grasp? The answer is "yes" *if* understanding or grasp is defined in terms of *conceptual* grasp or *propositional* knowledge (knowledge that). The answer is "no" if an affirmative answer is understood to imply the existence of a gap in understanding that could in principle be filled in, or that the sort of knowledge involved in this and other instances of knowledge by acquaintance isn't adequate to its object.

Are there two quite different senses of mystery,[93] then, which we might call epistemological mysteries and ontological mysteries, respectively? (The mysteries in question are epistemological when they are a function of the relation between God's nature or being, on the one hand, and the limitations of created intellects, on the other. They are ontological when they are an intrinsic aspect of God's own being rather than of human or divine knowledge of it.) These senses of mystery *are* at home in very different places. Discussions of epistemological mysteries are at home in philosophical theology, for example, and are the principal subject of this chapter's earlier sections. The ontological sense of mystery, on the other hand, is perhaps most at home in liturgical worship and the prayer of adoration.[94] But the two senses of "mystery" are not entirely equivocal. For both senses are partly defined by a lack of conceptual mastery.

Epistemological mysteries and ontological mysteries elude conceptualization in very different ways, however, and for very different reasons. Epistemological mysteries elude it because while adequate concepts are in principle available (if only to God), they are *not* available to *us*. Ontological mysteries elude conceptualization because *no* concepts can fully express it. Symbols, images, songs, poetry, and, perhaps ultimately, the silence of mystical prayer alone can do so.

The question raised by Rahner's claim that "mystery appertains to God's knowledge" of himself is thus roughly equivalent to this. Can God adopt the attitudes described by Otto toward himself? On the whole,[95] I don't see why not. Even if we understood everything about ourselves that can be conceptually grasped, we might still wonder at, or be amazed or astonished by, our own being. ("We are fearfully and wonderfully made" [Psalm 139:14].) Why, then, can't God wonder at, or be amazed by, *his* being. Moreover, that God can adopt these attitudes toward himself seems even clearer in a Trinitarian context. A standard Eucharistic prayer concludes "All this we ask through your Son Jesus Christ. *By him, and with him, and in him*, in the unity of the Holy Spirit, all honor and glory are yours, Almighty Father, now and forever" (my emphasis). Just as we adore or glorify God, so the Father and Son and Holy Spirit adore and glorify each other. Nor do I see why the Father's, the Son's, and the Holy Spirit's mutual adoration can't be tinged with awe, wonder, and (even) astonishment).

So in precisely what sense does mystery "appertain to God's knowledge" of himself? God, I suggest, knows everything that can be propositionally known about himself[96] through an analogue of propositional cognition. But other aspects of God's being (those that are mysteries in Marcel's or Rahner's sense) can't be grasped in this way even in principle, and God knows these by an analogue of appreciation or knowledge by acquaintance. Nothing about God is thus unknown to God. He is neither "baffled," "puzzled," nor "mystified" by his own being.[97] Nevertheless, God's nature is for him an object of an amazement, wonder, and awe that are the felt aspects, as it were, of a perfect experiential acquaintance with depths of his own being that necessarily elude even his own complete conceptual comprehension.[98]

Conclusion

I entered Kenyon College at eighteen as an aspiring poet with a strong interest in literary studies but encountered philosophy during my sophomore year. The departments at Kenyon and at the University of Michigan where I received my graduate training were largely analytic. I continue to regard myself as an analytic philosopher. The only text in my first course was Plato's *Republic*, however, and Plato remains my favorite philosopher. What initially struck me, and still does, is the way in which he weaves together closely reasoned pieces of analysis with myth, story, and symbol. Although Plato clearly believed that the latter are needed to express some truths or aspects of the truth, he employed them only after the resources of argument had been exhausted. This continues to seem to me the best way to do philosophy. I never lost the conviction that poetry, myth, symbol, and story can express truths and insights that can't be adequately expressed in other ways. Yet philosophy taught me that when poetry, story, symbol, and myth aren't tethered to reasoned argument and careful analysis, one runs the danger of falling prey to what Coleridge called "fancy" and distinguished from imagination. The latter, in his view, answered to something in reality. The former does not. These convictions have led to and shaped the understanding of the nature, role, and importance of religious argumentation expressed in this book.

Two facts are patently clear. As we saw in Chapter 2, philosophically sophisticated arguments are frequently deployed by adherents of the world's major religious traditions. What is equally clear, though, is that few of these arguments are universally persuasive. Not only do Christian arguments generally fail to convince Buddhists or atheists, for example, they often fail to convince many of their authors own co-religionists. In spite of the fact that both were Christians, Pelagius's arguments failed to convince Augustine, and Augustine's arguments failed to convince Pelagius. Chapter 2 argued that one of the main reasons for this is the person-relativity of most arguments. Two related sources of the person-relativity of religious proofs were explored in Chapters 3 and 4. The first is the embeddedness of the most interesting religious arguments in rich textual traditions. The second is that one's assessments of these arguments are deeply affected by one's possession of certain emotions, feelings, desires, and intuitions or by one's lack of them.

Plato thought that a proper education was a necessary condition of acquiring the moral and intellectual dispositions needed to ascertain and securely hold the most important truths and values. Ultimately, what was needed, in his view, was the existential appropriation of a way of life in which these truths and values were embedded. The major religious traditions have agreed with the broad outlines of Plato's position on this point but have differed on the most effective way of achieving their mutually desired goal.[1]

Plato's account of the desired education is found in the middle books of the *Republic*. The practices of the major religious traditions, on the other hand, clearly presuppose that the most effective way of inculcating the required intellectual, moral, and spiritual virtues is by immersion in rich textual traditions of the sort discussed in Chapter 3. The texts at the heart of these traditions provide models of the way of life they valorize[2] and are appropriated through memorization and the employment of the devotional and spiritual practices associated with them.

Chapters 4 and 5 explicated, defended, and explored the implications of the claim that our passional nature or heart is epistemically significant. Chapter 4 offered a variety of reasons in support of the claim that right emotions and right desires are necessary conditions of discerning truth about value-laden matters and defended that claim against charges of subjectivism and circularity.

Chapter 5 then argued that if the central claim of Chapter 4 is correct, philosophy must rethink its relation to rhetoric. Rhetoric is not only not opposed to philosophy, its carefully deployment is essential to sound reasoning in ethics, aesthetics, theology, and on many metaphysical topics.

The book's final two chapters examined ways in which reasoned religious argumentation may ultimately be limited. The textual traditions discussed in Chapter 3 differ. These differences reflect differences over the nature of the dispositions, emotions, and attitudes needed for right belief and the acquisition of ethical and spiritual knowledge and, ultimately, differences over the nature of the Good – whether it should be identified, for example, with the triune God of Christianity, the Nirvana of Thervada Buddhism, the One without a partner of Islam, or the Tao of Chinese philosophy. Up to a certain point, religious traditions can be defended by reason. Ultimately, however, their justification will almost invariably involve an appeal to revelation or the authority of a teacher. (Buddhism is merely an apparent exception. In principle, each person can discern the truths of the Buddha's teachings on his or her own. But in practice, his teachings are authoritative, and their authority derives from the impression that the Buddha is one who has seen the truth and found the way to escape from the world's woes, and not from one's own direct experience or argument.) The precise relation between reason and revelation is problematic, however. Chapter 6 explored different accounts of the relation between the two, but concluded that while revelation may transcend reason, it need not be opposed to it.

Chapter 7 examined the claim that the object of religious concern may ultimately transcend our conceptual grasp. Plato, for example, thought that dialectic or rational argumentation could only be pushed so far. It is ultimately left behind and superseded by a vision of the Good. The Good is not only "the cause of knowledge and truth," it is "beyond" them and "of still higher worth." It is also the cause of the "very being and reality" of objects, although it "is not the same thing as being, but even beyond being, surpassing it in dignity and power."[3]

The notion that the object of religious concern transcends reason is by no means peculiar to Plato. Advaita Vedanta, for example, said that the Brahman is *neti, neti* (not this, not that), and Chuang Tzu claimed that "the Tao is beyond all existing things, and neither words nor silence can convey its nature."[4] Chapter 7 focused on, and defended, the ways in which this theme was developed by the Fathers of the early Christian church and in Christianity's mystical traditions.

Notes

Introduction

1. Jonathan Edwards, "A Divine and Supernatural Light," in *The Works of Jonathan Edwards*, vol.17, *Sermons and Discourses, 1730–1733,* Mark Valeri (ed.) (New Haven, CT: Yale University Press, 1999), p. 422.
2. I am using "validity" here and elsewhere in this volume to refer not only to formal validity (the property an argument has when its premises logically entail its conclusion), but also to the property an argument has when it meets the appropriate logical standards for an argument of that type (e.g., the standards for a good inductive argument).
3. George Mavrodes, *Belief in God: A Study in the Epistemology of Religion* (New York: Random House, 1970).
4. John Locke, *An Essay Concerning Human Understanding*, book iii, chapter x, no. 34.

1 Four Examples of Religious Reasoning

1. Beings that are such that it is logically possible that they exist and logically possible that they not exist.
2. A being is essentially causeless if and only if it is causeless in every logically possible world in which it exists.
3. *Why* is its existence self-explanatory? Various answers have been suggested. Perhaps because it is being itself – being without limitation or qualification, as Aquinas thinks. Or perhaps because it is goodness or perfection itself and existence is a perfection, as Anselm and Christian Platonists believe.
4. A being is logically necessary if and only if it exists in every possible world. John Hick thinks that a being needn't be logically necessary to explain contingent being. Why? Because while we can raise causal questions about dogs, quarks, minds, or the space-time world as a whole, we can't raise causal questions about God. God can't have a cause, and so the search for causes must stop with him. God therefore provides a satisfactory ultimate explanation. John Hick, "God as Necessary

Being," *Journal of Philosophy* 57 (1960): 725–34; and Hick, *Philosophy of Religion* (Englewood Cliffs, NJ: Prentice Hall): 20–3.) But this is mistaken. Since God's existence isn't logically necessary on Hick's view, he might not have existed. Why, then, *does* he exist? The question has no answer. Since he isn't self-existent, his existence isn't self-explanatory. But since he is essentially causeless, no *other* being can explain it. His existence is thus contingent but inexplicable. As a consequence, his existence and activity can't adequately explain contingent existence. The question is, "Why are there *any* contingent beings at all?" It isn't answered by postulating the existence of yet another contingent being – not even an essentially causeless one.

5. The inference is sometimes accused of committing the fallacy of "composition," i.e., arguing from the assertion that something is true of each member of a set or each part of a whole to the conclusion that the same thing is true of the set or whole. But while some "compositions" are invalid, others are not. "Each part of the table weighs little" doesn't entail that the table weighs little. However, "Each part of the table is made of wood" does entail that the table is made of wood. Furthermore, Robert Koons argues that the world is a mereological whole. If it is and contains a contingent part, then it, too, is contingent. Koons, "A New Look at the Cosmological Argument," *American Philosophical Quarterly* 34 (1997): 193–211. (Cf. if *p* entails *q* and *p* is necessary, so too is *q*. Hence, if *p* entails *q*, and *q isn't* necessary, then neither is *p*.)

6. Cf. William Rowe, *The Cosmological Argument* (Princeton, NJ: Princeton University Press, 1976), chapter III.

7. Charles Hartshorne, *Anselm's Discovery* (LaSalle, IL: Open Court, 1965), 70–1.

8. Note that these alternatives aren't necessarily exclusive. Regulative principles can be necessarily true. (The principles of logic are an example.) Empirical generalizations can govern inquiry (though whether they can be constitutive of rationality is less clear).

9. It is sometimes objected that the principle of sufficient reason can't be an empirical generalization because, while it is empirically verifiable (and indeed verified every time we discover a reason for something), it is not empirically falsifiable. It is not empirically falsifiable because nothing we might experience or observe would entail its falsity. A failure to discover a sufficient reason for a contingent fact, for example, would not entail the principle's falsity since it is possible that there is a sufficient reason for the fact that we haven't yet discovered. This objection is mistaken, however. No finite set of observation statements would entail the falsity of empirical generalizations of the following form: for any x, there is a y such that y stands in relation R to x. Consider, for example, "For every substance, there is a substance that would dissolve it." While this is an empirical generalization, its falsity is not entailed by the fact that a particular substance is not dissolved by any of the solvents at our disposal – for even though we haven't yet found a solvent for that substance, one may nonetheless exist. Similarly, the most general form of the principle of sufficient reason could be expressed as follows: "For any fact, there is a fact which is a sufficient reason for it." Since it is of the required form, the fact that its falsity is not entailed by our failing to find a sufficient reason for a fact is not sufficient to show that it is not an empirical generalization. For while the principle of sufficient reason is not falsifiable in the strict sense, neither are other generalizations of the same form that clearly are empirical. Moreover, the principle

of sufficient reason *would* appear to be falsifiable in a less restricted sense. For suppose that as we learn more, the world begins to appear less amenable to rational investigation than it has in the past. New discoveries upset the old theories and we are unable to replace them with more adequate ones. New facts prove recalcitrant. While this state of affairs would not conclusively prove the falsity of the principle of sufficient reason, it would surely count against it. If any proposition is empirical that is such that empirical considerations can count for it and empirical considerations can count against it, then it would seem that the principle of sufficient reason is an empirical generalization after all.

10. W. Norris Clarke, "How the Philosopher Can Give Meaning to Language about God," in Edward H. Madden, Rollo Handy, and Marvin. Farber (eds.), *The Idea of God: Philosophical Perspectives* (Springfield, IL: Charles C. Thomas, 1968): 1–27 and 37–42.

11. However, it is hard to see how the rationality of trusting these principles could be *conclusively* established except by invoking the claim that God isn't a deceiver or something similar.

12. It may be worth observing that the fact that a *description* of a task is consistent is insufficient to show that the task is logically or metaphysically possible. Consider for example, "the task I am thinking of," where the task I am thinking of is making a round square, or "bringing it about that Troy is never destroyed," where the city referred to has already been destroyed.

13. This isn't entirely clear. Thomas V. Morris and Christopher Menzel ("Absolute Creation," *American Philosophical Quarterly* 23 [1986]: 353–62), for example, have argued that necessary states of affairs such as 2 = 2's equaling 4 *are* produced by God. Their necessity is accounted for by the fact that God exists in every possible world and produces the fact that 2 + 2 equals 4 in each world in which he exists. (Could God have produced 2 + 2's equaling 5, as Descartes seems to have thought? Not if producing 2 + 2's equaling 4 is one of God's essential features [i.e., a property he has in every world in which he exists].) Note too that even if God doesn't *produce* the fact that 2+ 2 = 4, it may nonetheless be grounded in his thinking it as a number of philosophical theologians have suggested. If it is, it depends upon him even if it isn't caused by him.

14. William James, "The Dilemma of Determinism," in *The Will to Believe and Other Essays in Popular Philosophy* (New York: Dover, 1956), 181–82.

15. Geach argues that attempts to define the latter tend to either be logically incoherent or have implications unacceptable to a Christian.

16. Peter Geach, "Omnipotence," *Philosophy* 48 (1973): 7–20.

17. Nelson Pike, "Omnipotence and God's Ability to Sin," *American Philosophical Quarterly* 6 (1969): 208–16.

18. Cf. Richard Swinburne, "Duty and the Will of God," *Canadian Journal of Philosophy* 4 1974): 213–17.

19. Jonathan Edwards, *The Freedom of the Will* (New Haven, CT: Yale University Press, 1957), pp. 165–6.

20. An important feature of God's righteous activity is its autonomy. Freedom from causal necessitation may be necessary if human righteousness is to resemble God's righteousness in this respect. Suppose that God constructed human beings in such a way that it was impossible for them to choose evil. While the immediate cause

of a person's righteous actions would lie within that person's own nature, its ultimate cause (namely, God's decrees) would not. And in that case the agent would
not be genuinely independent and its actions would not be genuinely autonomous.
In short, if God were to determine that rational creatures always act rightly, then,
while the agency of those creatures would resemble God's agency more closely
in one respect (namely, in its inability to sin), it would resemble it less closely in
another.

21. Paul J. Griffiths, *On Being Buddha: The Classical Doctrine of Buddhahood*
    (Albany: State University of New York Press, 1994), p. 59.

22. Ramanuja, *Vedarthasamgraha*, trans. S. S. Raghavachar (Mysore: Shri Ramakrishna
    Ashrama, 1956), pp. 4, 11.

23. Theravada is the only surviving "Hinayana" school. (While the term "Hinayana"
    continues to be fairly commonly used to refer to a set of similar Buddhist schools
    that once flourished in Southeast Asia, it is implicitly pejorative. "Hinayana" refers
    to the lesser vehicle [on the path to salvation] and is contrasted with Mahayana or
    the great vehicle.)

24. This would have seemed even more obvious in an Indian context where the self
    (*atman*) was typically believed to be permanent and unchanging, simple (not com-
    posed of parts), and uncaused. The argument doesn't depend on this conception of
    the self, however.

25. Trevor Ling, *The Buddha* (Harmondsworth, Middlesex, UK, and Baltimore, MD:
    Penguin, 1976), p. 164.

26. Walpola Rahula, *What the Buddha Taught* (New York: Grove Press, 1962), p. 36f.

27. *Udana* 80–81, in Edward Conze et al. (eds), *Buddhist Texts through the Ages*
    (New York: Harper and Row, 1964), p. 94f,

28. *Visuddhimagga* 507–09, in Conze et al., *Buddhist Texts*, p. 101.

29. Some Buddhists are reluctant to even say that nirvana exists, on the grounds that
    "x exists" entails that x is a causally conditioned object in *samsara*. They neverthe-
    less believe that nirvana is real: "Could it be said: 'Indeed, there is not Nirvana.
    It is like the horn of a hare; it is not to be got at?' No (this could not be said)
    for it is to be got at by (a certain) means [namely, meditation and wisdom]....
    Therefore, it should not be said: 'Because it is not to be got at (by more ordinary
    means) it is not'.... Because it has existence in the ultimate meaning, Nirvana is not
    non-existent" (Conze et al., *Buddhist Texts*, pp. 100–2) Indeed, if nirvana were *not*
    real, our situation would be hopeless since *samsara* alone would be real and *sam-
    sara* is *duhkha* (suffering, unsatisfactoriness). There *is* hope, however, and salvation
    is possible. (That is the good news or gospel of the Buddha.)

30. Trevor Ling, "Buddhist Mysticism," *Religious Studies* 1 (1966): 163–75.

31. The Sautrantikas (another historically influential Hinayana school) asserted "that
    Nirvana is not a real and distinct entity but the absence of one." It is nothing but
    "the absence of the tendency to act and the liability to be reborn." Nirvana, in their
    view, was a fact but not a "real separate entity." This very negative view of nirvana
    was atypical of the other Hinayana schools, however. Edward Conze, *Buddhist
    Thought in India* (Ann Arbor: University of Michigan Press, 1967), pp. 61–3.

32. Whether it adequately accounts for the self's unity, for example.

33. The first quotation is from *Shankara's Crest Jewel of Discrimination*, trans. Swami
    Prabhavananda (New York: Mentor, 1970), p. 101. The second is from The

Vedanta Sutras of Badarayana with the Commentary by Sankara, trans. George Thibaut (New York: Dover, 1962), part II, p. 158.

34. *Shankara's Crest Jewel,* p. 93.

35. *Vedanta Sutras,* part II, p. 281.

36. *Vedanta Sutras,* part I, pp. 329–30.

37. For this reason, referring to the nirguna and saguna Brahman as the higher and lower Brahman, respectively, is misleading since it suggests that there are two Brahmans when in reality there is only one.

38. Though there is a potential problem here. The concept of the saguna Brahman is presumably superior to other conceptions of ultimate reality such as the nirvana of Hinayana Buddhism or the collection of pure selves of Samkhya Yoga, because it is more like the nirguna Brahman than the latter conceptions. Yet how could the nirguna Brahman be more like one thing than another if it has no properties? A comparison with traditional Christian theology on this point is instructive. It maintains that God's nature is simple, utterly transcending plurality and division, and agrees that this implies that the divine nature is incomprehensible. According to Thomas Aquinas, for example, God can be described by negation (he is not finite, not composed of parts, not in space or time, etc.) and in terms of his relation to finite beings (he is their cause, their goal, and so on). But in this life, his nature must remain unknown. Part of the reason why traditional Christian theology has been able to combine these themes with theism, however, is because of the way it views the relation between ultimate reality and finite things. The space-time world is not an illusion in its view but a mirror of God's own being. Even though God infinitely transcends creatures, they are more or less like him, and the best images of God are provided by the most perfect creatures – angelic and human persons.

39. The formula "being-consciousness-bliss" is said to express the essence of the Brahman. Some Advaitins say that, strictly speaking, the formula doesn't describe the Brahman but, rather, our experience of the Brahman. Others conceded that the terms refer to the Brahman but are used in a negative sense. (The Brahman is not non-being, not nescient, and not the mere absence of pain.) Nevertheless, M. Hiriyana (*Essentials of Indian Philosophy* [London: Unwin, 1949], p. 22) talks as if the terms "belong to the object of the state of mind," and not the state of mind itself, while Karl H. Potter (*Encyclopedia of Indian Philosophies,* vol. III [Princeton, NJ: Princeton University Press, 1977], p. 342) claims that even though being, consciousness, and bliss are not "properties of the self [the Brahman] for the self [the Brahman] is without diversity and has no properties, it is *by nature* bliss, existence, and consciousness. It is non-dual" (my emphasis).

40. *Shankara's Crest Jewel,* p. 62.

41. Not all Hindu monotheists were Vaishnavas, however, and not all were Vedantins. Udayana, for example, was a Shaivite (a devotee of Shiva) and a follower of the Nyaya-Vaisheshika school rather than Vedanta. Again, while the views of Shaiva-Siddhanta are similar in many ways to the views of the theistic Vedantins, its adherents were devotees of Shiva rather than Vishnu, and they too weren't Vedantins.

42. Advaitins, too, engage in theistic devotional practices. Shankara, for example, wrote hymns to Shiva and Devi. These practices and their theistic presuppositions

are of secondary importance, however, and must ultimately be abandoned and transcended.

43. Robert F. Evans, *Pelagius: Inquiries and Reappraisals* (New York: Seabury, 1968), p. 92. What follows is heavily indebted to Evans's excellent book.

44. The moral law or "law of nature" is written in the human heart. A man or woman's action in conformity with this law is thus a conformity with his or her own nature, "which in turn is conformity with the will of God" (*Pelagius*, p. 93).

45. Evans, *Pelagius*, p. 96.

46. Evans, *Pelagius*, p. 97.

47. And, in particular, Pelagius objects to the idea (championed by Augustine) that sin is transmitted through procreation. In the first place, sin is the act of an individual, and an individual can be guilty only of deeds that spring from his or her own will. In the second place, if sin is transmitted through procreation, it is an inevitable or "necessary component of human nature" (Evans, *Pelagius*, p. 97), which is thus crippled or distorted. To assert this, however, is to effectually succumb to the Manichaean view that everything in human nature except the divine spark of light is evil and springs from the power of darkness.

48. Pelagius was thinking primarily of the law's moral aspects.

49. Evans, *Pelagius*, pp. 100–1.

50. Evans, *Pelagius*, p. 101. Presumably, our awareness of the content of the law, and of our own freedom, is dimmed or obscured as well.

51. Evans, *Pelagius*, p. 106.

52. Evans, *Pelagius*, p. 109.

53. Evans, *Pelagius*, p. 110.

54. Evans, *Pelagius*, p. 107.

55. That knowledge can save, can break the power of sin, is reminiscent of Rabbinic remarks about the healing efficacy of Torah study, the Gnostic notion of a saving gnosis, Plato's doctrine that vice is ignorance and virtue wisdom, and the like.

56. Paul Tillich, *A History of Christian Thought* (New York: Harper and Row, 1968), p. 126. Tillich suggests that "hubris" or "self-elevation" is a more apt expression for what Augustine intends than "pride," "because pride often has the connotation of a special psychological attitude. But that isn't what is meant here. The most humble people in a psychological sense [those who disparage themselves, who are unhappy with themselves, "take no pride in themselves," act as if they had no pride] can have the greatest pride" in the theological sense, i.e., can have the strongest drive toward autonomy and can be most self-contained.

57. The "ardor of concupiscence" (sexual desire as we experience it) shows that the soul is not fully master of its body. The body and the passions that depend on it move the will rather than the will moving the body, thus violating the proper order of nature.

58. Tillich, *History*, p. 127.

59. Tillich, *History*, p. 128.

60. Augustine, "On Marriage and Concupiscence" I. 27, quoted in Paul Lehmann, "The Anti-Pelagian Writings," in Roy W. Battenhouse (ed.), *A Companion to the Study of St. Augustine* (New York: Oxford University Press, 1955), p. 227.

61. Augustine, "On Marriage," quoted in Lehman, "The Anti-Pelagian Writings," p. 228.

62. Tillich, *History*, p. 128.
63. Augustine, "On the Grace of Christ and Original Sin" I. 13, 25, quoted in Lehmann, "The Anti-Pelagian Writings," p. 220.
64. Again, because our very nature has been corrupted, we are unable to extricate ourselves from the plight into which we have fallen. The divine omnipotence was necessary for the creation of our nature and nothing less than the divine omnipotence is needed if our nature is to be *recreated*. Etienne Gilson, *The Christian Philosophy of Saint Augustine* (New York: Vintage, 1967), pp. 153, 163.
65. Gilson, *Saint Augustine*, p. 160f.
66. Augustine, "On the Predestination of the Saints" 7, quoted in Lehmann, "The Anti-Pelagian Writings," p. 228.
67. Either for its own sake or for the sake of something else to which it is a means.
68. But note that free will in this sense is perfectly compatible with determinism.
69. Gilson, *Saint Augustine*, pp. 124–35, 157, 162.
70. Gilson, *Saint Augustine*, pp. 160–4.
71. Augustine, "On Rebuke and Grace" 7, 43, quoted in Lehman, "The Anti-Pelagian Writings," p. 227.
72. "Essence" is being used here in its traditional sense. The essence of x comprises not only its logically essential features but also those features of x that it would have to possess to be a good thing of its kind.
73. Namely, the movement of the soul is spontaneous or unconstrained, and it is able to and/or does act well.
74. It, arguably, isn't if genuine freedom is construed as freedom in the libertarian sense, i.e., as contra-causal freedom.
75. His "official" answer would be Paul's letters and other revealed scriptures. But of course, Pelagius can say the same. The real issue is just how those scriptures should be interpreted.
76. Gilson, *Saint Augustine*, p. 161.
77. Gilson, *Saint Augustine*, p. 159.
78. John Calvin, *Institutes of the Christian Religion*, vol. 2, trans. Henry Beveridge, (Grand Rapids, MI: Eerdmans, 1957), book three, chapter XI, section 2). References to Calvin in the following discussion are to this chapter and to chapter III of book three.
79. Calvin, *Institutes*, vol. 2, chapter XI, section 3.
80. Calvin, *Institutes*, vol. 2, chapter XI, section 16.
81. Calvin, *Institutes*, vol. 2, chapter XI, section 21.
82. Calvin, *Institutes*, vol. 2, chapter XI, section 22.
83. Calvin, *Institutes*, vol. 2, chapter XI, section 2.
84. Calvin, *Institutes*, vol. 2, chapter XI, section 23.
85. Calvin, *Institutes*, vol. 1, chapter III, section 5.
86. Calvin, *Institutes*, vol. 1, chapter III, section 6.
87. Calvin, *Institutes*, vol. 1, chapter III, section 9.
88. Calvin, *Institutes*, vol. 1, chapter III, section 8.
89. Calvin, *Institutes*, vol. 1, chapter III, section 16.
90. "Decrees Concerning Justification" chapter vii, in John C. Olin (ed.), *John Calvin and Jacopo Sadoleto: A Reformation Debate* (New York: Harper Torchbooks, 1966).

91. "Canons Concerning Justification," no. 8, in *Calvin and Sadoleto*. That is, it involves a real inward change. Note that Calvin too believes that God's gift to us includes sanctification but regards the gift as a *consequence* of justification, not as a *part* of it.
92. "Canons Concerning Justification," no. 1.
93. "Canons Concerning Justification," no. 5.
94. "Canons Concerning Justification," no. 4.
95. "Decrees Concerning Justification," chapter V.
96. "Canons Concerning Justification," no. 24 (my emphasis).
97. Calvin, *Institutes*, vol. 2, chapter XVI (my emphases).
98. Harry M. Tiebout, Jr., *Comparative Religion*, 3rd revised ed. (Champaign, IL: Stipes, 1980), pp. 106–7. A similar dispute arises between the Jodo ("Pure Land") sect and Jodo Shin-Shu (the "True Sect of Pure Land"). Pure Land Buddhism is quasitheistic, its adherents relying on the grace of the Buddha of the Western Paradise (Amida [Amitabha (Sanskrit)]. The founder of Jodo Shin-Shu (Shinran) argued that Jodo was inadequate since it relied in part on one's "own power" (*jiriki*) rather than entirely on the "other power" (*tariki*) of Amida.

2 The Purposes of Argument and the Person-Relativity of Proofs

1. As noted in the introduction, I use "validity" to refer not only to formal validity (the property an argument has when its premises logically entail its conclusion) but also to the property an argument has when it meets the appropriate logical standards for an argument of that type (for example, the standards for a good inductive argument).
2. George Mavrodes, *Belief in God: A Study in the Epistemology of Religion* (New York: Random House, 1970).
3. India "developed ... a tradition of public disputation that provided (at its best) an orderly procedure for representatives of the various competing standpoints to confront each other and to test the soundness of each other's claims before a mutually acceptable 'arbiter' or 'referee' (*saksin*) and a body of witnesses.... Indian logic in a formal sense – especially as systematized by the Buddhists and Naiyayikas – grew out of centuries of reflections on the rules which governed such disputations" and "the kinds of difficulties which can arise in the course of such debates." The rules required "amongst other things," that "the winner of a disputation both ... demolish the opponent's case and ... construct successful positive arguments in support of" his own position (John Clayton, *Religious Reasons and Gods: Essays in Cross-Cultural Philosophy of Religion* [Cambridge: Cambridge University Press, 2006], pp. 151–2f.). The Indian figures we will discuss in this chapter all followed these procedures.
4. Clayton, *Religious Reasons and Gods,* pp. 86–7.
5. Clayton, *Religious Reasons and Gods*, p. 128.
6. Anthony Pegis, "Introduction," *On the Truth of the Catholic Faith: Summa Contra Gentiles*, Book 1 (Garden City, NY: Image, 1955), p. 21.
7. Clayton, *Religious Reasons and Gods*, p. 93.
8. Roughly, Kalam proofs argue that the world must have a temporal beginning and that God's free decision alone can explain it. Aristotelian proofs do not assume that the world had a temporal beginning.

9. Clayton, *Religious Reasons and Gods*, p. 171.
10. Clayton, *Religious Reasons and Gods*, pp. 141–2.
11. Disputes between theists and Buddhists over the nature of ultimate reality are an example.
12. Clayton, *Religious Reasons and Gods*, p. 171f.
13. N. L. Tidwell, "Holy Argument: Some Reflections on the Jewish Piety of Argument, Process Theology, and the Philosophy of Religion," *Religious Studies* 32 (1996): 477–88, p. 477.
14. Tidwell, "Holy Argument," pp. 480–1.
15. Tidwell, "Holy Argument," p. 477. "For God as a student in the heavenly academy ... see [e.g.] the *Encyclopedia Judaica*, vol. 1, cols. 208–9, 'The Academy on High.'"
16. Louis Newman, *The Hasidic Anthology* (New York: Schocken, 1973), p. 23, n. 3.
17. *Babylonian Talmud*, vol. 2, trans. into English with notes, glossary, and indices under the editorship of Rabbi Dr. I. Epstein (London: Soncino Press, 1978), pt. 2, Pasahim 119a, p. 613. Thanks to Jerome Gellman for calling this passage to my attention.
18. Jerome Gellman, correspondence. Quoted with permission.
19. Clayton, *Religious Reasons and Gods*, p. 171.
20. Nicholas Wolterstorff, "The Migration of Theistic Arguments: From Natural Theology to Evidentialist Apologetics," in Robert Audi and William J. Wainwright (eds.), *Rationality, Religious Belief, and Moral Commitment: New Essays in the Philosophy of Religion* (Ithaca, NY: Cornell University Press, 1986): 38–81. Note that for Aquinas and other devout medieval theologians, the contemplative life was the highest form of life.
21. One hundred Brahma years equals 311,040,000,000,000 calendar years.
22. Though the "accumulated merits and demerits [of souls] will remain with them."
23. Clayton, *Religious Reasons and Gods*, p. 147.
24. Clayton, *Religious Reasons and Gods*, p. 148.
25. Clayton, *Religious Reasons and Gods*, pp. 153–5. This provides a further example of how one and the same argument can be deployed to serve different purposes. Yet another example is furnished by the arguments over omnipotence discussed in Chapter 1. These arguments can be used intramurally to settle disputes between those who agree that God is omnipotent but disagree about that property's nature. They can also be used extramurally to defuse attacks on the coherence of the concept of omnipotence by nontheists. Or they can be deployed in meditation in a prayerful attempt to more clearly understand what one already firmly believes.
26. Marilyn McCord Adams, "Praying the *Proslogion*," in Thomas D. Senor (ed.), *The Rationality of Belief and the Plurality of Faith* (Ithaca, NY: Cornell University Press, 1995): 13–39, p. 14.
27. In contrast with those he deploys in his *Cur Deus Homo*.
28. Anselm, *Monologion*, chapter lxviii.
29. Adams, "Praying the *Proslogion*," pp. 14–15.
30. Marilyn McCord Adams, "*Fides Quaerens Intellectum*: St. Anselm's Method in Philosophical Theology," *Faith and Philosophy* 9 (1992): 409–35, p. 414.
31. Adams, "Praying the *Proslogion*," pp. 19, 21.
32. Adams, "*Fides Quaerens Intellectum*," pp. 412, 418.

33. *Plato's Epistles*, trans., with critical essays and notes, by Glenn R, Morrow (Indianapolis, IN: Bobbs-Merrill, 1962), pp. 240–1. Lynceus was an Argonaut noted for keenness of sight.

34. Blaise Pascal, *Pensees,* trans. W. F. *Trotter* (New York: Random House, 1941). The numbers in the text refer to the number of the fragment (in the Brunschvicg ordering).

35. William James, *The Varieties of Religious Experience* (New York: Modern Library, c1902), pp. 429 and 422 (my emphasis).

36. While I have focused on the use of argument by Eastern and Western theists, the deployment of arguments is also an essential part of a number of nontheistic spiritual disciplines as well. The Madhyamikas are an example. Proofs are marshaled to demonstrate the incoherence of the concepts used to structure sense impressions (such as the concept of cause or the concept of substance) and thereby reveal the emptiness (*shunya*) of things. For when conceptual thinking is abandoned, the suchness of things (*tathata*) is then revealed in a nondual and nonconceptual intuition called "the perfection of wisdom (*prajna paramita*)" – an insight into the nature of reality that frees us from the ignorance (*avidya*) and thirst (*trishna*) that bind us to *samsara* (the wheel of birth and rebirth).

37. Austin Warren, *New England Saints* (Ann Arbor: University of Michigan Press, 1956), p. 24. Quotations from Stowe are from the Library of America edition of *Uncle Tom's Cabin, The Minister's Wooing, and Oldtown Folks* (New York, 1982, pp. 539f., 541, 565. Note that Mayhew and Hopkins were real persons. Hopkins, in particular, was, arguably, Jonathan Edwards's most distinguished student.

38. See, for example, the introduction to *The Works of Jonathan Edwards,* vol. 10, *Sermons and Discourses 1720–1723*, Wilson A. Kimnach (ed.) (New Haven, CT: Yale University Press, 1992), p. 33f.

39. Warren, *New England Saints*, p. 28f.

40. Perry Miller, *The New England Mind: The Seventeenth Century* (Boston: Beacon Press, 1961), p. 114.

41. George I. Mavrodes, "On the Very Strongest Arguments," in Eugene Thomas Long (ed.), *Prospects for Natural Theology* (Washington, DC: Catholic University of America Press, 1992).

42. Mavrodes, "On the Very Strongest Arguments," pp. 81–2.

43. Mavrodes, "On the Very Strongest Arguments," pp. 88–9.

44. "A propositional term is one that can reasonably fill the blank" in a sentence of the "form 'p ... is –,'" where p ranges over propositions. Mavrodes, *Belief in God*, p. 36.

45. Mavrodes, *Belief in God*, pp. 36–7, 39–40.

46. Mavrodes, *Belief in God*, p. 32.

47. Mavrodes, *Belief in God*, p. 34.

48. For the soundness of an argument is a function of the truth of its premises and its validity, and "truth" and "validity" aren't subjective propositional concepts.

49. "Knowledge" is a mixed concept because it contains both objective and subjective elements. "A knows that p," for example, entails that p is true and that A believes p.

50. Philosophically sophisticated contemporary nonbelievers, for example, typically reject the argument's first premise (that a thing's existence is either self-explanatory or explained by the causal action of another existent).

51. "In the relative sense, then, the sense in which we contrast reality with unreality, and in which one thing is said to have more reality than another, and to be more

believed, reality means simply relation to our emotional and active life. This is the only sense the word ever has in the mouths of practical men. In this sense, whatever excites and stimulates our interest is real" (William James, *Principles of Psychology*, vol. 2 [Cambridge, MA: Harvard University Press, 1981], p. 924). Again, "the *fons et origo* of all reality from the absolute or practical point of view, is thus subjective, is ourselves.... A whole system may be real if it only hangs to our Ego by one immediately stinging term." We feel "our own present reality with absolutely coercive force," and "ascribe an all but equal degree of reality, first, to whatever things we lay hold on with a sense of personal need, and second, to whatever further things continuously belong with these.... The world of living realities ... is thus anchored in the Ego, considered as an active and emotional term" (James, *Principles of Psychology*, vol. 2, pp. 925–6).

52. Arguments for solipsism are an example. If our interests and purposes are those of most normal men and women, arguments for solipsism will seem frivolous. (Cf. Samuel Johnson's response to Berkeley's arguments for subjective idealism.)

53. See my *Philosophy of Religion*, 2nd ed. (Belmont, CA: Wadsworth, 1999), pp. 178–87.

54. More accurately, I believe that some modal arguments, and a suitably qualified version of Clarke's argument, are sound.

55. Both Kant and Bernard Lonergan speak of reason's "unrestricted desire to know" (although Lonergan thinks that this desire can be partially satisfied by classical theistic proofs and Kant does not). And many modern Thomists believe that cosmological arguments such as Aquinas's Five Ways, are rooted in pre-philosophical experiences of the world's contingency. (See Jacque Maritain's *Approaches to God* [New York: Collier, 1962], for an example.)

56. John Henry Newman, "Love the Safeguard of Faith against Superstition," in *Fifteen Sermons Preached before the University of Oxford* (Oxford, 1843; reprint, Westminster, MD: Christian Classics, 1966), p. 226.

57. John Henry Newman, *An Essay in Aid of a Grammar of Assent* (London, 1870; reprint Notre Dame, IN: University of Notre Dame Press, 1979), p. 318.

58. See Adams, "Praying the *Proslogion*," p. 25, footnotes 148–50, for examples; or the scriptural citations listed on pp. 273–74 of *The Prayers and Meditations of St. Anselm with the Proslogion*, trans. and with an introduction by Sister Benedicta Ward (London: Penguin, 1973).

59. Clayton, *Religious Reasons and Gods*, pp. 172–3.

60. Clayton, *Religious Reasons and Gods*, pp. 173–4).

61. Buddhist or Mormon textual traditions, for example, or those of Advaita Vedanta.

62. Eileen Sweeny ("The Rhetoric of Prayer and Argument in Anselm," *Philosophy and Rhetoric* 38 [2005], pp. 357–60) argues that Anselm's prayers, on the one hand, and his theoretical works such as the *Monologion* and *Proslogion*, on the other, trace a similar trajectory – from a soul's infinite distance from the God for whom it yearns to intimacy or union with him. For example, with respect to prayer, "the very greatness of God, the absolute and infinite goodness of God that so separates the sinner from God, opens up the possibility of union with God." Anselm's prayers stress the depth of, and horror at, his own sin. Yet, "ultimately, the [very] condition that makes the sinner's salvation impossible," namely, the infinite distance between God's greatness and goodness and his own wretchedness, "is exactly what makes it possible, [for] to think his salvation impossible is to place limits on the mercy and

power of God." Analogously, while the theoretical works stress reason's inability to penetrate or comprehend the infinite and thus satisfy the demands of the pious intellect, they simultaneously insist that in establishing that (as the *Proslogion* XV has it) God is greater than can be thought, we at least in part achieve what we sought, namely, an understanding of God's unsurpassable greatness. In neither case is union fully achieved, however. "The prayers do not end in the ecstasy of union with God or even the calm certainty of future deliverance," but "instead in desire and tears." (Thus Anselm prays, "Give me O Lord, in this exile, the bread of tears and sorrow for which I hunger more than for copious delicacies." Similarly, the ecstasy of union Anselm has sought in his desire to know God is enjoyed only proleptically: "Let me progress in knowledge of you here, and there be full; so that here my joy may be in great hope, and there in full reality."

63. Thomas Nagel, *The Last Word* (New York: Oxford University Press, 1997), p. 130.

64. See also William James, who asserts that "among all sensations, the *most* belief-compelling are those productive of pleasure or pain." James, *Principles of Psychology*, vol. 2, p. 934.

65. *Plato's Phaedo*, trans., with an introduction and commentary by R. Hackforth (Indianapolis, IN: Bobbs-Merrill, 1955), p. 93 (*Phaedo* 83, C and D).

66. Mark Wynn, *Emotional Experience and Religious Understanding: Integrating Perception, Conception, and Feeling* (Cambridge: Cambridge University Press, 2005), pp. 135–6f. Wynn thinks that we can't simply set these pre-theoretical readings of the world aside since they "tend to be too deeply engrained for that and are anyway not readily accessible to consciousness." Nor would it be rational for us to do so even if we could. For that would mean approaching "situations without any preconception of their likely import; and that would imply that in each new circumstance, we would have no initial sense of what is at stake and what in particular deserves attention [which in turn would mean that in each new situation] we would ... need to work through an indefinitely extended review of" all its features "before reaching any conclusion about its overall character and what it may require of us in the way of action." The result would be paralysis and endless postponement of decision. The "*practically* rational" (my emphasis) course therefore "is to allow ourselves to be governed by affectively toned" readings of the general character of experience "in the first instance ... [T]hey provide a way of interpreting the world that is prima facie [although perhaps not ultima facie] justified" (Wynn, *Emotional Experience*, pp. 137–8). Wynn's book touches on many of the themes addressed in the present volume and is highly recommended.

67. Including alleged disproofs of the existence of God or any kind of "higher universe" (James).

3 Religious Reading and Theological Argument

1. Sister Benedicta Ward, S. L. G., introduction to *The Prayers and Meditations of Anselm with the Proslogion* (London: Penguin, 1973), p. 28f.

2. Quoted in Ward, *Prayers and Meditations*, p. 36. In both private prayer books, and choir psalters, the psalms "were copied with 'psalter collects,' short prayers in the form of a roman collect in which the Old Testament words were given a New Testament meaning."

3. Ward, *Prayers and Meditations*, pp. 43–4.
4. Paul J. Griffiths, *Religious Reading: The Place of Reading in the Practice of Religion* (New York: Oxford University Press, 1999), p. 43 (Griffiths's translation).
5. Ward, *Prayers and Meditations*, p. 44, where she also notes that the theology of the church fathers "was continually rising up into prayer, or rather there is no distinction between the two. In Cyprian, Irenaeus, and especially Origen, prayer welled up spontaneously as they wrote their commentaries. Their theology … was a hymn, a prayer, the point where knowledge and love become praise."
6. Griffiths, *Religious Reading*, pp. 42–3.
7. In the seventh century, the Buddhist monastery of Nalanda had a "permanent monastic population … in the thousands," and "about a … hundred separate classes were given each day … [T]he monastic complex contained a number of large, square courtyards, open in the center … with seven or eight [monastic] cells on a side." Classes "consisted of a discourse delivered by a teacher from a raised platform." While the teacher may have had a manuscript before him, he probably most often quoted "the work from memory, and then [gave an] oral exposition." The works were thus essentially stored and transmitted memorially (Griffiths, *Religious Reading*, pp. 118, 120–3).
8. Griffiths, *Religious Reading*, pp. 38, 128.
9. Griffiths, *Religious Reading*, pp. 161–3.
10. Griffiths, *Religious Reading*, p. 52. It is important to note that illiteracy was common among religious "professionals" as well as among the laity. See, for example, Douglas Burton-Christie, *The Word in the Desert: Scripture and the Quest for Holiness in Early Christian Monasticism* (New York: Oxford University Press, 1993). Although the Bible "as written word" had a "formative influence" on many of the desert fathers, it probably wasn't "the primary means of access to" it for most of them. "Rather, the monks most often encountered and appropriated the Word through *hearing* the scriptures at the weekly *synaxis* [or gathering] and from the lips of the elders. Beyond this, the monks were encouraged to prolong their encounter with the Word … through memorization, continual recitation, meditation, and rumination, appropriating the Word at the deepest level of their being." Indeed, scriptural meditation itself was a largely "oral phenomenon," consisting in "the utterance, or exclamation of words, which were gradually digested and interiorized" (pp. 117, 123; emphasis in the original text).
11. Griffiths, *Religious Reading*, pp. 46–7.
12. Griffiths, *Religious Reading*, pp. 103, 65, 167–8. Excerpts were not always short, however. The *Speculum de Scriptura Sacra* (*A Mirror of Sacred Scripture*), attributed to Augustine, contains a number of long excerpts, including almost the whole of the Sermon on the Mount (Matthew 5–7).
13. "Medieval Indian Buddhist works," for example, "often signaled excerpts by such devices as *sutrokta* ['it is said in a sutra'], or *ity eke* ['some say'].… Similarly, Latin Christian anthologies (at least until the twelfth century) … tend to signal their excerpts by such devices as *origenes dixit* ['Origen said'] with no indication of where or when." Griffiths, *Religious Reading*, p. 102.
14. Griffiths, *Religious Reading*, p. 55.
15. Francis X. Clooney, S. J., *Comparative Theology: Deep Learning across Religious Borders* (Oxford: Wiley-Blackwell, 2010), p. 6of.

16. Quoted from Santideva's anthology, the *Suksasamuccaya,* in Griffiths, *Religious Reading,* p. 66.
17. Griffiths, *Religious Reading,* p. 160. Why idolatrous? Presumably because they are assigned a truth and importance denied them by the Christian scheme of things.
18. John Clayton, *Religions, Reasons and Gods: Essays in Cross-Cultural Philosophy of Religion* (Cambridge: Cambridge University Press, 2006), pp. 158–9. For example, much of Udayana's case against the Buddhist *anatman* (no-self) doctrine is built on the fact that the Vedas (which are not accepted as authoritative by Buddhists) "clearly and consistently" teach an *atman* doctrine.
19. Francis X. Clooney, S. J., *Beyond Compare: St. Francis de Sales and Sri Vedanta Dasika on Loving Surrender to God* (Washington, D. C.: Georgetown University Press, 2008), p. 33.
20. Dasika, quoted in Clooney, *Beyond Compare,* p. 50f.
21. Pierre Hadot, *Philosophy as a Way of Life,* edited and with an introduction by Arnold I. Davidson (Oxford: Blackwell, 1995), p. 74.
22. Though not only that, for those who have ingested the tradition allegedly *experience* their intrinsic luminosity.
23. And if Hadot is right (as I believe he is), something like this is also true of major philosophical schools of late antiquity. Buddhism is sometimes said to be an exception, for the Buddha's teachings can be authenticated by argument and one's own experience. But in practice, the Buddhist sutras are treated as revelation. Note that (as we shall see in Chapter 6) revelation doesn't necessarily presuppose a revealer. The Mimansa school of Vedanta claims that the Vedas are an example.
24. Secular traditions arguably display analogues of the first and third features. Empirico-analytic traditions are buttressed by appeals to empirico-analytic arguments. Continental philosophical traditions are buttressed by the sorts of arguments valorized by continental philosophers. And both sets of arguments are arguably circular.
25. Richard Fox Young, *Resistant Hinduism: Sanskrit Sources on Anti-Christian Apologetics in Early Nineteenth-Century India* (Vienna: Publications of the De Nobili Research Library, 1981), p. 139.
26. Young, *Resistant Hinduism,* p. 136.
27. Francis X. Clooney, S. J., *Hindu God, Christian God: How Reason Helps Break Down the Boundaries between Religions* (Oxford: Oxford University Press, 2001), pp. 165, 8.
28. Clooney, *Hindu God,* p. 9.
29. "A home religion is the one you belong to if you belong to one at all," and "alien religions … are any you do not belong to." Paul J. Griffiths, *Problems of Religious Diversity* (Malden, MA and Oxford: Blackwell, 2001), p. xiv.
30. James L. Frederick, "Introduction," in Francis X. Clooney (ed.), *The New Comparative Theology: Interreligious Insights from the Next Generation* (London and New York: T. & T. Clark, 2010), pp. xii–xiv.
31. Nicholas of Cusa, *Nicholas of Cusa's De Pace Fidei and Cribratio Alkorani: Translation and Analysis,* by Jasper Hopkins, 2nd ed. (Minneapolis, MN: Arthur J. Banning Press, 1994), p. 34.
32. Thus, in support of the claim that, appearances notwithstanding, Islam's core doctrinal claims are essentially identical with Christian ones, Nicholas cites "excellent books" whose authors (e.g., Marcus Varo and Eusebius) suggest that religions are

divided by a diversity of rites rather than by a diversity of doctrines. Nicholas, *De Pace Fidei*, p. 68.

33. Clooney, *Hindu God*, pp. 10–11.
34. Clooney, *Beyond Compare*, p. 79.
35. Frederick, "Introduction," p. xiii (my emphases).
36. Clooney, *Hindu God*, pp. 173, 177.
37. Hugh Nicholson, "The New Comparative Theology and the Problem of Theological Hegemonism," in Clooney, *Comparative Theology*, p. 59.
38. Nicholson, "The New Comparative Theology," pp. 60–2.
39. Clooney, *Hindu God*, pp. 167, 26,
40. Clooney, *Hindu God*, pp. 103, 106, 108.
41. Either because God's bodies aren't composed of the three constituents out of which everything in the space-time world is woven, or because it is fashioned out of only one of them, namely, "pure-being [*sattva*] … without passionate energy [*rajas*] and dark lethargy [*tamas*]." Clooney, *Hindu God*, p. 117f.
42. Clooney, *Hindu God*, pp. 116, 119.
43. A Christian, for example, and a Shri Vaishnava or other Hindu monotheist.
44. Nicholson, "The New Comparative Theology," pp. 54–5 (my emphasis). The pandits who opposed Muir are one example. Some Christian and Muslim fundamentalists and a number of the Jewish "ultra-orthodox" provide others.
45. John Cobb, *Beyond Dialogue: Toward a Mutual Transformation of Christianity and Buddhism* (Philadelphia: Fortress Press, 1982), p. 30.
46. Doctrinal exclusivists maintain that the central claims of one's home religion are true and that the claims of alien religions that conflict with them are false. Doctrinal exclusivism should be distinguished from salvific exclusivism. Salvific exclusivists insist that salvation can be found only in their home religion. While doctrinal exclusivists *may* be salvific exclusivists, many are not. The practice of comparative theology doesn't foreground the issue of doctrinal truth. It also pays more attention than is customary to truths conveyed by images and poetry (and one might add, by meditational and devotional practice) that cannot be reduced to abstract doctrinal propositions. It does not follow that questions of doctrinal truth are denigrated or permanently set aside, however, or that some doctrinal claims aren't essential parts of the confessional packages to which the participants in these interreligious dialogues are committed, or that the claims in question don't sometimes conflict. Its confessional component thus does commit comparative theologians to a mild form of doctrinal exclusivism.
47. Cobb, *Beyond Dialogue*, pp. 30–1.
48. Roughly speaking, the equal weight view requires assigning as much weight to the opinion of one's epistemic peers as to one's own in cases of conflict. (One's epistemic peers are – again roughly – those whose intelligence, training, information, and experience in dealing with the subject matter are more or less on a par with one's own.)
49. *And* with respect to basic moral, aesthetic, political, etc., disputes.

4 Passional Reasoning

1. I owe this point to Stephen J. Wykstra. See his "Toward a Sensible Evidentialism: On the Notion of 'Needing Evidence,' " in William L. Rowe and William J. Wainwright

(eds.), *Philosophy of Religion: Selected Readings.* 3rd ed. (Fort Worth, TX: Harcourt Brace, 1998), pp. 481–91.

2. William Wainwright, *Reason and the Heart: A Prolegomenon to a Critique of Passional Reason* (Ithaca, NY: Cornell University Press, 1995).

3. John Locke's view is an example of the first. The views of Kierkegaard, Pascal, and William James are usually (and wrongly, in my opinion) regarded as examples of the second.

4. John Calvin, *Institutes of the Christian Religion,* vol. 1 (Grand Rapids, MI: Eerdmans, 1957), book 1, chap. 7, sec. 3.

5. Thomas Aquinas, *The Summa Theologica,* vol. 2 (New York: Benziger, 1947), part II–II, quest. 6, art. 1.

6. John Spurr, "Rational Religion in Restoration England," *Journal of the History of Ideas* 49 (1988), p. 580. The internal quote is from Robert South, *Sermons,* vol. 1 (Oxford, 1842), p. 116.

7. Jonathan Edwards, "Miscellany 782," in *The Works of Jonathan Edwards,* vol. 18, *The Miscellanies 501–832,* Ava Chamberlain (ed.) (New Haven, CT: Yale University Press, 2001), p. 457.

8. True benevolence consists in the "love of being in general," that is, of God and the things that depend upon God, in proportion to their worth.

9. The quotations are from Edwards, "Miscellany 782"; Edwards, *A Treatise concerning Religious Affections,* in *The Works of Jonathan Edwards,* vol. 2, *Religious Affections,* John E. Smith (ed.) (New Haven, CT: Yale University Press, 1959), pp. 260, 205; and Edwards, *The Nature of True Virtue,* in *The Works of Jonathan Edwards,* vol. 8, *Ethical Writings,* Paul Ramsey (ed.) (New Haven, CT: Yale University Press, 1989), p. 548.

10. Edwards, *Religious Affections,* pp. 272, 302; 274, 301; 302.

11. Edwards, "A Divine and Supernatural Light," in *The Works of Jonathan Edwards,* vol. 17, *Sermons and Discourses 1730–1733,* Wilson H. Kimnach (ed.) (New Haven, CT: Yale University Press, 1999), pp. 413, 422; Edwards, *Religious Affections,* p. 298.

12. Quoted in G. Nuttall, *The Holy Spirit in Puritan Faith and Experience* (Chicago and London: University of Chicago Press, 1992), pp. 23, 29.

13. Edwards, "A Divine and Supernatural Light," p. 413.

14. Edwards, *Religious Affections,* pp. 298–9.

15. Edwards, *True Virtue,* p. 620.

16. For a discussion of these arguments, see Wainwright, *Reason and the Heart,* pp. 34–8.

17. Jonathan Edwards, "Of Atoms," in *The Works of Jonathan Edwards,* vol. 6, *Scientific and Philosophical Writings,* Wallace E. Anderson (ed.) (New Haven, CT: Yale University Press, 1980), pp. 215–16.

18. Edwards, *Religious Affections,* p. 201 (my emphasis).

19. Edwards, *Treatise on Grace,* in *The Works of Jonathan Edwards,* vol. 21, *Writings on the Trinity, Grace, and Faith,* Sang Hyun Lee (ed.) (New Haven, CT: Yale University Press, 2003), p. 194 (my emphases).

20. God "is in effect being in general." Edwards, *True Virtue,* p. 621. Since God is the only true substance and the only true cause, created beings are no more than God's "shadows" or "images," absolutely and immediately dependent on him for both their being and their qualities.

21. Jonathan Edwards, "Discourse on the Trinity," in *Works of Jonathan Edwards,* vol. 21, pp. 123f, 125 (my emphasis).

22. Their acts *count* as the other's.

23. "Illative" was "defined in contemporary dictionaries [from 1864 and 1901] in terms of 'inference; deduction; conclusion.'" David A. Pailin, *The Way to Faith* (London: Epworth Press, 1969), p. 144.

24. John Henry Newman, *An Essay in Aid of a Grammar of Assent* (London 1870; reprint, Notre Dame, IN: University of Notre Dame Press, 1979), p. 284.

25. If we did not, "I do not see how we could conduct an argument at all; our way would be blocked up by extravagant principles and theories, gratuitous hypotheses, ... unsupported statements," and the like. Newman, *Grammar of Assent*, p. 293.

26. Newman, *Grammar of Assent*, p. 233.

27. John Henry Newman, "Love, the Safeguard of Faith against Superstition," in *Fifteen Sermons Preached before the University of Oxford* (Oxford, 1843; reprint. Westminster, MD: Christian Classics, 1966), p. 226.

28. Newman, *Grammar of Assent*, p. 294.

29. Newman, *Grammar of Assent*, p. 245.

30. Newman, "Love," p. 227.

31. Newman, *Grammar of Assent*, p. 281.

32. Newman, *Grammar of Assent*, p. 318 (my emphases).

33. Newman, *Grammar of Assent*, pp. 217–22, 235–7, 259.

34. Hugo M. de Achaval and J. Derek Holmes (eds.) *The Theological Papers of John Henry Newman on Faith and Certainty* (Oxford: Clarendon Press, 1976), p. 108.

35. Newman, *Grammar of Assent*, pp. 142–3.

36. Newman, *Grammar of Assent*, p. 82.

37. Newman, *Grammar of Assent*, p. 290.

38. Newman, *Grammar of Assent*, p. 283.

39. de Achaval and Holmes (eds.), *Theological Papers*, p. 27 (my emphasis).

40. Newman, *Grammar of Assent*, p. 300 (my emphasis).

41. de Achaval and Holmes (eds.), *Theological Papers*, pp. 70–9.

42. Newman, *Grammar of Assent*, p. 248.

43. Just as we "instinctively" infer "the fact of a multiform and vast world, material and mental" from the "phenomena of sense," and just as a child instinctively recognizes in the "smiles and frowns" of a face "not only a being external to himself but one whose looks elicit in him confidence or fear," so we spontaneously infer God's existence from "particular acts of conscience" (Newman, *Grammar of Assent*, pp. 67–8; see also pp. 97, 102). Our experience of guilt and moral inadequacy "instinctively" suggests the presence of a "moral governor" and "judge."

44. Newman, *Grammar of Assent*, p. 318.

45. Newman, *Grammar of Assent*, pp. 300–31.

46. Newman, *Grammar of Assent*, pp. 254–6.

47. de Achaval and Holmes (eds.), *Theological Papers,* p. 92.

48. Newman, *Grammar of Assent*, p. 270.

49. Newman, *Grammar of Assent*, p. 272.

50. Newman, *Grammar of Assent*, p. 273.

51. Newman, *Grammar of Assent*, p. 275.

52. Newman, *Grammar of Assent*, pp. 320–1.

53. Newman, *Grammar of Assent*, p. 275.

54. Newman, *Grammar of Ascent*, p. 252.
55. Newman, *Grammar of Ascent*, p. 253.
56. William James, *Essays in Philosophy* (Cambridge, MA: Harvard University Press, 1978), p. 11.
57. William James, *Principles of Psychology*, vol. II (New York, 1890; reprint, New York: Dover, 1950), p. 335.
58. William James, *The Meaning of Truth* (New York, 1907; reprint, Cambridge, MA: Harvard University Press, 1975), pp. 41–2.
59. William James, "The Dilemma of Determinism," in *The Will to Believe and Other Essays in Popular Philosophy* (New York, c1896; reprint, New York: Dover, 1956), p. 147; William James, "The Sentiment of Rationality," in *The Will to Believe*, p. 77.
60. James, "Sentiment of Rationality," pp. 92–3.
61. James, "Sentiment of Rationality," p. 70.
62. Roughly, the generally admitted facts of science and common sense; the facts about which there is no real dispute.
63. William James, *A Pluralistic Universe* (New York, 1909, reprint, New York: Longmans, Green, 1947), p. 23.
64. James, "Sentiment of Rationality," p. 89.
65. James, *Pluralistic Universe*, p. 10.
66. William James, *Pragmatism* (New York, 1907; reprint, New York: Meridian, 1955), p. 18.
67. James, *Pluralistic Universe*, p. 140.
68. Pluralism is the contradictory of monism.
69. William James, *Essays in Religion and Morality* (Cambridge, MA: Harvard University Press, 1982), pp. 61–2.
70. Mark Wynn has called our attention to the work of Ronald de Sousa. De Sousa believes that emotions "constitute patterns of salience. To register some feature of a situation emotionally is to accord that feature weight, or to judge it to have some importance." In this way, emotions select an "agenda" for thought by focusing our attention on a certain object and highlighting some of its features rather than others. Emotions thus "play a role akin to that of scientific paradigms [in Kuhn's sense]: 'paying attention to things is a source of reasons but comes before them' … they identify certain lines of enquiry, and certain kinds of question, as potentially more fruitful then others." Mark Wynn, *Emotional Experience and Religious Understanding: Integrating Perception, Conception and Feeling* (Cambridge: Cambridge University Press, 2005), pp. 102–3. (The internal quote is from de Sousa, "The Rationality of Emotions," in Amelie Rorty [ed.], *Explaining Emotions* [Berkeley, CA: University of California Press, 1980], p. 139.) See Thomas S. Kuhn, *The Structure of Scientific Revolutions*. 2nd ed. enlarged (Chicago: University of Chicago Press, 1970). Emotions can also affect our weightings of pieces of evidence, as Wynn notes on pages 140–1. An angry person, for example, may place more weight on the evidence that suggests that he has been wrongly offended and less weight on the evidence that exonerates or lessens the blame of the alleged offender. On the other hand, a person's anger may prevent her from treating the offending behavior more lightly than it deserves. Guy Kahane has recently drawn our attention to yet another way in which our affective-laden evaluations can affect our metaphysical views ("The Value Question in Metaphysics," *Philosophy and Phenomenological Research* 85 [2012]: 27–55). We can address

the question of the value of possible worlds (e.g., worlds in which God or objective moral values do or do not exist) "from the standpoint of a single person's good" or from the "standpoint of the universe," i.e., of what is good "*tout court*," and not just for me (Kahane, "The Value Question, pp. 41–2). Our evaluations of these worlds may then guide inquiry by determining what is and is not important, and therefore worth examining more carefully and in more detail. Our affectively laden evaluations differ, however, and even if some might track metaphysical truth, it is highly unlikely that they all do. As Kahane points out ("The Value Question," pp. 28f, 32–3) that dearly *wanting* something to be true isn't a good reason to believe that it *is* true. On the contrary, that we dearly want something to be true is a reason for making sure that our desires aren't causing us to misread the evidence for it. But while this is clearly true of most of the "retail" propositions that we want to be true (e.g., that my children are safe or innocent), is it clearly true of "wholesale" propositions about the nature of reality as a whole? If the world is (in James's words) "friendly" to us, then we might expect our reflective value intuitions to line up with reality. If, on the contrary, the universe is "alien" to us, we have no reason to think that our deepest intuitions about the nature of the world as a whole are trustworthy. The upshot is that not only may our evaluations partly determine what metaphysical systems we believe to be true, what metaphysical systems turn out to be true will determine which evaluations track the truth and which do not.

71. William James, "The Will to Believe," in *The Will to Believe*, p. 11.
72. James, "Will to Believe," p. 22 (my emphasis).
73. James, "Will to Believe," pp. 1–2 (my emphasis).
74. William James, *The Varieties of Religious Experience* (New York: Modern Library, c1902), pp. 424, 426, 428, 430 (my emphasis).
75. Hegelian dialectic or F. H. Bradley's logic, in which what is not included in a concept is excluded by it.
76. James, *Pragmatism*, pp. 57–8, 60.
77. William James, *Some Problems in Philosophy* (New York, 1911; reprint, Cambridge: Harvard University Press, 1979), pp. 70–4.
78. James, *Pluralistic Universe*, p. 49.
79. James, *Pluralistic Universe*, p. 52.
80. James, *Varieties of Religious Experience*, p. 475.
81. James, *Varieties of Religious Experience*, p. 505.
82. James, *Varieties of Religious Experience*, p. 506.
83. James, *Varieties of Religious Experience*, pp. 507, 515.
84. James, *Varieties of Religious Experience*, pp. 445–6.
85. James, *Essays in Religion and Morality*, p. 127.
86. James, *Varieties of Religious Experience*, pp. 414, 418. Why classify mystical experience as "subjective" evidence? The fact that I had a mystical experience should be distinguished from the mystical experience itself. The latter may be "subjective" evidence but the former is not. That I had a mystical experience (if I did) is as hard and objective a fact as the fact that I had measles. Furthermore, James himself believes that mystical states should have some authority over nonmystics and that interpretations to the contrary are mistaken. What he denies is that they "have a right to be *absolutely* authoritative over the" nonmystic; that nonmystics have "a *duty* ... to accept their revelations uncritically." Those who are not mystics must "sift and test" them as we sift and test "what *comes from the outer world of sense*"

(James, *Varieties of Religious Experience*, pp. 414, 417–18, my emphases). The only claim that James rejects is the claim that mystical experience's prima facie weight is sufficiently strong to *close* the issue for nonmystics.

87. James, *Varieties of Religious Experience*, pp. 427, 429.
88. The objective evidence does rule out some hypotheses, however. James thinks, for example, that "healthy-minded" religions such as Christian Science fudge the facts by denying the existence of real evil.
89. James, *Varieties of Religious Experience,* pp. 480–1.
90. James, *Varieties of Religious Experience,* pp. 489, 492.
91. James, *Varieties of Religious Experience,* p. 497.
92. James, *Varieties of Religious Experience,* pp. 495, 497.
93. James, *Varieties of Religious Experience,* p. 501.
94. James, *Varieties of Religious Experience,* p. 509 (my emphases).
95. James, *Varieties of Religious Experience,* p. 513.
96. As Peter Madden points out in his introduction to the Harvard edition of *The Will to Believe and Other Essays in Popular Philosophy*, James had a weak and strong version of his will to believe doctrine – that we have a *right* to believe either alternative in the cases in question; and that, because of certain features of our passional nature, we *should* believe one alternative rather than the other. He stresses the first when speaking to the "tough-minded" and the second when speaking to the "tender-minded." On the whole, James seems committed to the stronger version.
97. James, "Sentiment of Rationality," p. 93.
98. James, "Sentiment of Rationality," pp. 93–4 (my emphasis).
99. James, *Meaning of Truth*, p. 5.
100. James, *Meaning of Truth*, pp. 140–1.
101. James, "Will to Believe," p. 29.
102. James, "Sentiment of Rationality," p. 93.
103. James, *Pluralistic Universe*, pp. 328–9.
104. William James, "The Dilemma of Determinism," in *Will to Believe*, pp. 177–8.
105. Satisfactions include achieving consistency, fulfilled expectations, satisfied emotional needs, felt "congruity with our residual beliefs," and so on.
106. James, "Sentiment of Rationality," p. 88.
107. William James, "Is Life Worth Living?" in *Will to Believe,* p. 62. Cf. "It is more probable that to the end of time our power of moral and rational response to the nature of things will be our deepest organ of communication therewith that we shall ever possess" (William James, "Reflex Action and Theism," in *Will to Believe,* p. 141).
108. James, "Reflex Action, p. 125.
109. James, "Reflex Action, p. 116.
110. James, "Sentiment of Rationality," p. 89.
111. James, *Pluralistic Universe*, p. 33.
112. James, *Pragmatism*, p. 188.
113. Meliorism is the view that the world can be progressively made better by human effort.
114. Agreement with sense perception, logical coherence, congruity with our other beliefs, and so on.

115. "Our satisfactions" are "possibly true guides to [truer beliefs about reality], not ... guides true solely *for us*" (James, *Meaning of Truth*, p. 105).

116. Foundationalists claim that one is only rationally justified in believing self-evident propositions and propositions that can be validly inferred from them. Yet because this claim is neither self-evident nor entailed or inductively implied by self-evident propositions, it fails to meet its own standard.

117. *Pragmatism* and other late works clearly evince James's belief that the pragmatic method can do a better job of resolving outstanding metaphysical disputes. And in *The Varieties of Religious Experience*, James expresses the hope that the "science of religions" can "help to bring about consensus of opinion" on (at least some) religious issues.

118. All quotations in this and the next paragraph are from David W. Tien, "Warranted Neo-Confucian Belief: Religious Pluralism and the Affections in the Epistemologies of Wang Yangming and Alvin Plantinga," *International Journal for the Philosophy of Religion* 55 (2004): 31–55.

119. "The mind in its original state ... or the original mind."

120. "The Nature endowed in us by Heaven is pure and perfect. The fact that it is intelligent, clear, and not beclouded is evidence of the emanation and revelation of the highest good.... As the highest good emanates and reveals itself, we will consider right as right and wrong as wrong. Things of greater or less importance and situations of grave or light character will [then] be [appropriately] responded to as they act upon us" (Wang Yangming, *Inquiry on the Great Learning*, in *Instructions for Practical Living, and Other Neo-Confucian Writings: by Wang Yangming, 1472–1529*, Wing-tsit Chan [trans.], [New York: Columbia University Press, 1963], p. 274). Wang "referred to" the *liangzhi* "in negative terms, as the Taoist 'Void' (*hsu*) and the Buddhist 'Nothingness' (*wu*)," and identified it with the Great Void (*T'ai-hsu*) of the Sung philosophers, which he said "embraces all things without letting anything become a hindrance to itself" (Wang Yangming, *Wen-ch'eng kung ch'uan-shu* ["the so-called *Complete Works of Wang Yang-ming*"] 6:217). "The vacuity of *liangzhi* is [one with] the vacuity of the Great Void.... The nothingness ... of *liangzhi* is the formlessness of the Great Void. Sun, moon, wind, thunder, mountains, rivers, people, and things – all that have figure, shape, form and color – all operate within this formlessness of the Great Void. None of them ever becomes a hindrance to Heaven. The sage merely follows the function of his *liangzhi*. Heaven, Earth, and the myriad things are all contained in its functioning and operating. How [then] can there be anything else transcending the *liangzhi* which can become a hindrance [to it]?" (Wang, *Wen-ch'eng* 3; 142). Julia Ching, *To Acquire Wisdom: The Way of Wang Yangming* (New York: Columbia University Press, 1976), pp. 139–40.

121. Not just selfishness in the usual sense but any affective orientation that makes oneself the center of existence.

122. Louis Pojman, *Religious Belief and the Will* (London: Routledge and Kegan Paul, 1986), pp. 172–5.

123. For a fuller discussion of the charge of subjectivism, see Wainwright, *Reason and the Heart*, pp. 109–15.

124. William P. Alston, "Epistemic Circularity," *Philosophy and Phenomenological Research* 47 (1986): 1–30.

125. In an important recent paper, Danielle Sgaravatti has suggested that "an argument A is circular relative to an evidential state E if and only if in order for a subject S in E to have a justified belief in each one of A's premises, it is necessary that S has a justified belief in A's conclusion" (*"Petitio Principii*: A Bad Form of Reasoning," *Mind* 122 [July 2013]: 749–79, p. 759). Edwards's argument isn't circular in this sense. Having a justified belief in the argument's conclusion isn't a necessary condition of having a justified belief in the truth of its premises because those premises have other grounds, and these grounds are, arguably, sufficient. One *might* argue that a belief in Edwards's conclusion is a necessary condition of having a justified belief that his argument has sufficient force to make a belief in its conclusion reasonable. But even that is doubtful. For it is doubtful that I need to *believe* antecedently the conclusion (let alone *reasonably* believe it) to believe justifiably that Edwards's premises make his conclusion more probable than not. This does not mean that his argument is without problems, however, as we shall see in a moment.

126. Peter Kung and Masahiro Yamada ("A Neglected Way of Begging the Question," *American Philosophical Quarterly* 47 [2010]: 287–93) have recently shown that noncircular arguments can beg the question. They offer an example in which the question is begged because the *procedure* used in establishing the argument's conclusion presupposes its truth even though the *premises* of the argument do not. While this point is related to mine, it is distinct from it. True benevolence and other relevant affections are not procedures (such as arguing to the best explanation) but the cause of a way of deploying them.

127. As Louis Pojman and Richard Swinburne suggest. See Pojman, *Religious Belief and the Will*, p. 177; and Richard Swinburne, *Faith and Reason* (Oxford: Clarendon Press, 1981), p. 22.

128. True benevolence's assessment of the evidence is not a nonrational ground for belief. It does not lead the saints to construct new inductive or deductive standards, forget about some of the evidence, or engage in selective investigation. Nor does it provide them with a reason for doing so True benevolence is not a nonrational ground for belief because it is not a *ground* for belief at all, although its presence does partially explain why the saints hold the beliefs they do. In the same way, a good scientist's impartiality, intellectual honesty, and desire for the truth help explain why she holds the beliefs she does and not the views of some less scrupulous or more credulous colleague. But they are not grounds for her belief. (It should be noted, however, that Edwards does seem to regard his "new spiritual sensation" as a fresh piece of evidence. The perception of true beauty is nonetheless distinct from the new spiritual disposition [namely, true benevolence] that is the "mechanism" underlying it.)

129. And we cannot assume it is false without begging the question.

130. This sentence relies heavily on Alston, "Epistemic Circularity."

131. Michael Smith, "Virtuous Circles," *Southern Journal of Philosophy* 25 (1987): 207–20.

132. Cf. Andrew D. Cling, "Justification-Affording Circular Arguments," *Philosophical Studies* 111 (2002): 251–74. For this consideration to carry any weight with the theist's critics, however, they must concede that (1) there is a nonnegligible chance that the alleged fact obtains and that (2) the explanation has some plausibility

(although they need not concede that the fact *does* obtain or that the explanation is plausible *überhaupt*).

133. Appeals of this sort are usually implicit, of course.
134. Rowe put this objection in correspondence with me.
135. James, "Sentiment of Rationality," p. 105.
136. It may be possible in some cases to explain an opponent's resistance to an argument purporting to show that some defect places him in an inferior epistemic position without appealing to that defect. But (in the most interesting cases at least) the explanation will typically be provided by the defect that the conclusion of the disputed argument attributes to him.
137. That is, she has implicitly assumed that (e.g.) true benevolence is needed to assess properly the force of arguments to theological conclusions.
138. For a related but somewhat different point, see Michael Bergmann, "Epistemic Circularity: Malignant and Benign," *Philosophy and Phenomenological Research* 69 (2004): 709–27.
139. Does it infect all disciplines? Probably not mathematics and logic. But it does infect reasoning in the social sciences and humanities. It also infects reasoning in some of the hard sciences. Evolutionary biology and cosmology are examples.
140. Although some would. Richard Foley and Richard Fumerton are examples.

5 The Role of Rhetoric in Religious Argumentation

1. See Aristotle, *Rhetoric* 1356a, in Jonathan Barnes (ed.), *The Complete Works of Aristotle*, vol. 2 (Princeton, NJ: Princeton University Press, 1984), for a discussion of these devices. The effective speaker persuades by his "personal character," by stirring his hearer's emotions, and by "proof, or *apparent* proof" (my emphasis).
2. My account of Plato relies heavily on the work of A. E. Taylor and Gregory Vlastos. See especially the former's *Plato: The Man and His Work* (Edinburgh, 1927; reprint, New York: Meridian, 1956), and the latter's "Justice and Happiness in the Republic," in Gregory Vlastos (ed.), *Plato, a Collection of Critical Essays II: Ethics, Politics, and Philosophy of Art and Religion* (Garden City, NY: Anchor, 1971), pp. 69–95.
3. Augustine, *On Christian Doctrine*, trans. D. W. Robertson, Jr. (Indianapolis, IN: Bobbs-Merrill, 1958), pp. 118f, 121 (my emphasis).
4. Augustine, *On Christian Doctrine*, pp. 136–7.
5. Thomas Hobbes, *Leviathan* (Cambridge: Cambridge University Press, 1996), part I, chapter 4, p. 26, my emphasis.
6. Hobbes, *Leviathan*, part I, chapter 5, p. 35, my emphasis.
7. John Locke, *An Essay concerning Human Understanding* (London, 1690; reprint, New York: Dover, 1959), book III, chapter x, no. 34.
8. David Hume, "Of Miracles," part II, *An Enquiry concerning Human Understanding* (Oxford: Clarendon Press, 2000), p. 89.
9. Quoted in John Morgan, *Godly Learning: Puritan Attitudes towards Reason, Learning and Education, 1560–1640* (Cambridge: Cambridge University Press, 1986), p. 106.
10. Morgan, *Godly Learning*, p. 108.
11. Perry Miller, *The New England Mind: The Seventeenth Century* (Boston: Beacon Press, 1961), p. 300f.

12. John Edwards, *The Preacher* (London, 1705), quoted in Wilson A. Kimnach (ed.), *Sermons and Discourses 1720–1723 (The Works of Jonathan Edwards,* vol. 10) (New Haven, CT: Yale University Press, 1992), introduction, p. 33f.

13. From an ordination sermon on John 5:35 entitled "The True Excellency of a Minister of the Gospel" (1744), quoted in Kimnach, *Sermons and Discourses,* vol. 10, p. 25.

14. Jonathan Edwards, "Thoughts on the Revival of Religion in New England," in C. C. Goen (ed.), *The Great Awakening (Works of Jonathan Edwards,* vol. 4) (New Haven, CT: Yale University Press, 1972), pp. 387–8.

15. Aristotle, *Rhetoric* 1354a, in Barnes, *Complete Works,* vol. 2.

16. Robin Smith, "Dialectic," in Robert Audi (ed.), *The Cambridge Dictionary of Philosophy,* 2nd ed. (Cambridge & New York: Cambridge University Press, 1999), pp. 232–33.

17. Aristotle, *Rhetoric* 1404a, in Barnes, *Complete Works,* vol. 2.

18. Paul Ricoeur, "Between Rhetoric and Poetics," in Amelie Rorty (ed.), *Essays on Aristotle's Rhetoric* (Berkeley: University of California Press, 1996), pp. 340–41.

19. Aristotle, *Rhetoric* 1403ab, in Barnes, *Complete Works,* vol. 2.

20. Jamie Dow, "Aristotle on the Centrality of Proof to Rhetoric," *Logique & Analyse* 210 (2010): 101, 113, 109–10.

21. Ricoeur, "Between Rhetoric and Poetics," pp. 326, 342.

22. Amelie Rorty, "Aristotle on the Virtues of Rhetoric," *Review of Metaphysics* 64 (2011): 721–2.

23. Rorty, "Aristotle on the Virtues of Rhetoric," pp. 715–16, my emphasis.

24. Dow, "Aristotle on the Centrality of Proof to Rhetoric," pp. 117, 119.

25. Rorty, "Aristotle on the Virtues of Rhetoric," p. 731.

26. Namely, that the rhetorician, unlike the philosopher, isn't typically engaged in a disinterested quest for knowledge, following the argument wherever it leads.

27. The debates can of course be internal, with the investigator assuming the role of both advocate and critic.

28. Samuel Ijsseling, *Rhetoric and Philosophy in Conflict: An Historical Survey* (The Hague: Martinus Nijhoff, 1976), p. 50

29. So-called critical rhetoric "'rejects … not only universal reason, but also reason rooted in the deliberative practice of a community,' since any sort of reason whose telos is geared to 'consensus,' is tainted by the will to power.… The idea of reason has historically served the powers that be." (Satoru Aonuma, "Induction and Invention: The Toulmin Model Meets Critical Rhetoric," *The Uses of Argument: Proceedings of a Conference at McMaster University,* May 18–21, 2005, pp. 12–13.) In this connection, it is worth noting that Plato, in Book I of the *Republic* and elsewhere, associates *rhetoric* with the will to power and *opposes* it to reason or philosophy – precisely the opposite of what critical rhetoric maintains.

30. See Costica Bradatan, "Rhetoric of Faith and Patterns of Persuasion in Berkeley's Alciphron," *Heythrop Journal* 47 (2006): 544–61.

31. Matthew Sterenberg, "Tradition and Revolution in the Rhetoric of Analytic Philosophy," *Philosophy and Literature* 34 (2010): 161–72.

32. How should we live? How should we shape our political, social, and cultural institutions? Does God or a higher power exist? What is the meaning of life?

33. Two leading protagonists of this approach were R. M. Hare and P. H. Nowell-Smith.

34. I.e., their validity and the truth of their premises.

35. Except, as I shall argue, where the premises incorporate or presuppose value claims or value-laden points of view.

36. For a similar point, see William Rehg, "Reason and Rhetoric in Habermas's Theory of Argumentation," in Walter Jost and Michael J. Hyde (eds.), *Rhetoric and Hermeneutics in Our Time: A Reader* (New Haven, CT: Yale University Press, 1997), p. 368. These remarks do not, of course, apply to purely technical questions of validity, consistency, etc.

37. Desires distinct from those of "spirit" [*thymos*] and appetite.

38. Ernesto Grassi, "Rhetoric and Philosophy," *Rhetoric and Philosophy* 9 (1976), p. 210.

39. Augustine, *Letters*, vol. 2, trans. Sister Wilfred Parsons, *Letters 83–130* (*The Fathers of the Church*, vol. 18) (Washington, D.C.: Catholic University of America Press, 1953), p. 302. Moreover, teaching and speaking are themselves rooted in prayer and hence faith. The successful Christian orator who "speaks of the just and holy and good" in such a way "that he may be willingly and obediently heard" owes his success more "to the piety of his prayers" than to the skill of his oratory, so that *praying for himself* and for those whom he is to address, he is a petitioner before he is a speaker. And, indeed, insofar as his prayers are granted, the real speaker is the Holy Spirit, who speaks "in those who give over Christ to learners" (Augustine, *On Christian Doctrine*, p. 140f).

40. Precisely what "passional states" are epistemically needed? One's answer will depend on the subject matter and on one's philosophical anthropology and metaphysics. For example, whether a hunger for God is needed to do natural theology successfully depends upon whether God exists, what he is like, and the nature of the relationship between God, on the one hand, and human beings, on the other. (I have discussed this at some length in William Wainwright, *Reason and the Heart: A Prolegomenon to a Critique of Passional Reason* (Ithaca, NY: Cornell University Press, 1995).

41. As contrasted with what Edmund Burke called "just [i.e., reasonable] prejudice" or bias.

42. And, arguably, values are at stake in all basic philosophical and theological disputes.

43. The importance of imaginative and emotional appeals is often overlooked or underestimated by philosophers, but how many would pursue a life of philosophy whose imaginations weren't captured and hearts stirred by figures like Socrates or Augustine, or by projects like Descartes's or Hume's?

44. Arash Abizadeh, "The Passions of the Wise: Phronesis, Rhetoric, and Aristotle's Passionate Practical Deliberation," *Review of Metaphysics* 56 (2002): 294–5.

45. Grassi's conception of reason is too narrow. For reason also includes our immediate grasp of self-evident truths. His central point remains plausible, however.

46. Grassi, "Rhetoric and Philosophy," pp. 202f, 211, 213–15. This is similar in some respects to Stephen Pepper's claim that different "root metaphors" (e.g., mechanism, mind) generate different world hypotheses. (See, e.g., Pepper's "The Root Metaphor Theory of Metaphysics," *Journal of Philosophy* XXXII [1935]: 365–74.) The second part of the *Phaedrus*, "which has as its subject matter, the nature and subject of rhetoric begins with a solemn reference to the Muses.... In the activity of the Muses, order clearly plays a prevalent and unifying part. The order of

movements appears in the dance, the order of *tones* in song, and the order of *words* in verse." The Muses are thus implicitly linked with the objective order of the *archai* or forms that brings order into chaos so that a cosmos might appear. For Plato, "'true' rhetoric ... has its roots in the *nous* ... as the insight into [the] original 'ideas,' " which provide "the pre-requisite of *episteme*, in so far as *episteme* can only prove or explain something following an insight" into original forms, an insight that can be expressed only by images or metaphors.

47. Nicholas Rescher, "The Role of Rhetoric in Rational Argumentation," *Argumentation* 12 (1998): 315, 318, 320. The rhetorician enlists a "person's body of experience – vicarious experience included. Here providing information can help – but only by way of influencing their sensibility; the reader's [or auditor's] established way of looking at things and appraising them ... what matters is that agreement is elicited through a contention's being rendered plausible by its consonance with duly highlighted aspects of our experience," including our imaginative experience. One may appeal to "a collection of suitably" selected "illustrations and examples," for instance, or a telling fiction such as Voltaire's *Candide*, or "pure invective," if "cleverly articulated" (p. 321).

48. In this respect, comparisons with philosophical disputes over basic logical intuitions are instructive. While Rescher's central point (that rhetoric necessarily and legitimately comes into play in defending or establishing an argument's underlying presuppositions or assumptions) seems to me sound, other aspects of his essay strike me as questionable. (1) For example, Rescher says that "conscientious rhetoricians" don't appeal to emotions (Rescher, "The Role of Rhetoric," p. 317). But since evaluations are partly *based* on, or *expressive* of, emotions, this isn't consistent with his claim that rhetoric can legitimately be used to reinforce or change our evaluations. (2) The distinction between rhetoric and argumentation is less clear than Rescher makes out. For instance, on p. 319, he cites a passage from Nietzsche as a paradigmatic example of rhetoric, yet admits that it implicitly *contains* an argument. So must arguments be explicit to count as argumentation? And if so, why? (3) In comparing Spinoza and Bradley on p. 321, Rescher appears to claim that while there is an appearance of "close reasoning" in both, the appearance is specious in Bradley's case but not in Spinoza's. But the appearance of close reasoning appears to me to be neither more nor less specious in the one case than in the other. Again, in contrasting Hegel with Kierkegaard, Schopenhauer, and Nietzsche, Rescher suggests that Hegel, unlike the others, typifies "the scientific/ discursive" approach and, in general, appears more or less to equate a "demonstrative" approach with a "scientific" one. But if Hegel's approach is "scientific/ discursive," then surely so too is Bradley's. And why on earth should we equate a "demonstrative" approach with a "scientific" one?

49. Aristotle, *Poetics* 1459a, in Barnes, *Complete Works,* vol. 2.

50. Aristotle, *Rhetoric* 1412a, in Barnes, *Complete Works,* vol. 2.

51. Paul Thargard and Craig Beam, "Epistemological Metaphors and the Nature of Philosophy," *Metaphilosophy* 35 (2004): 513.

52. Thargard and Beam, "Epistemological Metaphors," p. 514.

53. James M. Farrell, "The Rhetoric(s) of St. Augustine's Confessions," *Augustinian Studies* 39 (2008): 271.

54. Farrell, "The Rhetoric(s)," pp. 267–9.

55. Farrell, "The Rhetoric(s)," pp. 275–6.
56. Farrell, "The Rhetoric(s)," p. 277.
57. It is significant that the first three books of *On Christian Doctrine* were completed immediately before the composition of the *Confessions*.
58. Farrell, "The Rhetoric(s)," pp. 278–83.
59. Farrell, "The Rhetoric(s)," pp. 284–6f.
60. Farrell, "The Rhetoric(s)," pp. 287–9.
61. Farrell, "The Rhetoric(s)," p. 290, my emphasis. The quoted passages in this paragraph are from *On Christian Doctrine*. Augustine's personal confessions seem to end with Book X, however. The *Confessions'* final three books are primarily dialectical, consisting in "tortuous and abstractly impersonal exposition of *Genesis* and philosophical analysis of such matters as the notion of time, the multiple meanings of scripture, and how an earth 'without form and void' (Gen 1,1) can exist." (Donald G. Marshall, "Rhetoric, Hermeneutics, and the Interpretation of Scripture: Augustine to Robert of Basevern," in Jost and Hyde (eds.), *Rhetoric and Hermeneutics in Our Time,* p. 278.) Marshall suggests, however, that the last three books are nonetheless connected with what has preceded it and, in particular, with the desire to praise God, which Augustine expresses at the outset of the *Confessions*.
62. Immanuel Kant, *Critique of Judgment,* trans. Werner S. Pluhar (Indianapolis, IN: Hackett, 1987), #53 (p. 197f.), my emphasis.
63. Ijessling, *Rhetoric and Philosophy*, p. 85.
64. Kant, *Critique of Judgment*, p. 198.
65. Immanuel Kant, "What Is Enlightenment?" in *Foundations of the Metaphysics of Morals and What is Enlightenment?*, trans. Lewis White Beck (Indianapolis, IN: Bobbs-Merrill, 1959), p. 85.
66. In Edmund Burke's sense, namely established biases of the mind, valuations that have become settled habits or sentiments.
67. Note that Kant too sometimes talks as if "feeling" (respect for the moral law, our sense of the sublime, and the like) plays a legitimate role in reasoning about morality, religion, and aesthetic issues, and clearly does *not* think that this threatens our autonomy. All that saves Kant from inconsistency is the rather dubious claim that such feelings actually belong to *reason*. (They are no more than the affective resonance of pure rational judgments in beings with inclinations, and are therefore *necessarily* felt by all rational beings with animal natures.)
68. Samuel T. Coleridge, "Biographia Literaria," in *The Selected Poetry and Prose of Samuel Taylor Coleridge* (New York: Modern Library, 1951), p. 263.
69. Stephen Halliwell, "Pleasure, Understanding, and Emotion in Aristotle's Poetics," in Amelie Rorty (ed.), *Essays on Aristotle's Poetics* (Princeton, NJ: Princeton University Press, 1992), p. 247.
70. Amelie Rorty, introd. to *Essays on Aristotle's Poetics*, p. 8.
71. Halliwell, "Pleasure, Understanding, and Emotion," p. 252f.
72. Although the sentence was not carried out. Only the leaders were executed.
73. Which are "fully compatible with general goodness of character."
74. Martha Nussbaum, "Tragedy and Self-Sufficiency: Plato and Aristotle on Fear and Pity," in Rorty (ed.), *Essays on Aristotle's Poetics,* pp. 282f., 263.
75. A vice to which people in competitive societies such as Athens are especially prone.

76. Precisely what Aristotle means by this term is controversial, but arguably it involves correcting and refining the value judgments incorporated in the emotions – that the object of pity or fear is worthy of pity or fear, for example.

77. Aristotle claims that comedy and tragedy are distinguished by the fact that "the one would make its personages worse, and the other better, than the men of the present day" (Aristotle, *Poetics* 1448a, in Barnes, *Complete Works*). When coupled with the fact that it aims at the universal, that tragic poetry ennobles its protagonists and their actions may also have epistemic implications. Classical philosophy aims at grasping the essence of things. But the pre-modern concept of a thing's essence includes not only those properties that are necessary and sufficient conditions of its being a thing of that kind, but also the properties it needs to be a *good* thing of its kind.

78. Henry W. Johnstone, Jr., *Validity and Rhetoric in Philosophical Argument: An Outlook in Transition* (University Park, PA: The Dialogue Press of Man and World, 1978), pp. 15–19, my emphasis. Note that this is one of Johnstone's earlier essays. In later essays in this collection, Johnstone disavows the sharp distinction between rhetoric and philosophy he draws here – but not for the reasons I will give shortly.

79. The hearer might appeal to a mutually shared sense of justice, for example, to temper the speaker's approval of a policy motivated by their mutually shared compassion.

80. A. N. Whitehead, for example, argued that Christian theism cleared a metaphysical space within which modern science became possible. Since the Christian God is a God of reason and order, any world he creates will exhibit pattern and regularity. But because he *freely* creates the world, its order will be contingent. So the world's structures can't be deduced a priori but must be discovered by observation and experiment. Others claim that, because of their insistence that God alone is holy, Christian cultures desacralized the world, which thereby became an appropriate object for manipulation and detached observation. There may be some truth in these views, though, in my opinion, they are overstated. (For example, early Buddhism also "desacralized" the world, and Islam's and Indian theism's picture of God is quite similar to the Judeo-Christian one.)

81. This may be doubted. Robin Horton ("Tradition and Modernity Revisited," in Martin Hollis and Steven Lukes [eds.], *Rationality and Relativism* [Cambridge, MA: MIT Press, 1982]) suggests that the intellectual virtue in question is peculiar to pluralistic cultures. But while these cultures are more likely to encourage the development of this virtue, I am not convinced that it is essentially tied to them.

82. Correspondence from Roger T. Ames. Quoted with permission.

83. Nietzsche, and perhaps Kierkegaard, provide modern Western counterparts. Since values are at stake, divesting their texts of their rhetorical components distorts them. Their expression of and appeal to passions are an integral part of the cases they are making. For an apposite Chinese work from the Warring States period (453–221 BCE) see Carine Defoort, *The Pheasant Cap Master (He gaun zi): A Rhetorical Reading* (Albany: State University of New York Press, 1997).

84. Edwards's true benevolence, for example, is intrinsically tied to his brand of theistic metaphysics. True benevolence is an epistemic virtue if and only if the latter is basically sound.

85. This presupposes, of course, that world views aren't essentially tied to specific cultures. The success of Islam and Christianity in Africa, for example, or of Buddhism in America and Europe suggests that many of them, at least, are not.

6 Reason, Revelation, and Religious Argumentation

1. And even those that aren't depend heavily on texts that *are* believed to be revealed.
2. Even if they aren't revealed, they might still have some weight if there are independent (of revelation) reasons for believing the allegedly revealed propositions to be true.
3. Down to their very letters.
4. K. Satchidananda Murty, *Revelation and Reason in Advaita Vedanta* (New York: Columbia University Press, 1959), pp. 40–2.
5. What is the force of "must" here? I take it that it is: "it is only fitting or appropriate that they be."
6. Murty, *Revelation and Reason,* pp. 33–5. The Nyaya school (which was theistic but not Vedantin) objected that from the fact that no one remembers who dug a particular disused well, we cannot infer that no one dug it. Mimamsa-Vedanta replied that the cases aren't parallel, for the well was never of importance to more than a few people and is no longer of importance to anyone, whereas the Vedas are "a living book ... on which the religious lives of millions depends."
7. Murty, *Revelation and Reason,* pp. 44–8.
8. Murty, *Revelation and Reason,* pp. 230–1.
9. John Clayton, *Religions, Reasons and Gods: Essays in Cross-Cultural Philosophy of Religion* (Cambridge: Cambridge University Press, 2006), p. 149.
10. H. H. Farmer, *The World and God* (London: Nisbet, 1942), p. 82.
11. C. H. Dodd, *The Authority of the Bible* (Glasgow: William Collins Sons, 1978), chapter 1.
12. Farmer, *The World and God,* chapter V.
13. For a brief introduction to Barth's views on revelation, see G. W. Bromily (trans. and ed.), *Karl Barth, Church Dogmatics: A Selection* (New York: Harper Torchbooks, 1961), pp. 29–92. One of the more interesting features of Barth's account is his attempt to combine an orthodox (Protestant) conception of revelation and the authority of scripture with an acceptance of the methods and results of modern Biblical scholarship.
14. This is a bit oversimplified. The works of genius sometimes cause us to modify our standards. For example, the paintings of Picasso and Matisse altered our conception of what constitutes a good painting.
15. This movement should be distinguished from charity, however. Charity is a movement of the will toward God as *the* supreme good, and not just as *my* supreme good. That is, it is a love of God for his own sake (i.e., for what he is in himself) and not merely for what he can do and has done for me.
16. Thomas Aquinas, *The Summa Theologica,* vol. 2, trans. Fathers of the English Dominican Province (New York: Benziger Bros., 1947), part II–II, question 1, article 2; question 2, article 2; question 4, article 7, reply to objection 5; question 5, article 2, reply to objection 2.
17. Aquinas, *The Summa Theologica,* vol. 2, part II–II, question 2, article 5.
18. For example, the notion that temporal things are the most important things, that financial and social success is necessary for a good life, that a good appearance is more important than a good character, and so on.
19. Samuel Clarke, *A Discourse Concerning the Unchangeable Obligations of Natural Religion and the Truth and Certainty of the Christian Revelation* (London: Printed

by W. Botham, for James Knapton, 1706; reprint Stuttgart-Bad Cannstatt: Friedrich Frommann Verlag, 1964), pp. 193–240.

20. Founder of the Bhamati school of Advaita Vedanta.

21. Murty, *Revelation and Reason,* pp. 27–33.

22. For example, no proposition can be true which conflicts with self-evident truths. Divinely revealed propositions can't, then, conflict with the laws of logic. On the other hand, we can mistakenly believe something to be self-evident when it isn't. To illustrate: Locke and Leibniz agree that *if* the doctrine of transubstantiation conflicts with necessary truths, it is false and so can't be divinely revealed. They also agree that the doctrine conflicts with the proposition that no body can exist as a whole in two distinct places at the same time. But they *disagree* about the necessity of this proposition.

23. John Locke, *An Essay concerning Human Understanding*, vol. 2 (New York: Dover, 1959), book 4, chapters 18, 19.

24. George H. Joyce, "Revelation," in *The Catholic Encyclopedia*, vol. 13 (New York: Robert Appleton, 1907–12).

25. They can therefore be appealed to in disputes between Christians and Vaishnavas, say, or Jews and Muslims, without begging the question of the truth of propositions on which they disagree.

26. John Calvin, *Institutes of the Christian Religion*, vol. 1, trans. Henry Beveridge (Grand Rapids, MI: Eerdmann's, 1957), book 1, chapter 7, section 4.

27. As we have seen, this motion of the will takes God as one's end.

28. Thomas Aquinas, *Summa Theologica*, vol. 2, part II-II, question 6, article 1; and *The Disputed Questions on Truth*, vol. 2, trans. James V. McGlynn (Chicago: Henry Regnery, 1953), question 14, article 1.

29. Locke, *Human Understanding*, book 4, chapter 19. Nothing is a reliable sign of truth appeal to which yields a wide diversity of conflicting results. Since people are subjectively certain of many incompatible things, subjective certainty isn't a reliable sign of truth.

30. As well as phenomenologically distinct from each other.

31. Charles Blount, *Oracles of Reason*, pp. 198–9. Quoted in Peter Byrne, *Natural Religion and the History of Religion: The Legacy of Deism* (London: Routledge, 1989), pp. 53–4.

32. Byrne, *Natural Religion*, pp. 54, 71.

33. Michael Tindal, *Christianity as Old as the Creation* (London, 1730; repr. New York: Garland, 1978), pp. 13–21. (I have modernized Tindal's spelling and capitalization.)

34. Byrne, *Natural Religion*, pp. 72–4. But even if God's justice and reasonableness were to preclude his making human salvation *depend* on assent to such revealed truths as the doctrine of the Trinity or the doctrine of the Incarnation, why should it preclude either the possibility that some truths about God are irreducibly mysterious or his communicating those truths to us? Perhaps it wouldn't. But the deists' confidence in the transparency of a just and reasonable religion doesn't comport well with either the existence or communication of irreducibly mysterious truths. In any case, if knowledge of them isn't necessary for salvation, then (from the deists' point of view) their communication is superfluous at best and, at worst, a distraction from what is truly important.

35. Terence Penelhum, *God and Skepticism* (Dordrecht: D. Reidel, 1983), p. 27.
36. Pierre Bayle, *Historical and Critical Dictionary: Selections*, trans. Richard H. Popkin (Indianapolis, IN: Bobbs-Merrill, 1965), p. 414.
37. Bayle, *Historical and Critical Dictionary*, pp. 435, 423. My emphasis.
38. Penelhum, *God and Skepticism*, p. 28.
39. Bayle, *Historical and Critical Dictionary*, p. 298.
40. Penelhum, *God and Skepticism*, pp. 56–9.
41. John Toland, *Christianity Not Mysterious* (London, 1696; repr. New York: Garland, 1978), p. 24.
42. Toland's first response is this: to the claim that while doctrines such as the Trinity are indeed "not contrary to sound reason,.... *no man's reason is sound*," Toland objects that even though the reason of most people is indeed unsound, the de facto defects of human reason can be remedied without divine assistance. For we can learn to "compare ideas, distinguish clear from obscure conceptions, suspend our judgments about uncertainties, and yield only to evidence" (Toland, *Christianity Not Mysterious*, pp. 57, 60, my emphasis). One may reasonably doubt whether these measures are sufficient to restore an impaired or fallen intellect. But more on this later in the chapter.
43. Toland, *Christianity Not Mysterious*, p. 34. My emphasis.
44. Jonathan Edwards, "Miscellany 1340," *The "Miscellanies," 1153-1360 (Works of Jonathan Edwards*, vol. 23), Douglas Sweeney (ed.) (New Haven, CT: Yale University Press, 2004), p. 371.
45. David Hilbert described a hotel with an infinite number of rooms, each of which is occupied. Yet even though the hotel is full, its proprietor can accommodate an infinite number of new guests. If Jones requests a room, for example, the proprietor can simply move the guest in room number 1 to room number 2, the guest in room number 2 to room number 3, the guest in room number 3 to room number 4, etc., and assign Jones room number 1. And the process can be repeated for each new arrival.
46. Jonathan Edwards, "The Mind," section 35, *Scientific and Philosophical Writings (Works of Jonathan Edwards*, vol. 6), Wallace E. Anderson (ed.) (New Haven, CT: Yale University Press, 1980), p. 355. He also adds the following corollary: "No wonder, therefore, that the high and abstract mysteries of the Deity, the prime and most abstract of all beings, imply so many seeming contradictions."
47. Toland, *Christianity Not Mysterious*, pp. 30, 32.
48. This is discussed in greater detail later in this chapter.
49. Tindal, *Christianity as Old as the Creation*, p. 179.
50. Tindal, *Christianity as Old as the Creation*, p. 187.
51. That is, theism as abstracted from the peculiarities of any particular religious tradition.
52. That is, given only the hypothesis that an all-powerful, all-knowing, and all-good being has created whatever worlds happen to exist.
53. That is, of theism *alone* without Christian, Muslim, or Hindu embellishments.
54. See Marilyn M. Adams, *Horrendous Evils and the Goodness of God* (Ithaca, NY: Cornell University Press, 1999).
55. Paul Tillich, *Systematic Theology*, vol. 1 (Chicago: University of Chicago Press, 1951), p. 105.

56. Frederick Ferré and Kent Bendall, *Exploring the Logic of Faith* (New York: Association Press, 1963), p. 171.

57. William James, "The Will to Believe," in *The Will to Believe and Other Essays on Popular Philosophy* (New York: Dover, 1956), p. 25f.

58. The same is, of course, true of many professed Christians.

59. John Owen, *Phronema tou Pneumatou, or the Grace and Duty of the Spiritually Minded* (London: Printed by J. G. for Nathaniel Ponder, 1681), pp. 102–5.

60. Roughly, God is simple if and only if his existence and essential properties are ontologically identical.

61. Though not necessarily ultima facie.

62. John Henry Newman, *An Essay in Aid of a Grammar of Assent* (Notre Dame, IN: University of Notre Dame Press, 1970), p. 237.

63. Toland, *Christianity Not Mysterious*, pp. 37–8.

64. Tindal, *Christianity as Old as the Creation*, p. 190.

65. Jonathan Edwards, "Miscellaneous Observations," in *The Works of President Edwards*, vol. 8 (New York: B. Franklin, 1968), p. 227.

66. It should be noted, however, that these dispositions should be distinguished from anything like Jonathan Edwards's "new spiritual sensation." The latter *is* a new piece of evidence. The former is not. (See Chapter 4, footnote 128.)

67. John Smith, *Select Discourses* (London, 1660; reprint New York: Garland, 1978), p. 382.

68. Henry More, *A Collection of Several Philosophical Writings*, 2nd ed., vol. 1 (London, 1662; reprint New York: Garland, 1978), p. viii.

69. Cf. the following remark by Henry More: "Surely it is not for nought that the Spirit of God so frequently in Scripture names the Heart for the chief seat of Wisdom; which is yet less the marvelous, considering that the Wisdom which the Scripture driveth at, is Practical Wisdom, Moral or Divine, wherein the Heart is much concerned.... For what the Eye is in reference to Colours, that is the Heart in reference to the discrimination of Moral Good and Evil." (Henry More, *Discourses on Several Texts of Scripture* [London, 1692, p. 39]. Quoted in Aharon Lichtenstein, *Henry More: The Rational Theology of a Cambridge Platonist* [Cambridge, MA: Harvard University Press, 1962], p. 63.)

70. Alexander Roberts and James Donaldson (eds), *The Ante-Nicene Fathers* (Edinburgh and London, 1867–72; Grand Rapids, MI: Eerdmans, 1950), vol. 3, p. 246.

71. Roberts and Donaldson (eds.), *The Ante-Nicene Fathers*, vol. 3, p, 535.

72. Quoted in Etienne Gilson, *Reason and Revelation in the Middle Ages* (New York: Charles Scribner's Sons, 1938), pp. 12–13. Emphasis in the original text.

73. Roberts and Donaldson (eds.), *The Ante-Nicene Fathers*, vol. 2, p. 305.

74. Roberts and Donaldson (eds.), *The Ante-Nicene Fathers*, vol. 1, pp. 193, 178.

75. Roberts and Donaldson (eds.), *The Ante-Nicene Fathers*, vol. 1, p. 191.

76. Robert Bolton, quoted in John Morgan, *Godly Learning: Puritan Attitudes towards Reason, Learning and Education, 1560–1640* (Cambridge: Cambridge University Press, 1986), p. 47.

77. Quoted in C. A. Patrides, *The Cambridge Platonists* (Cambridge, MA: Harvard University Press, 1970), p. 9.

78. The quotations from Perkins and Rous are found in Morgan, Morgan, *Godly Learning*, p. 51.

79. Quoted in Frederick J. Powicke, *The Cambridge Platonists: A Study* (London, 1926; Westport: Greenwood Press, 1970), p. 23.
80. Quoted in Morgan, *Godly Learning*, p. 59.
81. Quoted in Geoffrey F. Nuttall, *The Holy Spirit in Puritan Faith and Experience*, 2nd ed. (Chicago: University of Chicago Press, 1992), p. 47.
82. Richard Bernard, quoted in Morgan, *Godly Learning*, p. 55.
83. Quoted in Morgan, *Godly Learning*, p. 113.
84. Quoted in Morgan, *Godly Learning*, p. 106.
85. Perry Miller, *The New England Mind: The Seventeenth Century* (New York, 1939; reprint Boston: Beacon Press, 1961), p. 114.
86. Quoted in Morgan, *Godly Learning*, p. 74.
87. Quoted in Morgan, *Godly Learning*, p. 71.
88. Quoted in Morgan, *Godly Learning*, p. 125.
89. Quotations in Morgan, *Godly Learning*, p. 127.
90. Cotton Mather, *Reasonable Religion: Or the Truths of the Christian Religion Demonstrated* (London, 1713), p. 37. The last emphasis is mine.
91. Quoted in Morgan, *Godly Learning*, p. 54.
92. Powicke, *Cambridge Platonists*, p. 30.
93. Smith, *Select Discourses*, p. 384.
94. Smith, *Select Discourses*, pp. 1–2, 4, 12.
95. Nathanael Culverwel, *An Elegant and Learned Discourse on the Light of Nature, with Several Other Treatises* (London, 1652; New York: Garland, 1978), pp. 167–8.
96. Culverwel, *Elegant and Learned Discourse*, p. 168.
97. Culverwel, *Elegant and Learned Discourse*, pp. 169–70.
98. Charles Taliaferro and Alison J. Teply (eds.), *Cambridge Platonist Spirituality* (New York & Mahwah NJ: Paulist Press, 2004), p. 35. The internal quotes are from Peter Sterry, *The Spirit's Conviction of Sinne – a Sermon before the Honourable House of Commons* (1645), p. 27.

7 Theology and Mystery

1. David Hume, *The Natural History of Religion* (London: Adam and Charles Black, 1956), p. 54.
2. John Toland, *Christianity Not Mysterious* (London, 1696; New York: Garland, 1978 [reprint]), p. 73.
3. Toland ultimately explains it by the activity of "cunning priests" who exploited people's gullibility for "their own advantage" (Toland, *Christianity Not Mysterious*, p. 70). Hume traces its origin to people's fear of God and of his ill favor; and who, "supposing him to be pleased, like themselves with praise and flattery," spare "no eulogy or exaggeration … in their addresses to him…. Thus they proceed; till at last they arrive at infinity itself…. And it is well, if, in striving to get farther … they run not into inexplicable mystery, and destroy the intelligent nature of their deity, on which alone any rational worship or adoration can be founded" (Hume, *Natural History*, p. 43).
4. *Dionysius the Areopagite on the Divine Names and the Mystical Theology*, trans. with introduction by C. E. Rolt (London and New York: Macmillan, 1957), p. 191.

5. John Chrysostom, *On the Incomprehensible Nature of God*, trans. Paul W. Harkins, (Fathers of the Church, vol. 72), (Washington, DC: Catholic University of America Press, 1984), p. 100.

6. Chrysostom, *Incomprehensible Nature*, pp. 65–6. Again, in commenting on Psalm 139, Chrysostom says, "we wonder at the open sea and its limitless depth: but we wonder fearfully when we stoop down and see how deep it is. It was in this way that the prophet stooped down and looked at the limitless and yawning sea of God's wisdom. And he was struck with shuddering. He was deeply frightened, he drew back, and said in a loud voice: 'I will give you thanks for you are fearfully wondrous; wondrous are your works. And again: 'Your knowledge is too wondrous for me; it is too lofty and I cannot attain it'" (p. 60). He then cites Paul (Romans 11: 33) and observes: "As he looked at" but a "small part" of God's providence, "it was as if he were shuddering at a limitless sea and were peering into its yawning depth. And immediately he drew back and, with a loud shout exclaimed: 'How deep are the riches and the wisdom and the knowledge of God! How inscrutable are his judgments'" (p. 63). And note that the mystery here is not God's essence or inmost nature, but rather an attribute of God which, in some sense, we (and presumably Chrysostom) believe that we know and at least partially understand – the point, I take it, being that even what we know and understand of God has a dimension of mystery that both repels and enraptures the mind.

7. Jonathan Edwards, "Discourse on the Trinity," in *The Works of Jonathan Edwards*, vol. 21, *Writings on the Trinity, Grace, and Faith,* Sang Hyun Lee (ed.) (New Haven, CT: Yale University Press), pp. 134, 139.

8. And not only to Christian worship and reflection. Maimonides believed that God can only be described negatively, and the Kabbalists thought that while "the God of religion … has many names, the *deus absconditus,* the God who is hidden in his own self, can only be named … with the help of words which … are not real names at all." The early Spanish "Kabbalists, for example, used terms like … 'Great Reality,' 'Indifferent Unity,' and above all, *En Sof* [the Infinite]." Isaac the Blind called the hidden God "that which is not conceivable by thinking," and thus *"not* He who is not, etc." Gerrshom G. Scholem, *Major Trends in Jewish Mysticism* (New York: Schocken, 1954), pp. 11–12. Emphasis in the original text. Nor are themes like these restricted to theists. The bodhisattva, Vimalakirti, once asked a host of bodhisattvas who were led by Manjushri to express their views on nonduality. Some said, because I say "I am," I think some things are mine. But as there is no "I am" (the no-self or *anatman* doctrine), there is no mine. Others said, to long for release and to shun bondage is dualism. But there really is no bondage (since fundamentally we already are Buddhas, i.e., our real nature is the Buddha nature), and if there is no bondage, there is no release. Many similar answers were given until all but Manjushri had spoken. At this point, Vimilakirti asked him to give his own view, and he responded that nonduality is that which is beyond all words and signs, "all questionings and answerings." Manjushri then asked Vimilakirti if *he* had anything to add about nonduality, "but the latter kept completely silent and uttered not a word. Thereupon Manjustri admiringly exclaimed 'Well done! Well done!'" Vimalakirti's "answer" or nonanswer, is known as the "Thunderous Silence." D. T. Suzuki, *Outlines of Mahayana Buddhism* (New York: Schocken, 1963), pp. 106–8.

9. Among many Protestants but also among some Catholics.

10. Bernard McGinn, *The Foundations of Mysticism: Origins to the Fifth Century* (New York: Crossroad, 2003), pp. 180–1.

11. Johannes Scotus Erigena, *Periphyseon: The Division of Nature*, trans. I. P. Sheldon-Williams, revised by John J. O'Meara (Dumbarton Oaks: Bellarmin, 1987), chapter 4, section 13.

12. John the Scot, *Commentary on John*. Quoted in Bernard McGinn, *The Growth of Mysticism: Gregory the Great through the 12th Century* (New York: Crossroad, 2004), p. 108.

13. Andrew Louth, *The Origins of the Christian Mystical Tradition from Plato to Denys* (Oxford: Clarendon Press, 1981), p. 176.

14. Even though Plotinus does sometimes use personal as well as nonpersonal pronouns to refer to the One, and, even though ultimately for Dionysius, "God is person" *and* "God is not a person" must both be negated. Just as, according to Dionysius, God transcends and is more than being or goodness (is "superbeing" or "supergoodness"), so, presumably, God transcends and is more than personal (i.e., is "superpersonal").

15. The fact that the soul is in permanent contact with the "intellect" (the world of intelligences or forms), which is, in turn, in permanent contact with the One, and that everything tends to revert to it.

16. I. P. Sheldon-Williams, "The Greek Christian Platonist Tradition from the Cappadocians to Maximus and Eriugena," in A. H. Armstrong (ed.), *The Cambridge History of Later Greek and Early Medieval Philosophy* (Cambridge: Cambridge University Press, 1967), p. 470.

17. Dionysius, "The Divine Names," chapter 4, sections 12–14, in *Pseudo-Dionysius: The Complete Works* (Mahwah, NJ: Paulist Press, 1987).

18. The author of the first (and highly influential) Latin translation of the Dionysian corpus.

19. There is "a long tradition in Latin exegesis" that prepares for this. Gregory the Great, for example, claims that "love itself is knowledge," and refers to the "Seraphim and their fiery love ... as an exegetical commonplace" (although he never claims that Dionysius understood the Seraphim in this way). The quotations are from Boyd Taylor Coolman's "The Medieval Affective Dionysian Tradition," and Paul Rorem's "The Early Latin Dionysius: Eriugena and Hugh of St. Victor," respectively, in Sarah Coakley and Charles M. Stang (eds.), *Rethinking Dionysius the Areopagite* (Oxford: Wiley-Blackwell, 2009), pp 89, 78–9.

20. Rorem, "The Early Latin Dionysius and Hugh of St. Victor," pp. 78–81.

21. In his Middle English paraphrase of the *Mystical Theology*, entitled *Denis's Hidden Theology*.

22. Coolman, "Medieval Affective Dionysian Tradition," pp. 86–7.

23. Coolman, "Medieval Affective Dionysian Tradition," pp. 90–1, 94. My emphasis. It is worth noting that, for Gallus, while "in the darkness of seraphic union [with God] ... the soul lacks 'mental eyes,' that is, reason and understanding," it is able to ... taste and touch the beloved." "This refreshment does not occur through a *mirror*, but through the experience of divine sweetness, because taste and touch are not accomplished through a mirror, ... though vision is." And Gallus notes that while scripture says that no one can see God and live, it does not say that no one can taste or touch God and live. (Coolman, "Medieval Affective Dionysian Tradition," pp. 94–5).

24. See Luis M. Giron-Negron, "Dionysian Thought in Sixteenth-Century Spanish Mystical Theology," in Coakley and Stang (eds.), *Rethinking Dionysius*, pp. 163–76.
25. An anonymous fourteenth-century product of Rhineland mysticism.
26. Cf. e.g., W. R. Ward, *The Protestant Evangelical Awakening* (Cambridge: Cambridge University Press, 1992), p. 48, and elsewhere.
27. William P. Alston, "Two Cheers for Mystery," in Andrew Dole and Andrew Chignell (eds.), *God and the Ethics of Belief: New Essays in Philosophy of Religion* (New York: Cambridge University Press, 2005), p. 99.
28. So-called because he displayed the *hiera* or sacred objects to the worshipers.
29. Milton K. Munitz, *The Mystery of Existence: An Essay in Philosophical Cosmology* (New York: Appleton-Century-Crofts, 1965), pp. 15–20, 23–5.
30. Michael B. Foster, *Mystery and Philosophy* (London: SCM Press, 1957), p. 46, my emphasis.
31. Foster, *Mystery and Philosophy*, p. 41, my emphasis.
32. Foster, *Mystery and Philosophy*, p. 47.
33. G. S. Hendry, "Reveal," in Alan Richardson (ed.), *A Theological Word Book of the Bible* (New York: Macmillan, 1951), p. 198.
34. Andrew Louth, *Discerning the Mystery* (Oxford: Clarendon Press, 1983), p. 70. Dale Tuggy in correspondence denies that Biblical passages describing Moses's encounter with God on Mt. Sinai, Isaiah's vision in the temple, or the visions of God's throne in (e.g.) Ezekiel, Daniel, and Revelations, the claim that God dwells in unapproachable light, and so on support the "mystery thesis." In his view, Toland and other eighteenth-century deists have successfully shown that God is mysterious only in the same sense that nature is – there are truths about both which we don't know and doubtlessly many which we will never know. But that God is only a mystery in the same sense in which nature is seems to be a very reductive sense of "mystery." Nor does it capture what the church fathers, and the Christian spiritual tradition on the whole, have meant by the term. It is true that I read scripture in the light of this tradition and Tuggy does not. But note that reading scripture in the light of a tradition doesn't distinguish Catholic from classical Protestant or from Tuggy's own uses of the Bible. Reformed and Lutheran theologians read Paul in the light of Augustine. Many contemporary Christian fundamentalists read Revelations in the light of Meade and various nineteenth-century dispensationalist schemes. And Tuggy reads the Bible in the light of seventeenth- and eighteenth-century deists whose own readings of scripture were infused by the presuppositions and values of the early modern enlightenment. What I strongly doubt is that the Bible itself, *abstracted from all traditions of reading*, clearly speaks for one of these interpretations rather than another.
35. Jonathan Edwards, "Miscellany 1340," in *The Works of Jonathan Edwards*, vol. 23, *The "Miscellanies," 1153–1360*, Douglas A. Sweeney (ed.) (New Haven, CT: Yale University Press, 2004), p. 368.
36. Paul Gavrilyuk, *The Suffering of the Impassible God: The Dialectics of Patristic Thought* (New York: Oxford University Press, 2003), pp. 81–3. "Many apologists considered an open attack upon the prevailing [sentiments and] social conventions to be the most successful defense strategy." They admitted "that the divine birth, suffering, and crucifixion were unseemly, scandalous, and offensive in the eyes of the world," but insisted that what the world deemed shameful and offensive is in

fact a most God-befitting way of securing the redemption of a ruined creation since it was only by assuming flesh, suffering, and death that God could redeem them (p. 87). I would only add that scandals in this sense don't entirely disappear upon conversion. For old sentiments and habits of evaluation linger on even if they no longer dominate one's life and outlook. Insofar as they do, the sense of offense and scandal isn't entirely eradicated. (Cf. Kierkegaard, for whom the sense of scandal or offense is *constitutive* of the Christian faith as he understands it.)

37. Jonathan Edwards, "Miscellany 654," in *The Works of Jonathan Edwards*, vol. 18, *The "Miscellanies," 501-832*, Ava Chamberlain (ed.) (New Haven, CT: Yale University Press, 2000), pp. 195–6.

38. At least when well formed.

39. A mystery, in this sense, should be distinguished from the "unknowable," for the latter is a purely negative notion. "The recognition of mystery," on the other hand, "is an essentially positive act of the mind." (Gabriel Marcel, *Being and Having* (New York: Harper and Row, 1965), p. 118.

40. Rudolf Otto, *The Idea of the Holy*, trans. John W. Harvey (New York: Oxford University Press, 1958), p. 26.

41. Otto, *Idea of the Holy*, p. 30. Emphasis in the original text. Although it *can* be expressed in images and symbols. Otto is explicitly speaking in this passage of the concepts of transcendence and the supernatural. The context makes it clear, however, that what Otto says of the concepts of transcendence and the supernatural also applies to the concept of mystery.

42. Alston, "Two Cheers for Mystery," pp. 104–6. The last quotations are from Thomas Merton, *New Seeds of Contemplation* (New York: New Directions, 1961), pp. 1–2, 135.

43. Alston, "Two Cheers for Mystery," pp. 100–1. Alston asks us to consider, in this connection, how difficult it is to even craft "a picture of the physical world … the complete correctness of which we can be assured" (p. 100).

44. Edwards, "Miscellany 1340," pp. 370–1, my emphasis.

45. Thomas Aquinas, *On the Truth of the Catholic Faith, Book Four: Salvation*, trans. Charles J. O'Neil (Garden City, NY: Doubleday, 1957), pp. 35–7, my emphasis.

46. So there is nothing God has that God doesn't know, and no task that someone could perform (such as defining God's essence) that God cannot do.

47. Johannes Scotus Erigina, *Periphyseon*, book II, pp. 585A–590D. The idea here is presumably this. Finitude and infinity contrast with, and hence circumscribe, each other. An infinite line or quantity isn't a finite line or quantity, and vice versa, and is, in that sense, limited. Infinite lines or quantities are thus only limitless in certain respects. God, by contrast, is limitless in *all* respects.

48. Mixed perfections are good-making properties that entail an imperfection.

49. John's claim that God has no essence also rests upon the traditional notion that a good definition states a thing's genus and differentia and/or proceeds by locating the definiendum within the Aristotelian categories. If God is simple and/or transcends the Aristotelian categories, then neither of these requirements can be met. What is unclear, however, is just why definitions must meet either of these requirements. Does "God = df. a being greater than which none can be thought" do so, for example? I doubt that it does, but a traditionalist could reply that it doesn't capture God's essence either and, for that reason, isn't a "real definition."

50. Anselm, *St. Anselm's Proslogion, with a Reply on Behalf of the Fool by Gaunilo and the Author's Reply to Gaunilo*, trans. M. J. Charlesworth (Oxford: Clarendon Press, 1965), p. 137.

51. Anselm, *Proslogion*, p. 81, my emphasis.

52. Anselm, *Proslogion*, p. 189.

53. Matter for Plotinus, for example, is "not an independently existing principle, but the point at which the outflow of reality from the One fades away into utter darkness"; or, alternatively, the point at which the process of fragmentation reaches its logical limit, a plurality without any unity at all – and hence not even a real plurality, since a real plurality is "always a plurality of [determinate] things, each of which is one." Matter is thus sheer formless indeterminacy. Matter is below being (although not nonexistent) just as the One is above it. Since only what has being and form can be conceptualized, both matter and the One elude our intellect. R. T. Wallis, *Neoplatonism* (New York: Charles Scribner's Sons, 1972), pp. 48–50.

54. Not only is God's joy or happiness greater than any finite joy or happiness, no finite joy or happiness is half as great, two-thirds as great, or almost as great as God's.

55. Alston, "Two Cheers for Mystery," p. 101.

56. If simplicity *supervenes* on the relations between God's first-order properties, being greater than can be thought would be a third-order divine property: being greater than can be thought supervenes on God's simplicity, which supervenes in turn on the relations between his first-order properties. If, however, God's simplicity is simply *identical* to the relations between his first-order properties, then being greater than can be thought would presumably be a second-order divine property.

57. Strictly speaking, the latter two cases are also cases in which being greater than can be thought is a consequence of God's first-order properties. For (as we saw in note 56), since God's simplicity depends on his first-order properties, so too does the property of being greater than can be thought that is a consequence of it; and mystery, in Rahner's view, is presumably a first-order property of the divine essence (?).

58. George Mavrodes "'It Is Beyond the Power of Human Reason,'" *Philosophical Topics* 16 (1988), p. 77.

59. Thomas Aquinas, *Summa Theologica,* vol 1, trans. by the Fathers of the English Dominican Province (New York: Benziger Brothers, 1947), pt. 1, Q. 32, A. 1, my emphases.

60. Indeed, if we follow Locke, Swinburne, and others who believe that a rationally compelling case can be made for the authority of the Christian revelation, and that that revelation includes the doctrine of the Trinity, and if we broaden the concept of proof or demonstration to include proofs from testimony, then reason *can* prove or demonstrate that God is triune. As Jonathan Edwards says, "divine testimony" cannot be opposed to reason, evidence, and argument because it is a *rule* of reason, a *kind* of evidence, and a *type* of argument like the "human testimony of credible eye-witnesses," "credible history," "memory," "present experience," or "arithmetical calculation." Jonathan Edwards, "Miscellaneous Observations," *The Works of President Edwards*, vol. 8 (New York: B. Franklin, 1968; reprint of the Leeds edition reissued with a two-volume supplement in Edinburgh, 1847), p. 228.) While Edwards doesn't clearly distinguish between evidence, argument, and rule of reason, the distinction is presumably this: apparent memories, for example, are a type of evidence, justifying claims by appeal to memory is a type of argument, and

the appropriate rule is that "one's memories are normally reliable." Similarly, the contents of scripture are a type of evidence, justifying claims by appealing to scripture is a type of argument, and the appropriate rule is "scripture is trustworthy." "Scripture is reliable" resembles such rules as "The testimony of our senses may be depended on," "The agreed testimony of all we see and converse with continually is to be credited," and the like. Edwards, "Miscellany 1340," p. 361. Principles like these can be established, or at least certified, by reason and then used to establish other truths that cannot be established without their help. (As we saw in Chapter 6, that reason can appropriately be used to establish the credentials of a rule of reason, and that that rule can in turn be used to establish other truths that can't be demonstrated without it, does *not* imply that opinions formed by a reason that does not employ that rule can be used to determine the truth or falsity of opinions established only *by* its means.)

61. As we shall see, for example, John Chrysostom clearly thinks that God's essence can't be known by even the most exalted of creatures. The cherubim and seraphim themselves know God only by "figures."

62. Jonathan Edwards, "The Mind," in *The Works of Jonathan Edwards*, vol. 6, *Scientific and Philosophical Writings*, Wallace E. Anderson (ed.) (New Haven, CT: Yale University Press, 1980), p. 385.

63. Jonathan Edwards, "Miscellany 1100," in *The Works of Jonathan Edwards*, vol. 20, *The "Miscellanies," 833–1152*, Amy Plantinga Pauw (ed.) (New Haven, CT: Yale University Press, 2002), p. 485. Propositions about infinities and, perhaps, quantum mechanics provide other examples.

64. Edwards, "Discourse on the Trinity," p. 134.

65. James Kellenberger, "God and Mystery," *American Philosophical Quarterly* 11 (1974), p. 99.

66. Edwards, "Discourse on the Trinity," p. 140.

67. Edwards, "Discourse on the Trinity," p. 139.

68. Edwards, "Miscellany 839," in *Works of Jonathan Edwards*, vol. 20, pp. 54–5.

69. Edwards, "Miscellany 1340," p. 371.

70. Jonathan Edwards, "Miscellany 83," in *The Works of Jonathan Edwards*, vol. 13, *The "Miscellanies," a–500*, Thomas E. Schafer (ed.) (New Haven, CT: Yale University Press, 1994), p. 249.

71. The two are not unrelated, of course.

72. See, e.g., William J. Danaher, Jr., *The Trinitarian Ethics of Jonathan Edwards* (Louisville, KY: Westminster John Knox Press, 2004). Cf. Amy Plantinga Pauw, *The Supreme Harmony of All: The Trinitarian Theology of Jonathan Edwards* (Grand Rapids, MI: William B. Eerdmans, 2002).

73. Or, more cautiously, have said things that imply that it doesn't.

74. Thomas Aquinas, *de Pot*, q. 7, a. 5. Quoted in Karl Rahner, "The Concept of Mystery in Catholic Theology," *Theological Investigations*, vol. 4 (New York: Seabury, 1974), pp. 58–9.

75. Namely, that our minds are "not proportionate to the divine substance."

76. Rahner, "Concept of Mystery,: p. 59. Aquinas, of course, thinks that the redeemed in heaven have a direct vision of God's essence. Yet how is this possible if "no proportion exists between the created intellect and God" because of the "infinite distance between them?" His answer is that while there is no *quantitative*

proportion between God and created intellects (God isn't twice as great, or four times as great, or a thousand times as great, or … and so on, as created intellects), "*every* relation of one thing to another is called proportion," and created intellects are related to God as effects to their cause. (Aquinas *Summa Theologica*, vol. 1, pt. I, q. 12, a. 1, my emphases.) Whether this response is adequate seems to me doubtful. It may be sufficient to show that created intellects are capable of knowing *that* there is a first cause and that that cause must have those properties entailed by its being first cause. It isn't clearly sufficient to show that created intellects are capable of directly beholding God's *essence*. But even if they are, Aquinas is clear that the lack of "quantitative" proportion between created intellects and God implies that God's essence can't be known by created intellects *as God himself knows it*, namely, "in an infinite degree." The beatified see God "wholly," and there is nothing "of him [which] is not seen." But he is not seen "perfectly." Aquinas illustrates the distinction between knowing a whole in its entirety yet not knowing it perfectly by contrasting two ways of knowing that a triangle's angles are equal to two right angles, the first resting on a "probable reason" and the second on a "scientific demonstration." A person possessing the latter "*comprehends*" the truth while someone who only possesses the former does not. Yet it "does not follow that any part of [the truth] is unknown [to the former], either the subject, or the predicate, or the composition; but [only] that it is not as perfectly known as it is capable of being known." (Aquinas, *Summa Theologica*, vol. 1, pt. I, q. 12, a. 7) Aquinas's point, I think, is not that certain truths about God's essence necessarily elude the saints in heaven, but rather that their apprehension of them is unavoidably imperfect or obscure to one degree or another. The *object* of the saints' vision (the divine essence) is apprehended directly (without a medium) and in its entirety, but the *manner* in which they behold it is necessarily imperfect. None of this, as far as I can see, is inconsistent with the thesis of this section, namely, that there are aspects of God that can't be fully captured by the propositional or conceptual intellect.

77. Edwards, "Miscellany 654," p. 196.
78. Jonathan Edwards, "Miscellany 765," in *Works of Jonathan Edwards*, vol. 18, p. 411.
79. Jonathan Edwards, "Miscellany 1340," pp. 370–1, my emphasis.
80. Chrysostom, *Incomprehensible Nature*, p. 97, my emphases.
81. Chrysostom, *Incomprehensible Nature*, p. 101. "God condescends whenever he is not seen as he is, but in the way one incapable of beholding him is able to look upon him," that is, by images, visions (including, presumably, so-called intellectual visions), and the like (p. 101).
82. Rahner, "Concept of Mystery," p. 41.
83. Namely, the Bible, creeds, and the like.
84. Rahner, "Concept of Mystery," p. 56.
85. Rahner, "Concept of Mystery," p. 58.
86. That is, to concepts or their divine analogues.
87. Rahner, "Concept of Mystery," p. 48f.
88. That is, he doesn't know himself by any analogue of propositional knowledge.
89. I owe this suggestion to Alvin Plantinga.
90. See, e.g., Foster, *Mystery and Philosophy*, chapter II.

91. Note that appreciation should not be construed as a purely subjective reaction to something that can, in principle, be fully captured in concepts. The taste of strawberries, for example, or the nature of first love elude adequate conceptualization, although both *can* be expressed in poetry or song.

92. Otto, *Idea of the Holy*, pp. 26, 28, 30.

93. As Plantinga also suggested to me.

94. See, for example, the Eucharistic hymn adapted from the Liturgy of St. James, which begins, "Let all mortal flesh keep silence and with fear and trembling stand."

95. On the whole, because God presumably isn't "numbed" or "chilled" by the sight of his own being.

96. That he is omnipotent, say, or good.

97. Reactions that, notice, are only appropriate to puzzles in Marcel's sense, i.e., to problems that would be resolved by the acquisition of the right propositional knowledge.

98. Thus, to put the point in terms of the distinction introduced earlier, God is not an epistemological mystery to himself, but does regard his own being as an ontological mystery.

Conclusion

1. Namely, the existential appropriation of the way of life in which the desired truths and values are incorporated.

2. Imaginative depictions of Radha's love for Krishna, for example, or of Teresa of Avila's love of God, stories of the Desert Fathers or of the great Hasidic rabbis, and tales of the Buddha and his followers or of heroic Christian or Islamic preachers and evangelists.

3. Plato, *Republic*, trans. with introduction and notes by Francis MacDonald Cornford (New York and London: Oxford University Press, 1941), p. 220 [Book vi, 508]. The Form of the Good, or Goodness Itself, is usually identified with the Form of Beauty, or Beauty Itself, which the *Symposium* describes as being seen "suddenly," recalling "the culminating revelation of the Eleusinian mysteries – the disclosure of sacred symbols or figures of the divinities in a sudden blaze of light." F. M. Conford, "The Doctrine of Eros in Plato's *Symposium*," in Gregory Vlastos (ed,), *Plato II: Ethics, Politics, and Philosophy of Art and Religion* (Garden City, NY: Anchor, 1971), p. 127.

4. *Chuang Tzu*, chapter 25, Laurence G. Thompson (trans.), in Laurence G. Thomson, *The Chinese Way in Religion* (Encino and Belmont, CA: Dickenson, 1973), p. 50.

Index